The Politics of Group Rights

The State and Multiculturalism

Edited by
Ishtiaq Ahmed

UNIVERSITY PRESS OF AMERICA,® INC.
Lanham • Boulder • New York • Toronto • Oxford

4501 Forbes Boulevard
Suite 200
Lanham, Maryland 20706
UPA Acquisitions Department (301) 459-3366

PO Box 317
Oxford
OX2 9RU, UK

Printed in the United States of America
British Library Cataloging in Publication Information Available

Library of Congress Control Number: 2005927668
ISBN 0-7618-3246-7 (paperback : alk. ppr.)

∞™ The paper used in this publication meets the minimum requirements of American National Standard for Information Sciences—Permanence of Paper for Printed Library Materials, ANSI Z39.48—1992

Contents

Foreword v

1 Making Sense of Group Rights 1
Ishtiaq Ahmed

2 Group-Specific Rights as Political Practice 35
Ulf Mörkenstam

3 The Muslim Presence in Sweden 60
Jan Hjärpe

4 Group-Rights Theory Meets Balkan Secessionism 76
Kjell Engelbrekt

5 Crisis in the Identity Politics of Turkey 101
Sahin Alpay

6 Kabyles in History and the Crisis of Contemporary Algeria 129
Inga Brandell

7 Democracy, Religion and Minority Rights in Nigeria 149
Jibrin Ibrahim

8 Hindu Nationalism and the Quest for a Uniform Civil Code 169
Henrik Berglund

9 The Politics of Group Rights in India and Pakistan 189
Ishtiaq Ahmed

Index 215

Foreword

This book originates in a conference called by the Politics of Development Group at Stockholm University (PODSU) on 21–22 September 2001. The aim of the conference was to discuss the challenges to the post-World War II human-rights regime from cultural relativism, multiculturalism and claims to communal separatism and special group rights.

The general assumption underlying the founding of the United Nations, and the Universal Declaration of Human Rights, was that economic development, joined to liberal democracy and respect for individual human rights, would result in a friendlier, fairer and more peaceful world. At the beginning of the 21st century, however, this optimism no longer seemed warranted. The world was unmistakeably more restive, and the nation-state model appeared to be waning under the impact of globalization, both in the industrialized North and the more volatile South. Just before our conference opened, the terrorist attacks of 11 September took place in the USA. One need not emphasize that such a traumatic event added further urgency to our desire to examine how tensions between culture, religious convictions and the need for identity would affect an increasingly heterogeneous world.

After our initial discussions in Stockholm in 2001 it was decided that we ponder the idea of group rights in greater depth. In the process the writing and editing of our essays took longer than foreseen. Peter Lomas was drafted in last autumn to help expedite the process and has rendered invaluable assistance to the project.

The book which we have now brought to fruition examines, in different political, geographical and cultural contexts, the politics of group rights in relation to the overall question of democracy, the survival of the state and the integrity and rights of the individual. Pervading all the essays is an awareness that there is no reason to abandon a commitment to individual human rights. Group-based rights can, however, be justified as a way to combat historical disadvantage and to enable vulnerable ethnic and cultural minorities to assert their claims as citizens to a share of political power within the recognized borders of states. Some of the concrete manifestations of this process, together with their theoretical underpinnings, are explored here.

I would like to take this opportunity to thank PODSU for the generous grant it gave for the initial conference in 2001 and for covering the subsequent expenditures on the way to preparing the manuscript for publication. PODSU receives its funding from the Swedish International Development Cooperation Agency (SIDA).

Magnus Lembke helped me greatly in successfully arranging the 2001 conference in Stockholm, and the Department of Political Science at Stockholm University has as usual stood solidly behind the latest PODSU venture.

Ishtiaq Ahmed

Sollentuna, 24 February 2005

Chapter One

Making Sense of Group Rights

Ishtiaq Ahmed

The notion of groups as repositories of privileges, or conversely burdened with duties, depending on their place in society, is older than the idea of individuals as autonomous bearers of rights. Both secular and religious legal systems in, for example, ancient and medieval Europe and Asia were premised on the naturalness of the community, with hierarchy within it being taken for granted.

The citizen of the Greek city-states was without exception male, and a member of a small, closed group, which alone provided political leadership and partook in the making of laws and public decisions. Women simply were not citizens, just as they were treated as inferior by Christian, Islamic and Hindu law. Another key feature of ancient and medieval social order was the institution of slavery, including under Hinduism, where casteless people were treated as virtually sub-human. Classical slavery is now almost extinct, though stigmatized groups like some indigenous peoples are often held in forms of bonded labor. In South Asia today, most of the people tied down by this oppressive practice belong to the untouchable castes and tribal peoples whose forebears were conquered by the Aryan tribes and later by Muslims (Ahmed 2002a: 2).

In contrast with these traditional practices, equality is a defining feature of modern political ethics. It is associated with the rise and growth of democracy and universal citizenship. At least from the time of the French Revolution, disenfranchized sections of the population—women, poor and uneducated individuals, non-Christian minorities—began to demand equal civil and political rights. In the face of their protracted petitioning and agitation, the democratic process was gradually expanded, and after the Second World War, universal democracy and inclusive citizenship were given recognition in formal international agreements. In practice, however, discriminatory laws continued to apply, the most notorious being those which upheld racial segregation in some southern states of the USA.

It is now increasingly recognized that ethnic and religious minorities, indigenous peoples, stigmatized or disadvantaged ethnic groups (used here to include religious, cultural, sectarian and other such ascriptive groups), and women, should enjoy equal political rights with members of the majority population. Alongside this process, the idea of cultural heterogeneity within the bounds of law and public order is gaining widespread acceptance. A politics of identity is at work within, and to some extent in competition with, the application and assertion of liberal notions of equal citizenship rights. Constitutional and legal changes have been introduced to reflect such developments. In actual terms, however, such provisions apply in a rather small portion of the world, the Western industrialized societies, where they are sometimes called 'models of differentiated citizenship'.

Closely related to differentiated citizenship is the generic concept of multiculturalism, which roughly means equality of all cultures and the need to enshrine that principle in law and social practice. Some Western states which contain several historically-distinct cultural groups have adopted consociational models of democracy. Such models combine the devolution of powers within a federal framework with communal autonomy deriving from denominational and linguistic differences. The Netherlands, Belgium and Switzerland are cases in point. The Dutch political system, while firmly upholding individual human rights and universal citizenship, has traditionally been organized around the so-called Catholic, Protestant and secular 'pillars' of separate institutions like political parties, trade unions, schools, and even media and leisure-time organizations. This arrangement was premised on the idea of mutual communal tolerance or 'live and let live'. In the past few decades, secularization processes have weakened the old arrangements; the pillars have been crumbling as religious affiliation has weakened. Trade unions merged, for example, and newspapers discontinued the practice of telling readers whom they should vote for. At the same time, Jewish and Islamic organizations benefited from the idea of 'pillarization' and they too established schools and other communal institutions.

Such arrangements have been presented as extensions of human rights—complementing, rather than contradicting, political gains on the individual level. They have not, however, been without complications. Some principles of law and procedure may appear to conflict, and if they are applied in the same territorial domain can lead to tensions and, indeed, real injustices.

ISLAMIC EXCEPTIONALISM AND WESTERN RESPONSES

A prominent recent example of this is the series of claims to communal autonomy made by some Muslim organizations in Western Europe since the late 1960s. Many of these have centred on the application of Islamic law, or *sharia*, to their family or personal matters. In 1975, for example, Sheikh Syed Darsh, the head cleric of the Regent's Park Mosque in London, said:

> [Muslims] firmly believe that the British society, with its rich experience of different cultures and ways of life, especially the Islamic way of life which they used to see in India, Malaysia, Nigeria and so many other nations of Islamic orientation, together with their respect for personal and communal freedom, will enable the Muslim migrants to realize their entity within the freedom of British society. When we request the host society to recognize our point of view we are appealing to a tradition of justice and equity well established in this country. The scope of [Islamic] family law is not wide and does not contradict, in essence, the law here in this country. Both aim at the fulfillment of justice and happiness of the members of the family. Still, there are certain Islamic points which, with understanding and the spirit of accommodation, would not go so far as to create difficulties in the judiciary system (quoted in Nielsen 1993: 1–2).

Sheikh Darsh's argument in favor of communal autonomy needs to be understood in terms of the traditional Islamic *dhimmi* system sanctioned in the Qur'an. Islamic jurisprudence defines the *dhimmi* as non-Muslims recognized by the Qur'an as 'People of the Book' (that is, Jews, Christians and a now-extinct group called the Sabaeans; Shia Islamic law recognizes even Zoroastrians as People of the Book).

The *dhimmi* system recognized non-Muslims as legitimate residents in Islamic societies if they paid the protection tax, *jizya*, for which they were exempted from military service. They were allowed to practice their religion and maintain business and commerce and own property. They were not included among the political community, although they could make a representation to the state about their specific religious and other interests. Political power remained in the hands of Muslims. Some pragmatic Muslim jurists in the very beginning of the Islamic expansion into India applied the jurisprudential principle of *qiyas*, or analogy, to Hindus and recognized them too as believers in the true God (Naqvi 1995: 45). This decision remained controversial in the eyes of dogmatic experts of Islamic law since they considered Hindus as polytheists, but most of the time Muslim rulers preferred to follow the interpretation of the pragmatic scholars, and some even waived the *jizya* tax.

The *dhimmi* system was further developed by the Ottoman Empire as the *millet* system (Faruki 1971: 81). The Ottomans classified not only Muslims but also Jews and different Christian churches as *millets*, or nations. Thus there was the Muslim nation, from which the ruling class was derived, and the Greek, Armenian, Jewish and other *millets* which enjoyed substantive communal autonomy. Such a system, however, did not recognize the secular individual human rights emerging in the West. In particular, non-Muslims could not convert Muslims to their faith.

Thus, contrary to Sheikh Darsh's assertions, any autonomy based on 'Islamic points' of family law seems destined to cause serious legal, philosophical-theoretical and political problems with prevailing Western notions of justice and equality. Among these are matters of marriage, divorce and inheritance. *Sharia* allows a Muslim male, for example, to be married simultaneously to up to four wives, while it does not allow any Muslim, male or female, to marry a polytheist or an atheist; and a Muslim man may marry a Jewish or Christian woman, but a Muslim woman cannot marry a non-Muslim man. Moreover, under Islamic law inheritance favors male descendants; the rule is that female children inherit one-half of the shares of male children. Children born out of wedlock are disinherited. Children of a deceased son are excluded from inheriting property from their grandfather; it is distributed instead among the deceased's siblings. Further examples could be given (Doi 1984: 289–91).

Thus, it is quite clear that *sharia* laws pertaining to family matters differ radically from Western family-law systems. Moreover, serious procedural questions arise with regard to the practical application of *sharia*. Who would be competent to interpret and enforce it in respect of family law? Could non-Muslim judges do so, or should the state set up separate courts with Muslim judges to try disputed cases? Even more intractable would be problems stemming from mixed marriages. Additionally, there is a distinct possibility that some Muslims may prefer to seek redress from the mainstream legal system, or worse still that the conflicting parties may appeal to the two different legal systems. Who should decide then which court is appropriate for a Muslim? The complications are legion, for *sharia* provisions are underpinned by values which identify divine revelation and community as superior to reason and the individual, and this view conflicts directly with the Western trend over the last two centuries towards growing secularism and individual rights in the legal-social order. Nor, incidentally, is *sharia* applied universally to family and inheritance matters in the Muslim world: in Turkey, for instance, and the former Soviet republics of Central Asia it is completely absent from the legal system (Ahmed 2002b: 32).

With the liberalization of naturalization procedures, post-Second World War South-to-North migration has been in the millions. Religious freedom, one should note, is now granted in all Western democracies. In general, Western governments have responded sympathetically to immigrant communities seeking to establish places of worship and cultural organizations for themselves. However, the assumption has been that in the event of conflict or dispute, fundamental national law, based on secular principles, will apply to both civil and criminal matters no matter what the religious affiliation of the parties.

The possibility, therefore, that the Ontario provincial government in Canada may allow civil disputes to be settled in special *sharia* courts has triggered a lively debate in the country, not least among Muslims. Such a possibility arises out of the 1991 Arbitration Act in Ontario, which permits any citizen of Ontario to offer his services as a private arbiter, and there are indeed many other individuals (of many religious faiths) offering their services in this way since 1991, including several Muslims. For example Canadian Jews have been taking their disputes to rabbinical courts to settle them according to Jewish law. The problem is that some conservative Muslim organizations have been campaigning for the application of *sharia* (Jiménez 2003) to other sectors of life, claiming they enjoy the support of the estimated 1m Canadian Muslims. Such moves have been opposed from sizeable sections of the Muslim community; especially women's organizations and intellectuals have been vocal. They have stressed that in the face of social pressures and actual physical threats, Muslim women will not dare to refuse the application of *sharia* in family disputes; it will thus reinforce the traditional subordination of women (Hurst 2004). However, such speculation has been partly dispelled by the Boyd Report (2004), which was set up to see what amendments should be made to the 1991 Arbitration Act to make it more difficult for people to set up private arbitration services.

It is interesting to note that the European Court of Human Rights in Strasbourg gave a ruling on 29 June 2004 (*Case of Leyla Sahin v. Turkey*) that state-run Turkish educational institutions which banned Muslim headscarves did not violate their students' freedom of religion. The decision came following an appeal by a Turkish student who was barred from attending Istanbul University's medical school because her headscarf violated the official dress code. The ban on headscarves in Turkey applies only to students in educational institutions and to state employees. The headscarf is worn widely in the countryside and also by older women in traditional families. The worldwide Islamic revival of recent years, however, has helped to cause a lively debate in Turkish politics, with Islamists and conservative Muslim parties supporting the right to wear the headscarf in all places and the secularists, comprising social democrats, modern-educated Turks, the military and left-leaning intellectuals, remaining steadfast in supporting the existing ban.

In their unanimous judgment, the seven judges of the ECHR noted that wearing the Islamic headscarf to school and university was a relatively recent phenomenon in Turkey. They held that headscarf bans were appropriate when issued to protect the secular nature of the state, especially against extremist demands; and further that the principle of secularism in Turkey was undoubtedly one of the fundamental principles of the state, which was in harmony with the rule of law and respect for human rights. The judges added: 'The court does not lose sight of the fact that there are extremist political movements in Turkey which seek to impose on society as a whole their religious symbols and conception of a society founded on religious precepts' (sec. 109). Bans issued in the name of the separation of church and state could, in the judges' view, be considered necessary in a democratic society; and in consequence, 'measures taken in universities to prevent certain fundamentalist religious movements from pressuring students who do not practice the religion in question or those belonging to another religion can be justified' (*ibid.*).

The decisions of the European Court of Human Rights take precedence over national court rulings and will have implications for similar cases elsewhere in Europe. Earlier the French government imposed a ban on headscarves in state high schools, which came into effect during autumn 2004. In the Swedish city of Gothenburg two Somali girls came to attend college during the autumn term of 2004, completely covered from head to foot, with their faces concealed. Teachers objected that it was impossible for them to know who was behind that strange dress. In response, the Swedish government has chosen a compromise, leaving it up to the head teacher of a school to decide whether a form of dress obstructs normal educational activities (and to ban it, if he or she so inclines). In Germany, Muslim teachers have appealed against provincial laws in several *länder* which bar Muslim women from covering their heads. In all such cases it seems that governments in the respective member-states of the Council of Europe will establish a clear policy barring headscarves.

The varying responses in the West to these demands for Islamic exceptionalism are indicative of considerable disagreement over the implications of multiculturalism and the scope and limits to which it can be practiced in democracies. It is therefore necessary that the notion of a politics of identity, or what some others describe as the politics of recognition, be carefully analyzed against the overall background of societal peace and order. Particularly after the terrorist attacks of September 11, 2001 in the United States, the large Muslim minorities in Western Europe and North America have become objects of suspicion and fear. At the same time, some Muslim clerics have been preaching *jihad* or violent struggle to their congregations. Cases of female circumcisions being illegally carried out by some African Muslims have been reported from different parts of Western Europe. Such a practice has no basis in Islamic law; it was prevalent among some sub-Saharan African tribes long before they converted to Islam. Moreover, it has survived among both Muslim and Christian tribes, but the media usually presents such incidents as proof of Islamic barbarism. Under the circumstances any concessions to Muslim cultural and legal separateness is likely to heighten tension between Muslims and the majority communities in which they live. Indeed, in several otherwise liberal and tolerant countries such as France, the Netherlands, Denmark and Norway, there has been a rise in support for anti-foreigner and anti-Muslim parties.

THE BROADER PICTURE

Before the Second World War, the lives of ethnic and religious minorities in the West were usually socially and culturally segregated from mainstream society, and such segregation was underlined by patently-discriminatory laws. Even today, immigrant communities in general almost always belong to the underclass and are culturally on the periphery of society. It is therefore also important that Western democracies continue to seek to integrate and assimilate immigrants into the main political process. Otherwise, instead of a pluralist society of equal citizens and a tolerant, open democracy, a society with deeply-rooted economic, social and cultural cleavages may begin to take shape.

Moreover, regimes which are committed to an ethnic or organic conception of the nation simply exclude individuals or groups from the category of equal citizen on the basis of their religion, sect, colour, ethnic origin or gender. Until 1999 Germany drew a distinction between ethnic Germans and others for the purposes of citizenship. Ethnic Germans (for example, from parts of the former Soviet Union) could seek it as a birthright, while non-German residents of long standing (for example, of Turkish origin) were granted citizenship only on a very restrictive basis. These restrictions, however, have now been eased. In Israel, the so-called Law of Return qualifies Jews from any part of the world to come and settle in the country, but Palestinians who fled their homes and villages on the territory of Israel during 1948 and thereafter are virtually denied re-entry (Ahmed 1997: 162).

In the developing world, many societies are deeply divided, discrimination in law and practice is widespread and a strict social hierarchy is entrenched by the force of tradition. Theocratic Islamic regimes, like those in power today in Saudi Arabia, Iran and the Sudan, include only Muslims in the nation although nominal representation can be granted to non-Muslims in parliament, as is the case in Iran (Ahmed 1994: 43–44). Even in states which are claimed to be Islamic democracies, such as Pakistan, discriminatory laws are maintained against non-Muslims. In the case of Saudi Arabia only native Saudis normally acquire citizenship. In Muslim society in general, moreover, women are subjected to multiple forms of discrimination.

In all societies that employ discriminatory criteria for citizenship, the policy of differentiated citizenship is simply a means of lending dubious legitimacy to unequal treatment under the law, whereas minorities routinely expect inclusion in the general category of citizens. The question of group rights, therefore, has added complexity there.

Historically the worst treatment has been meted out to defeated peoples by invaders and conquerors. In this connection the liquidation through war and disease of the indigenous populations in much of the Americas is especially noteworthy. In those countries where the indigenous inhabitants have survived in substantial numbers, they are systematically denied political influence and robbed of what they regard as their ancestral lands, while a small ruling class dominated by the descendants of Europeans controls the levers of power (Sieder 2002). Elsewhere they are practically confined to so-called reservations as in the USA. In Africa the legacy of European conquests, the slave trade and other iniquities survived until recently in the form of racist white regimes in South Africa and Rhodesia. Similarly, in the rigidly hierarchical and oppressive social structures of India, derived from notions of caste, ethnicity and race, the stigmatized castes and ethnic groups find little relief in formal human rights; special group rights, therefore, have been given them under the constitution. Unsurprisingly, perhaps, these provisions are resented by many in the upper castes. But the Indian example at least illustrates the political feasibility of formally asserting group rights—the necessary condition being that the subordinate sections of society benefit demonstrably from them.

Even in nominally-liberal Western societies, there are anomalies which lead directly to injustice for certain groups. Under the federal dispensation of the USA, for example, the death penalty is statutory in some states of the Union but not in others. Years of research, moreover, on the use of the death penalty in that country have shown its application to be at the expense of ethnic and racial minorities.

In the world as whole, then, the concept of differentiated citizenship needs to be approached with care. Issues of rights and citizenship in general should be analyzed in the light of practices within particular states. As yet, there is nothing approaching a system of global citizenship. Many people, in the characteristic manner of the natural-law school, come close to it by ascribing a universal character to liberal-democratic concepts of human rights, but in everyday terms the freedom to interpret and apply rights is restricted to the governments of states.

Cross-border migration, including from South to North, provides an illustration of this. Most international borders are jealously guarded through routine patrols and checkpoints. These provide the most effective means of preventing the admission of unwanted aliens or ensuring their expulsion. Such individuals, nominally citizens in their own countries, may be members of oppressed political groupings or ethnic minorities, victims of sovereign state power unjustly applied; for the governments of states enjoy considerable freedom too in dealing with internal challenges and conflicts. It is only when massive human-rights violations take place that significant outsiders feel compelled to act, but actual intervention in the internal affairs of states remains a rare response, for 'domestic jurisdiction' remains a sacrosanct principle of international relations.

Despite all these discouragements, states have come under pressure, in recent years, from self-defined groups—in two political directions. One of these is the time-honoured route of breakaway and secession, which has led since the end of the Cold War to an independent East Timor and an independent Eritrea, as well as some unrecognized statelets like Somaliland. Centralized state governments tend, for a variety of reasons, not only to resist such pressures but to claim legitimacy for doing so, and by the invocation of domestic jurisdiction and the preservation of order, both internal and international, they often succeed.

The other political direction is followed by groups seeking to remain within existing state entities but to assert their particular rights there. Worldwide, we can note two sub-categories within this tendency. The first concerns groups that have suffered historical disadvantage and injustice. Among them the indigenous peoples' movement has been using world-wide co-ordination in international fora such as the United Nations to make their voices heard. Such a strategy is quite helpful in offsetting the disadvantage most of them suffer because of their small numbers within the confines of particular states. The indigenous peoples are demanding greater respect for their cultures and history and effective control over the natural resources in their traditional habitats (Minde 1995: 9–25). In 1995 the UN Commission on Human Rights set up a Working Group, comprising governments and organizations representing indigenous peoples, to produce a Draft Declaration on the Rights of Indigenous Peoples within the timeframe of the International Decade of the World's Indigenous Peoples, due to end in 2004. A similar but more widespread movement is that of disadvantaged minorities seeking greater access to universal citizenship rights as well as special cultural space to practice their own peculiar traditions and customs (Phillips and Rosas 1997).

The second category contains movements which base themselves on idealized versions of high cultures deriving from major world religions. They call into question the legitimacy of universal norms and standards prescribed by the UN-based treaties and conventions concerning human rights of individuals and groups, and instead seek to promote 'culturally-authentic' models of rights. Currently, worldwide revivalist movements are to be found among the adherents of Islam, Hinduism, Buddhism, Judaism and Christianity (Marty and Appleby 1993). In political terms, their main concern is to propound the alternative rights and obligations of their members based on scriptural texts and religious authority. Such movements, especially where they form a real or perceived majority, are manifestly hostile to religious minorities and to ideas of minority rights. It is perhaps not unusual that they seek to repress minorities through constitutional and legal devices, though it is not without paradox either, in the context of the modern, culturally-neutral or secular model of the state which is perceived to play a central role in supranational bodies and their legal frameworks, and to that extent in international relations in general.

Western modernity, as the pace-setter of change over the past two centuries, may be said to be partly responsible for the contradictions and conflicts in the contemporary world, between the power inherent in states and the development and general spread of a human-rights culture. 'Globalization', especially since the fall of the Berlin Wall in 1989 and the disintegration of the Soviet bloc, may have made this leading role even more pronounced. Globalization denotes a sense of increased interconnectedness, immediacy and simultaneity in the way things happen in the world. In this context one may note that the Internet has been an invention of particular use to historically-disadvantaged groups, generally the most powerless and marginalized sections of any population. They have begun to communicate and network world-wide through the UN, as well as with other solidarity movements and non-governmental organizations militating for the rights of women, minorities and indigenous peoples. The Untouchables of South Asia, the diverse assortment of indigenous peoples such as the Adivasis of South Asia, the Sami people of Scandinavian countries, Australian aborigines, and indeed the descendants of pre-Columbian natives of the Americas, suffer from long-standing historical disadvantage. Closely following such stigmatized groups are those dispersed at all levels of mainstream society but socially and culturally considered inferior. Women belong to that category in almost all traditional 'high cultures'. A group which almost universally suffers from persecution is that of gays. For such groups, globalization furnishes an opportunity to connect with world-wide solidarity and gain the assistance and protection of UN agencies.

While some observers see globalization as the definitive triumph of capitalism and individualistic liberal values, others warn that the pervasive influence of the West may actually decline, and that in order to preserve world peace and stability it would be wise to let non-Western cultural and belief-systems develop freely and independently of the West, notably in their apparent preference for group rights over individual ones (Huntington 1998: 183–206). I shall examine below whether universalism necessarily implies, under all circumstances, individual rights and thus a negation of group rights.

EUROPEAN MODERNITY AND THE RIGHTS OF INDIVIDUALS AND GROUPS

The philosophical origins of the modern notion of rights can be traced to the twin intellectual movements of the European Enlightenment and Romanticism. From the former descends the legacy of individual rights. The Enlightenment, notwithstanding its various strands and contradictory offshoots, sought to supplant the Christian paradigm with the Cartesian one of abstract universalism, derived from the assumption that the rational mind had the ability to reach correct conclusions through critical analysis of all issues. In principle this meant that all matters were to be subjected to questioning, and received or conventional wisdom was not to be accepted as authoritative. Thus, nothing was beyond the scope of suspicion and thorough scrutiny (Popkin and Stroll 1995: 232–239; Toulmin 1990: 107–117). Immanuel Kant added reciprocal equality in human dealings through his notion of the categorical imperative, which meant primarily that all individuals were entitled to respect as a duty and not as a tactic or calculation (Popkin and Stroll 1995: 41–47).

The social-contract philosophers—Hobbes, Locke and Rousseau—portrayed the state as the creation of free individuals who wished to preserve interests that were threatened in the so-called state of nature. Typically, the ends which the state was supposed to protect were safety and security of the human person (according to Hobbes), liberty and property (Locke), or emancipation from superior authority through direct democracy (Rousseau). Thenceforth, the individual in the role of a citizen was presumed to be at the centre of the political community.

It was, however, the French Revolution in 1789 which in a dramatic manner ushered in the era of citizenship. Hitherto, despite the expansion of trade and commerce, the old feudal order remained the principal edifice on which social structure and political authority were raised. The peasant and various categories of poor urban workers and petty artisans were considered subjects with obligations towards the superior tiers of society. The king and the nobility extorted many tithes and taxes, thus creating an oppressive and exploitative way of life. The Revolution did away with the duty-bound subject and created instead the rights-bearing citizen. True, women were excluded from the category of citizens, but for men, at least, citizenship was a liberating legal transformation. The French Revolution furnished a new model of nationhood—one based on the rights of citizens but limited within the territorial boundaries of the state (Hobsbawm 1990: 18–21). In an ideal sense, this can be described as the civic model of nationalism because citizens were the ideological centrepiece of the free French nation.

Still, the repercussions of the French Revolution were not entirely positive for the growth of citizenship and the equal rights of individuals. The reign of terror let loose by the Jacobins made a mockery of rights and citizenship, and in a curious manner the French Revolution became the stepping-stone for a policy of expansionism by Napoleon, who sought to spread the rationalism of the European Enlightenment, especially French philosophy and science, to the whole of Europe, and even embarked on a naval adventure to Egypt with the same mission in 1798. In Western Europe, the Napoleonic wars caused considerable suffering and bloodshed. The German peoples were particularly fearful of losing their cultural identity. In reaction, several variants of cultural and ethnic nationalism deriving from Romantic roots cropped up in Europe. In the place of the abstract citizen, the Romantic thinkers emphasized language and ethnicity as the basis of social solidarity and nationalism. Individuals bound together by language and blood were conceived as one nation irrespective of whether they lived together in one state. Such ideas of organic unity, however, were not understood as any reason for the abolition of 'natural' divisions of sex, religion and region within the cultural nation (Hutchinson 1994: 122).

The early Romantics, such as Herder, argued that all cultural nations should be treated as equals and accorded separate states. Later, right-wing parties gave birth to aggressive nationalist movements and some acquired patently racist overtones. Consequently the roots of the Italian fascist and German Nazi parties are traceable to the Romantic mind-set of the nineteenth century. In general the cultural ethno-nationalists, both moderates and extremists, spoke of a pristine past and/or lost homeland, for whose revival they longed. By the beginning of the 19th century much of Western Europe had been reorganized into so-called nation-states, based either on the French or German model or often a vague, eclectic combination of both. Not surprisingly, citizenship deriving from ethnic and cultural nationalism was invariably based on discriminatory criteria, which comes into conflict today with the individualistic universal citizenship upheld by the United Nations.

Majoritarian Nationalism and Minority Rights

The creation of so-called nation-states was primarily a triumph of the majoritarian principle. A process of recognizing minority rights, mainly dealing with religious freedom, had begun as early as the Peace of Augsburg in 1555, and was given greater recognition in the Peace of Westphalia in 1648. It continued to be mentioned in all European treaties leading to the Congress of Vienna (1815). However, the relevant clauses were not enforced with a view to creating political equality; rather, rulers treated them as means of limiting religious strife (Krasner and Froats 1998: 231–235).

This policy left minorities vulnerable to discrimination and persecution in some places. Thus, between 1815 and 1914, conflicts involving minorities were widespread in all parts of Europe but particularly in the central and eastern regions (*ibid.*: 236–239). On the one hand, the liberal and socialist thought of those times was generally supportive of the right of large nations to independence, while deriding as divisive and reactionary the demands of petty ethnic groups to separate states. The general assumption was that these groups should seek assimilation into the larger nations (Hobsbawm 1990: 31–32). On the other hand, the prevailing balance-of-power doctrine of the times enabled the governments of big powers to justify interference in the affairs of weaker ones and of empires, ostensibly in the interest of minorities. Typically the minority-rights idea was manipulated by several European regimes to invade Ottoman territories in defence of Christians (Krasner and Froats 1998: 236–239). Ironically the recognition of the principle of sovereign nation-states in Europe did not prevent Europeans from pursuing the most lawless colonial expansion in Asia and Africa. The infamous ‘Scramble for Africa’, formalized by the European powers in 1884–85 at the Conference of Berlin, gave free reign to expansionism in that continent within agreed spheres of influence. The First World War was indeed a manifestation of competing ambitions for global empire on the part of Western powers.

The Treaty of Versailles and the League of Nations gave recognition to the right of self-determination of peoples and nations, as advocated by President Woodrow Wilson and the Soviet leader Lenin, albeit with differences of emphasis: the former wanted it applied to central and eastern Europe while the latter wanted to employ it in opposition to colonialism in Asia and Africa. It was the Wilsonian emphasis which received practical application during the inter-war period, and empires in central and eastern Europe either ceased to exist or were drastically reduced. Such dramatic changes did not affect the British, French and other empires in Africa and Asia. However, the establishment of new states in central and eastern Europe and the reorganization of boundaries still left ethnic and religious minorities in exposed situations.

Under the Versailles settlement after the First World War, President Wilson insisted upon minorities being given protection. This resulted in new polities and required those whose borders had been altered to sign minority-rights treaties or to make unilateral pledges with regard to minority rights. The Versailles arrangements provided for monitoring and enforcement of the treaties and declarations through the League of Nations and the International Court of Justice (*ibid.*: 239–43). The League, however, was never able to develop effective instruments to enforce compliance. For instance, when a country renounced its obligations to its minorities, there was little the international community could do but protest. It was such weaknesses that Adolf Hitler exploited to justify aggression, first against Czechoslovakia, and then against Poland in 1939, under the pretext of acting on behalf of the German minorities in those countries, which he claimed were being ill-treated. The result was the outbreak of the Second World War, which wreaked havoc with all notions of communal harmony and peaceful co-existence of nations and peoples.

The Individualistic Post-War Perspective on Human Rights

The Second World War was a watershed in the evolution of international perspectives on human rights. The new standpoint rested on individualistic assumptions, though the most appalling aspect of the war had been the demonization and annihilation of minorities such as Jews and Roma (commonly known by the derogatory name of Gypsies).

The Slavic peoples had also been subjected to genocidal aggression, and their losses in absolute numbers were greater than those of the target minorities of the Nazis. It was in these circumstances that the United Nations Organization was established in 1945, as its founding Charter asserted, to save the world from the scourge of another world war and establish a framework for lasting peace. Among the preconditions considered necessary for maintaining the peace was respect for human rights. Thus Articles 1:3 and 55 of the Charter obliged all member-states to respect human rights. On this, the UN clearly and explicitly adopted an individualistic perspective. The reason seems to have been that minority rights had been abused in the past to justify aggression and invasion against weaker states by powerful ones. Consequently the doctrine of state sovereignty was raised to a higher, universal level. Thus, Article 2:7 of the UN Charter legally placed all states, big and small, on a par with each other and declared interference in their domestic spheres illegal under international law. Exceptions were situations threatening world peace and massive human-rights violations such as genocide. In most other matters, states were assured of sovereign power over their territories.

An elaborate statement on human rights followed in the Universal Declaration of Human Rights of 1948. It referred to civil, political, social, economic and cultural rights which individuals were to enjoy. The Declaration was a compromise document agreed mainly by the new great powers of the post-World War period, the USA and the USSR. Such typical liberal rights as freedom of expression, belief, religion, association, marriage, and participation in the political process were adequately covered. Among the social and economic rights were included the right to work, adequate wages for labor, the right to form trade unions and to negotiate over working conditions. Thus, the right to establish trade unions was a collective right but the working class was not seen as a social or cultural group as such. The general thrust was undeniably to establish a framework of human rights based on the individual.

The Declaration also made clear that in order to enjoy rights, individuals had to render duties and obligations to the state. On the whole, the UN approach prescribed a liberal/welfare-oriented state based on the rule of law, an open civil society, elected government in the domestic sphere and peaceful and friendly relations in the regional and international spheres. Article 1:2 of the UN Charter referred to the right of self-determination of peoples and nations, although it was not clearly spelled out how this principle was to apply to the clauses that explicitly referred to colonial and mandate territories (Ahmed 1998: 9–10). The post-war decolonization which began in Asia and continued into the mid-1970s was invariably invoked as a fulfillment of the right of self-determination by freedom movements and was welcomed in the UN bodies.

In brief, one can assert that the UN recognized the territorial nation-state, primarily fashioned on the French civic model of nationhood and nationalism, as the organizing unit of the international system. Consequently, the biases of conventional political science and international law implied that the permanently-domiciled population of a state constituted its nation —that is, a body of citizens who could legally claim equal rights and freedoms. Economic development and modernization were expected to do away with the remnants of parochial loyalty and narrowly-defined group solidarity and create, instead, a cohesive nation sharing an overriding interest in the preservation of the state. Within such a general model of citizenship, federal states allow for some variation in law and practice. Thus some constituent states in the USA apply capital punishment, while others do not. Similarly, abortion was considered a right in some states but not in others until 1973, when the landmark Supreme Court ruling *Roe v. Wade* legalized abortion across the USA. Yet despite some discrepancies, the overall liberal ideology of the United States does not allow matters of national security to be decided by the will of the member-states of the Union.

Such a prerogative is enshrined in the US Constitution and the power to uphold it is vested in the Federal Government.

The United Nations, Regional Human-Rights Regimes and Group Rights

Although the UDHR adopted an individualistic approach on human rights, it would be quite wrong to infer from this that group rights have not been considered legitimate bases for rights. In the UN Charter as well as in the two main treaties on human rights, the UN Covenants on Civil and Political Rights and on Economic, Social and Cultural Rights (1966), the right of self-determination for peoples is mentioned. Although it is not clearly stated, the general interpretation of this right is that it applies to people living under colonial and mandate systems. Other major instruments relating to group rights adopted by the General Assembly of the United Nations are the United Nations Convention on the Prevention and Punishment of the Crime of Genocide (1951); the International Convention on Elimination of All Forms of Racial Discrimination (1969); the International Convention on the Suppression of the Crime of Apartheid (1973); the Convention on the Elimination of All Forms of Discrimination Against Women (1979); the Convention on the Rights of the Child (1989); and the Declaration on the Elimination of all Forms of Intolerance and Discrimination Based on Religion and Belief (1995).

It should be noted that insofar as rights of cultural groups are concerned, a cautious line has been adopted. In general, member-state governments have been reluctant to agree to such rights, on the grounds that they can be subversive of the unity and integrity of the state. Moreover, there are strict republican traditions that are most hostile to the recognition of cultural minorities: those of France and Turkey are cases in point. They incline towards an assimilatory model of universal citizenship (although pressure has been growing of late for a liberalization of minority policies in these two countries and changes are under way). It should be noted that minorities have some recognition in the national constitutions of most states, but each state retains its own historical-ideological way of defining and recognizing minorities. Consequently progress on minority rights (as group rights) has, overall, been slow and cautious.

On 18 December 1992 the Declaration on the Rights of Persons Belonging to National or Ethnic, Religious and Linguistic Minorities was finally adopted by the General Assembly of the United Nations. Certain of the clauses read as follows.

> Article 1:1: States shall protect the existence and the national or ethnic, cultural, religious and linguistic identity of minorities within their respective territories, and shall encourage conditions for the promotion of that identity.

> Article 2:1: Persons belonging to national or ethnic, religious and linguistic minorities . . . have the right to enjoy their own culture, to profess their own religion, and to use their own language, in private and in public, freely and without interference or any form of discrimination.

An important qualification is introduced in Article 4:2:

> States shall take measures to create favorable conditions to enable persons belonging to minorities to express their characteristics and to develop their culture, language, religion, traditions and customs, except where specific practices are in violation of national law and contrary to international standards (emphasis added).

Another qualification, or at least a complication, is added in Article 8:2:

> The exercise of rights set forth in this Declaration shall not prejudice the enjoyment of all persons of universally recognized human rights and fundamental freedoms.

And Article 8:4 further cautions:

> Nothing in this Declaration may be construed as permitting any activity contrary to the purposes and principles of the United Nations, including sovereign equality, territorial integrity and political independence of States.

A declaration is the weakest form of agreement in the UN system, because it is not binding. Moreover, the bias in favor of the integrity and sovereignty of states is retained, and there is no recognition of any right to secede. Although minorities are accorded certain cultural and economic rights, it is 'persons' who are recognized as the claimants of these rights in their individual capacities, rather than minorities in their own (group) right. What one can easily discern is that minorities are to be enabled to retain their cultural distinctiveness, and to that extent, forced assimilation is delegitimized. Further development towards a proper convention or treaty has, however, been slow because many regimes consider the recognition of minority rights subversive. The most advanced international instrument is the Framework Convention for the Protection of National Minorities adopted by the Council of Europe on 1 February 1995. This follows the practice of recognizing 'persons' belonging to minorities, rather than the minorities themselves, as the bearers of rights;

but at least the member states are obliged to undertake necessary measures to ensure that minorities are enabled substantially to enjoy their cultural rights as well as being full and equal participatory citizens.

The African Charter on Human and Peoples' Rights (1986) differs from the other regional human rights systems such as the European Convention on Human Rights (1950) and the American Convention on Human Rights (1969), in that it explicitly includes peoples' rights. The liberal approach of mentioning the individual as bearer of rights is maintained but historical tradition and the values of African culture and civilization are invoked to assert that the individual has duties towards his family, parents and indeed community and nation. One can therefore notice a vague notion of group rights modifying the apparently liberal language of the African Charter.

CONTEMPORARY PERSPECTIVES ON GROUP RIGHTS

In terms of political theory, the individualistic standpoint on rights has received the most sophisticated and persuasive justification in the work of John Rawls (1971), who argued that although all individuals were egoists they were also intuitively and rationally attuned to recognize that justice means fairness. Therefore the purpose of the just polity is to ensure that two principles underlie its procedures and practices of dealing fairly with individual citizens: a principle of equal basic rights and liberties and a principle of economic justice. The latter principle required that the least-advantaged should benefit most from any change in the structure of distributive justice with regard to economic rewards and benefits. Thus, while preferring egalitarianism to the reigning utilitarian notions of rights, Rawls remained steadfastly loyal to mainstream political liberalism based on an individualistic and egoistic conception of human nature.

Those who are critical of the individualistic standpoint on rights allege that the ideal of a liberal democracy that respects the human rights of all individuals, maintains a universal, inclusive and non-discriminatory citizenship, and metes out justice fairly according to objective laws, rules and procedures, is a norm applicable only to Western cultural milieux. Some feminists go further, criticizing the liberal approach for expressing the biases of majoritarian, white, male, middle-class persons. Some of these theorists emphasize difference rather than similarity between the sexes and demand special rights for women (Baumeister 2000: 24–30).

This change in emphasis as to who should be entitled to rights, and on what basis, is partly reflective of the new modes of political assertion emerging in different parts of the world. Ethnic, or ethno-cultural, groups are increasingly asserting their demands in cultural terms and lacing them with cultural imagery and jargon. Identity (in the sense of feelings of mutual affection and solidarity, an uncritical or blind submission to sacred texts, and a general adulation for inherited culture and tradition), rather than interest (rational claims arrived at through critical analysis and argument), is the hallmark of the new politics. Writing in the context of the diversity resulting from immigration into the West from Asia and Africa, Bhiku Parekh (2000) argues in favor of a politics of recognition. This would assert that, while human beings share some basic dispositions, desires and capacities, they are simultaneously shaped by geography and the specific historical epoch into which they are born, together with the relationships that typically occur in those specific circumstances. Consequently, human beings are both natural and cultural beings, sharing a common human identity but in culturally-mediated environments. In contrast to the monist view of human nature which assumes universal rationalism as its distinguishing feature, Parekh argues in favor of including the formative role of culture in a theory of cultural rights. On this view, the claims of human beings should combine both universal and culturally-specific sets of rights.

Yet a question arises here: how can the tensions and conflicts that are bound to occur in a multicultural society be managed within a democratic polity? John Rex (1996: 29) identifies, among other characteristics, several essentials of a multicultural society.

1. A multicultural society should distinguish between, on the one hand, the public domain in which a single culture, deriving from the notion of equality between individuals, should prevail and, on the other, the private domain, which permits diversity between various groups.
2. The public domain should include the world of law, politics and economics. It should include education in so far as it is concerned with the inculcation, selection and transmission of skills and the sustenance of civic culture.
3. Moral education, primary socialization and the teaching of religious beliefs should belong to the private domain.

Rex admits that conflicting ideas about what belongs to the public and what to the private sphere can create considerable tension and even conflict in multicultural societies, but argues that such problems can be overcome through discussion and negotiation. He does not consider a properly-functioning multicultural society to have emerged anywhere yet and admits that the entire idea might fail.

In opposition to such reasoning, liberals have classically objected to rights being conferred on groups at the expense of individualistic, universal rights.

They argue that not all cultures are in agreement on what constitutes fundamental civic values and rights. Consequently, group rights could result in exceptions and exemptions from the universal category of citizens and lead to discriminatory and arbitrary rules and procedures being tolerated or even promoted by the state. They have also called into question the basic conceptualization of culture, and the group constituted around it, as an undifferentiated whole. Within cultures, tensions and conflicting interpretations exist on social and moral issues, and large stable groups almost invariably contain a social hierarchy. Consequently, tensions and conflicts of interest occur between classes and at the individual level (Baumeister 2000; Gutmann 1993: 173–206). Moreover, groups armed with superior rights over their individual members in the shape of oppressive rules and traditions can threaten them in different ways, up to and including the use of physical violence. For these reasons liberals have tended to argue that participation in group activities should be voluntary and confined to the private sphere, while within the private sphere individuals can associate with one another on the basis of religious belief or cultural traditions and practices.

The recognition of certain collective rights is compatible with this approach —such as the right to collective bargaining of wages, or to secure work conditions, which trade unions generally advocate on behalf of their members. These rights-claims are based on rational self-interest and not something as vague and subjective as cultural identity. North American liberals have also accepted, on similar lines, ideas of affirmative action or positive discrimination enshrined in temporary measures to rectify historically-derived disadvantages.

The Communitarian Critique of Neo-Liberalism, and Liberal Responses

During the 1970s and 1980s, aggressive theories of the free market advocated by neo-liberal or libertarian thinkers demanded that democracy be hedged about by legal and constitutional guarantees ensuring an inalienable individual right to private property. Such ideas gained great influence in the corridors of power through political leaders such as Margaret Thatcher and Ronald Reagan. Thereafter began the world-wide onslaught on the welfare state. Its devastating consequences have been reported from many parts of the Third World, but even in the successful industrialized countries of the West the social cost of unbridled egotism was considerable.

One response emanating from North America, associated with communitarian thinkers, was to stress the primacy of the community, calling into question the premise of abstract individualism—atomized, calculating and self-centred—which allegedly underpinned neo-liberal theories. According to the communitarians, the methodology of studying individual behaviour in terms of an unfettered and unconcerned actor, prioritizing his/her self-interest and ignoring the general social good, was flawed. The correct way to understand human behaviour was to study human beings in their social attachments constituted by communal, cultural and historical contexts.

In normative terms, communitarian theory found the notion of a selfish individual morally unsatisfactory because it militated against the need for a genuine community of caring members and legitimized an unjust distribution of goods in society. Also, the idea that equality of opportunity through the abolition of discriminatory laws created 'a level playing-field' for individual members of society was described as unconvincing. Furthermore, it was objected that 'unencumbered individualism' failed to explain why individuals were willing to fight for the defence of the state or fulfill related societal obligations (Tam 1998: 1–30). Communitarians have argued in favor of a more differentiated but inclusive citizenship and for negotiated power-sharing solutions to inter-group relations. The main thrust of their reasoning is that the love and affection which individuals need are possible only through the membership of groups; therefore education, work and the protection of individuals is best realized through the efforts of communities (Tam 1998; Etzioni 1998).

Despite the efforts of some communitarian writers, it is by no means self-evident that promoting social solidarity within given communities is as distinct or innovatory a philosophy as they would like us to believe, or even that this necessarily represents a critique of internationalism or universalism, as opposed to being, at worst, simply parochial or mildly conservative. Much depends on the context. In such a large and heterogeneous society as the United States communitarianism has aspects simultaneously of liberalism, emphasis on difference and nation-building. This is expressed in the work of Michael Walzer in his discussion of an American welfare state (Walzer 1983: 84–94).

Will Kymlicka's Theory of Group Rights

The Canadian philosopher Will Kymlicka takes on these paradoxes directly, asserting that the current communitarian critique is premised on a misconception of liberal thought. Classical liberal thinkers, most notably John Stuart Mill, in his view, envisaged the freedom (and, by implication, equality) of the individual as a possibility only within a cultural community (Kymlicka 1995: 49–57). However, contemporary societies are multicultural. Modern liberal-democratic societies have been successful in separating religion and state, but not ethnicity and state. Consequently, unequal power relations between the dominant ethnic majority and the various minorities are a fact.

Therefore, according to Kymlicka, individuals belonging to minority cultures need the support of their groups in order to feel secure and free and to function properly as citizens. Liberals should be willing to provide resources and legal and structural support for the maintenance of cultural identities. Such a policy would entail, on the one hand, ethnic representation at decision-making levels and, on the other, provision of support for the sustenance of minority languages and their religious and aesthetic values. In the case of national minorities, i.e., those groups who were conquered, with their land and resources taken from them, by a colonial, now-dominant majority, not only ethnic representation and support for their cultural identity should be envisaged but also the restoration of substantial control over their land and resources. The only restriction permissible on group rights in a democratic society is one that concerns illiberal cultures and the practices associated with them. Under no circumstance should groups be allowed to oppress their members, and members should have the freedom to opt out of their groups (*ibid.*: 131–172).

It is worth emphasizing that both Kymlicka and the communitarians theorize against the backdrop of liberal notions of tolerance and accommodation achieved through dialogue based on values and rules shared by all groups. Such a civic culture, however, may not be well-established in many non-Western parts of the world. Moreover, while pursuing a basically normative line of argument, Kymlicka makes concessions to realist biases. For example, on the one hand he asserts that nations organized in states have a right to restrict the entry of outsiders. Therefore the system of border controls is legitimate (he refers to a general consensus prevailing in favor of such a system). On the other hand, he thinks that the right to opt out by members of a nation-state should be absolute, so that a group of people aspiring to secede should have the possibility of doing so even if this means the territorial diminution of the original undivided state. He urges liberals to accept such a demand on a principled basis. Surely the case he has in mind is the movement for secession among the French Quebecois. Granting such a demand may not be very difficult in the rather secure and stable North American environment, but in many other parts of the world the claim to secession in the name of national self-determination is likely to be treated as anathema by central state authorities.

There are other problems with some of Kymlicka's theoretical premises. He believes that Western societies have successfully separated religion and state, but separating ethnicity and state has not occurred and cannot occur. This is a peculiar formulation insofar as ethnicity is a blanket term, covering not simply racial-cultural but also religious and other groups. In practice, following Kymlicka's approach, group divisions will be considered politically-meaningful *a priori* in any given situation, and only empirically will one be able to determine which specific 'ethnic' difference is relevant for the approval of particular group rights. Certainly, if religion is no longer relevant in Western democracies, while group differences based on appearance and/or 'culture' are still prevalent one has to look for solutions in this somewhat arbitrary way.

It is, however, debatable whether a separation between religion and state has been achieved in all Western societies. Trends in north America, especially in the USA, point to the continuing relevance of religion in politics. Especially since George W. Bush became President in 2000, and the terrorist attacks of 11 September 2001, the Christian Right has become a very important factor in US elections. The re-election of Mr Bush in 2004 was attributed by some commentators to this factor.

Therefore it is doubtful whether the socio-political relevance of religion can be dismissed so lightly as regards Western countries. In the case of many Third World societies, and most certainly in South Asia, one cannot proceed from such an assumption at all. Religion and culture deriving from religious myths and beliefs pervade group consciousness in South Asia and are at the bottom of many current conflicts, in which massive violence is involved. In such situations, religious or culture-based identity politics can prove to be particularly resistant to civic culture-based values and rules regulating group rights in the polity. Majoritarian versions of religious nationalism in particular can prove to be inimical to equal rights and universal citizenship.

Unlike in Western societies, where cultural heterogeneity has increased significantly only since the Second World War when immigration from Asian and African countries was allowed, South Asia has a long record of cultural and ethnic diversity. Consequently, the politics of identity in the contemporary era are complicated by group tensions and conflicts deriving primarily from differences in religious culture. Right-wing Hindu nationalists in India, for example, have demanded an unambiguously-privileged position for Hindu culture and identity within the state. Thus, the 'differentiated' group rights they support simply mean unequal rights for other groups than their own. Although the Hindu nationalist party, the BJP, was defeated in 2004 and the secularly-oriented Congress Party has been returned to power, sectarian movements within the nominally-secular Indian polity are far from new. We should not forget that Gandhi's assassin was not from another ethno-cultural group, but a Hindu extremist.

There are of course moderate academic versions of cultural authenticity as well, which aspire to anchor intercommunal understanding and accommodation within the historical traditions of South Asia. For example, the Indian scholar Ashis Nandy asserts that all efforts to transcend the politics of faith and culture in South Asia are futile. In reality the modern-educated ruling elite groomed in rationalism or Marxist radicalism has always compromised on secularism in order to retain power and influence. Therefore, he prescribes a model of governance which seeks to incorporate the reality of faiths and cultures into formulae of negotiated power, resource-sharing and communal understanding. Such an approach would ostensibly lead to more authentic and durable solutions to the infinite variety of faiths, sects, castes and ethnic groupings in South Asia (Nandy 1999: 135–66).

The more secular-minded academics writing in India tend to stress the need to maintain the identity of universal citizenship at a higher level than membership in cultural groups. However, they accept that minority rights are needed to augment the general rights of citizens. Neera Chandhoke argues that four universal individual-based rights should always be respected: the right to life, the right to equality, the right to freedom, and the right to assert rights. These rights all people should have, she says, 'even when they are in the minority'. The second type consists of those 'that people have only because they are members of a certain minority group', that is, they concern people's need to preserve their identity.

Minority rights, according to Chandhoke, include two kinds of rights. 'Forbearance' rights should include protection from hostile propaganda, from interference by outsiders in communication between group members, from threats to their existence and from subjection to alien culture. 'Positive' rights oblige the state to undertake positive measures to support the effort of groups to maintain their culture. However, Chandhoke also acknowledges the need to prevent culture groups from truncating the freedom and equality of their own members in the furtherance of group identity (Chandhoke 1999: 288–290).

In Pakistan and Bangladesh, regrettably, there is no significant academic discussion of group rights. The fundamentalists would like to redefine all rights in the light of dogmatic Islamic law or *sharia*. This would mean replacing the Western idea of individual human rights with 'differential' rights deriving from religious affiliation and, moreover, limited by *sharia*. Against this, the Human Rights Commission of Pakistan has demanded the implementation of all UN conventions and treaties ratified by Pakistani governments hitherto.

The Left and Group Rights

From the Left, demands for exclusive group rights have generally been held in suspicion, but simultaneously prescriptions to the effect that a minority should abandon its religion in order to enjoy political rights have been derided. For example, Karl Marx opposed Bruno Bauer's idea that in order to gain equal political rights in Germany, the Jewish minority should renounce its religion and join the general struggle for a secular democratic state. Marx argued that political emancipation was not enough; human emancipation had to be achieved too, and that required an end to the system of capitalism and private property. These, he alleged, had become the 'religion' of bourgeois society, irrespective of the theology to which people nominally gave their allegiance (Marx 1978: 26–52).

Later socialists have continued to be critical of capitalism and wary of demands for exclusive cultural rights. However, they seem increasingly to have become reconciled to the welfare-state model of rights. Consequently they have generally supported a more comprehensive package of civil, political, social, economic, cultural and environmental rights for all citizens without exception. Eric Hobsbawm points out an irony in the contemporary left project. In practical terms, parties of the left attract, in addition to working-class people, oppressed minorities and other self-identifying and possibly partisan groups, such as feminists, environmentalists and homosexuals. In ideological terms, however, the Left project cannot be partisan or particularistic, but must apply to all:

> Let me state firmly what should not need restating. The political project of the Left is universalist: it is for all human beings. However we interpret the words, it isn't liberty for shareholders or blacks, but for everybody. It isn't equality for all members of the Garrick Club or the handicapped, but for everybody. It is not fraternity only for all old Etonians or gays, but for everybody. And identity politics is essentially not for everybody but for the members of a specific group only. This is perfectly evident in the case of ethnic or nationalist movements. Zionist Jewish nationalism, whether we sympathize with it or not, is exclusively about Jews, and hang—or rather bomb—the rest. All nationalisms are. The nationalist claim that they are for everybody is bogus (Hobsbawm 1997: 277–8).

TOWARDS AN EMANCIPATORY PERSPECTIVE ON GROUP RIGHTS

The question of individual or group rights in the contemporary period cannot be examined separately from the overall question of human rights. A person's ability to enjoy, individually or in association with others, freedom, equality, identity, protection and security is inseparable from the doctrines of human rights that prevail (even when imperfectly applied) in modern societies. At its most basic level, a concern with human rights derives from a normative conviction that an individual should not be a passive object who simply complies with the dictates of other entities. He/she should be able to enjoy a measure of autonomy so as to act as a subject who can exercise his/her preferences and discretion rationally in private and public matters. Within this context, group-rights policy is one major means of promoting a particular version of citizenship.

Equally, while some groups may seek greater rights under the aegis of states, others may seek an exit-route with a view to establishing a separate state. Usually a group of people describing itself as a nation invokes the right of self-determination and tries to wrestle its way to independence. Central governments almost invariably react by trying to prevent secession. International lawyers have pointed out the irony of this, in the wake of the universal cause of anti-colonialism which contributed so forcefully to founding our current intergovernmental institutions. Rosalyn Higgins succinctly puts it:

> International law provides no right of secession in the name of self-determination. At best, the people's right to self-determination connotes the right of all citizens to participate in the political process, but this gives power to majorities and not minorities (quoted in Robertson 2002: 160).

The 'true meaning' of self-determination, in Geoffrey Robertson's view, is 'a right conferred on peoples against their own governments'. He goes on:

> The reason why international law has made so little contribution to the reduction of ethnic strife is because of its positivist composition: it constructs its rules as a synthesis of what states in fact do, rather than by reference to what they should do according to principles of fairness and justice. This approach has denied to minorities all but the bare rights to exist and to maintain innocuous cultural differences (*ibid.*: 164).

On the other hand, it is perhaps not unreasonable to expect little of state governments in the direction of a general policy on group rights, which would inevitably have secessionist overtones. Hence it is with regard to citizenship within the confines of the state that a general perspective on group rights is examined here.

Hobsbawm's model is of a modern, democratic state that recognizes one major identity as legitimate and overriding all others—that of individual citizens, consisting of the whole, permanent and bona fide population of a country entitled to universal rights. This can be considered the developmental ideal that societies should strive for within the framework of territorial nation-states (although some theorists are already thinking beyond the state in terms of global citizenship). It can work well in societies which have achieved a fairly high level of economic development, practice substantial distributive justice and, most importantly, have achieved an egalitarian civic culture which is attuned to the fact of cultural diversity as a more or less normal situation. Very few societies have in fact achieved such a degree of pluralist cultural harmonization.

Fairly high levels of egalitarian socio-economic standards, alongside significant levels of cultural pluralism, are to be found almost entirely in the post-Second World War Western democracies. However, the presence of a permanent and growing immigrant population from non-Western societies, particularly from the Muslim world, is bringing into being a more complex and contested type of cultural pluralism. Therefore a consensus on general social and economic values may be in the process of erosion even in the West. In this situation, it seems all the more important that central governments uphold universal citizenship and equal rights and hold to an inclusive ethos. The current human rights were won by deprived and disenfranchized people through long-drawn-out mass struggles. It would be ironic and tragic if in the name of communal autonomy or dubious claims to recognition of identity asserted by Islamic or other religious organizations, men and women were to be deprived of rights which other citizens or permanent residents of Western societies enjoy.

Arend Lijphart (1977: 1–52), writing against the background of his native Netherlands, developed a model of consociational democracy as a possible solution to the risk of instability in societies marked by social, ethnic and political differences. His main recommendations are 1) a high degree of co-operation, up to and including a grand coalition, between the leaders of the different segments of society, to counteract separatist tendencies; 2) mutual veto, to give additional protection to minority interests; 3) proportional representation governing the allocation of political office, civil-service appointments and public funds; and 4) a high degree of autonomy for each segment to govern its own affairs.

Although such a model can be useful to offset a majoritarian monopoly over state power, and has worked well in the Netherlands and some other Western societies, it is not yet clear whether the same principle of representation in the political system will apply to immigrant minorities as a distinct, new group in society. These minorities comprise, after all, a great diversity of cultures and religious beliefs. As for Third World societies, consociational democracy can be useful there, but will work only if all groups share a strong sense of common nationhood. Otherwise it is likely to prove divisive in these highly-complex societies where religious conflicts, sectarian affiliations and regional loyalties abound. To objectify group identities as a basis of power-sharing can therefore prove to be counter-productive. Certainly, majoritarian indifference to minorities' cultural concerns can be perceived as a form of tyranny; but it would be wrong to go to the other extreme, and allow, for example, cultural distinctiveness to inhibit individuals' freedom to voluntarily join political parties.

In a general sense, therefore, though recognition of cultural distinctions is necessary to bolster minorities' self-esteem, choosing which aspects of culture need be recognized as worthy of support by the state is an empirical matter. Certain things which strictly belong to the religious or spiritual dimensions of a culture should arguably be granted, such as the right to slaughter animals for meat in accordance with Islamic and Jewish ritual requirements, preferably if agreement can be reached with Western societies' prevailing laws and norms proscribing unnnecessary pain to animals. Of course such an arrangement may still be unacceptable to animal-rights activists, but as long as animal slaughter is generally permitted it should be possible to do so in a socially-acceptable manner. This is in consonance with the general liberal approach to resolving conflicts that prevails in the Western democracies. On the other hand, issues related to marriage, inheritance, divorce and the like should be the same for all citizens and permanently domiciled aliens. Barbaric practices such as female circumcision, or using religious pulpits to incite hatred for people of other cultures, can under no circumstances be tolerated.

It is crucial therefore that a deeply-divided society is not allowed to develop and consolidate in Western democracies (even through the best of intentions). Some features of such a society do exist, however. Immigrants in general, particularly Muslims, in Western Europe belong to the economically weaker sections of society. Ted Gurr and Barbara Harff (1994: 65–75), for example, describe the Turks in Germany as an ethno-class that is at the bottom of the social stratification obtaining in that country. Additionally the Turks are culturally alienated from the mainstream. The situation elsewhere in Western Europe is similar.

In light of such a situation, we can argue that granting group rights to cultural and religious communities that sharpen social cleavages and cultural alienation may prove subversive of democracy. Although Western European states are strong, societies afflicted by economic and cultural cleavages can implode under stress and even lead to violent conflict. It is important that a vibrant and pluralist democracy of equal citizens of diverse cultural backgrounds does not practice forced assimilation or forced segregation, but it must simultaneously reject a minority's self-imposed isolation and insulation.

In any event, Third World societies are marked by persistent and pervasive cleavages deriving from racial, ethnic and religious differences, which are compounded by the fact of economic and political deprivation. In addition, oppressive cultural practices and symbols underline the inequalities between the different groups. Leo Kuper (1982: 57–83) describes such societies as plural and not pluralist societies. He asserts that the colonial encounter exacerbated divisions, and created a pathological type of political relationship, based on suspicion and hostility, among the various groups. This observation is most incisive: prior to the colonial intervention, indigenous societies had devised cultural and social practices that maintained both hierarchy and heterogeneity on a stable basis, but the colonial policy of divide-and-rule deliberately sought to exploit social cleavages and often resulted in greater alienation and estrangement between competing cultural or religious groups. Thus post-colonial plural societies are often riddled with recurring riots, and despite a formal constitutional bill of equal individual rights and other democratic values being incorporated into the political system, hegemonic groups in advantageous positions almost invariably retain their dominant position. This they do not only in the economic and political domains but also through cultural practices which reinforce their social pre-eminence in relation to subordinated cultural groups and religious and ethnic minorities, which then either suffer open discrimination and stigma or are generally held in low esteem. Individuals belonging to the latter groups clearly need to be assisted in becoming substantive, rather than simply nominal citizens. In such situations the question of identity carries ramifications across the whole spectrum of human rights because cultural affiliation affects not simply people's formal identity but also their ability to enjoy the normal civil, political, social and economic rights that are the entitlements of the mainstream, typical citizens of a state. In other words, policy inputs aiming at the inclusion of vulnerable groups into the nation through a wide range of legal and educational measures are needed to create a democratic and egalitarian order.

It can further be argued that in order to become active and confident individual citizens, individuals belonging to religious and ethnic minorities and depressed or stigmatized groups in plural societies need the support and protection of their groups to assert their rights in relation to the super-ordinate groups. The communitarians of the liberal societies of the West have a point in emphasizing the need for locating individuals in communities rather than as free-floating self-centred atoms. This becomes even more important for individuals who belong to oppressed cultural groups in cleavage-ridden plural societies of the Third World. However, unlike the communitarians, who wish to restrict the role of the state in the mediation of societal tensions, I would argue for a more active central-government intervention in the form of firm and explicit policy inputs to foster a culture of individual autonomy and respect. This is in my view a precondition for developing a strong civic culture of individual liberty and freedom, which nevertheless does not negate the principle of group rights for the vulnerable of any social or cultural definition.

Indeed both dominant and dominated groups need to be groomed into a culture respectful of all individuals, regardless of their origins.

Therefore democracy in the Third World requires a strong state committed to an active policy of democratization and promotion of egalitarian change. The formal description given to such a state is unimportant, but it must try to be secular and neutral in relation to the right to equal treatment of disparate groups constituting its permanent population. Civil society in general, and civil-society actors such as NGOs committed to human rights, women's rights and group rights of minorities and indigenous peoples can play a very important role in augmenting the state's efforts, but they cannot replace it in bringing about the dissolution of rigidly-hierarchical social structures and cultural mores. This will be achieved only through the state and the democratic elements of civil society co-operating and co-ordinating their activities in favor of democracy.

In the final analysis, therefore, it is only through an empirical investigation of concrete situations that one can determine whether, and if so to what extent, individual autonomy is enhanced or inhibited through rights being conferred on individuals or groups or both. In some situations only membership in a group allows an individual access to citizenship rights; in other situations group membership may restrict his/her freedom of choice. Consequently group rights conferred within a state can be justified only if they enhance an individual's autonomy. As a substitute for individual rights, group rights can prove to be a negation of the purpose of rights. Only as a complement to individual rights can they be considered appropriate and justified.

The fundamental premise, then, on which I wish to ground an emancipatory perspective on citizenship, comprising both individual and group rights, is that the dichotomization between individual and group rights is misplaced. Rather, the two need to be harmonized. In principle, some core fundamental rights should be non-discriminatory, universal and egalitarian and conferred on individuals. These should include the right to life, including such basic rights as food and shelter (Shue 1980); the right to freedom of conscience, belief and expression; to form trade unions and other institutions of collective bargaining; and to form political organizations and contest public office. However, special group-based affirmative action or positive discrimination may be needed to help cultural groups who stand no chance of taking advantage of formal equal opportunities. This applies not only to minorities but also to oppressed majorities. In some Latin American countries the native population is greater in number than the white ruling class which dominates all the organs of power; and where they are menaced, the culture, language, script and other aesthetic heritage of such groups may need to be given constitutional and legal protection, and recognized as a legitimate basis for claiming a reasonable share in political power. In other cases, particularly those of the indigenous Amazon peoples, one would need to confer special and exclusive rights, including to ancestral land. As Richard Falk has pointed out, this is the only conceivable way in which these defenceless peoples' desire *to exclude themselves* from modern polities can be respected, and their uniquely-valuable culture can be preserved (Falk 1988: 27–31).

As a general approach to rights, there is of course much to be said for Rawls' principle of altering existing laws and procedures to allow the least advantaged to benefit the most. The benefit, it should be stressed, results in both material and cultural terms. The policy of affirmative action in the USA is one such input to rectify historical disadvantages suffered by, for example, African-American and Hispanic groups. Similarly India's policy of reserving seats for the Dalits and aboriginal tribes in political representation and employment, and in admission to educational institutions, can be defended as a necessary group right because it helps alleviate the suffering of perhaps the most degraded group of human beings in history. This policy also has the potential to affect adversely the rights of more talented individuals from the upper castes, many of whom may also be poor, but for some time to come India will need to continue with affirmative action in order to achieve anything like an acceptable level of social and economic equality. One can in addition argue in favor of recognizing women in the Third World as an historically-disadvantaged group. With some minor exceptions, all historically-evolved cultures uphold male chauvinist traditions, but in the Third World there is very little awareness of the cultural roots of misogyny. A policy of reservations should therefore be introduced in favor of women in poor developing countries, both in parliament and in other government-service employment. Similarly, the right to religious freedom of religious minorities and deviant sects needs to be given special attention in the democratization processes of Third World states.

CONCLUSION

In conclusion, one can say that whatever the policy chosen to realize a balanced individual and group-based political culture, the fundamental aim of all such inputs should be to bring about the emancipation of individuals and groups from all fetters of exploitation and oppression, cultural as well as structural. As Kymlicka correctly points out, illiberal tendencies within disadvantaged groups can prove to be oppressive to individual members who may not in fact subscribe to outmoded traditions and customs within their own nominal group. Many minority religious sects, which otherwise suffer persecution at the hands of majority sects, are themselves inclined to be extremely intolerant of internal dissent, and penalize their own members, especially those who attempt to leave. Thus the recognition and categorization of groups qualifying for special rights should take into account the need to uphold the basic civil and political rights of individuals and groups recognized by the UN, and also incorporate the main features on group rights presented in the 1992 Declaration on the Rights of Persons Belonging to National or Ethnic, Religious and Linguistic Minorities. In recognizing the principle of group rights, governments must under all circumstances uphold standards of social justice which, on the one hand, aim at integrating citizens into a common category of universal rights-bearers and, on the other, acknowledge cultural diversity and the need to accommodate it through constitutional safeguards and specific policies.

REFERENCES

Ahmed, I. (1994). 'Western and Muslim perceptions of universal human rights'. *Afrika Focus* 10, no. 1–2.

—— (1997). 'Exit, voice, citizenship' in Hammar *et al*. eds.

—— (1998). *State, Nation and Ethnicity in Contemporary South Asia*. London and New York: Pinter.

—— (2002a). 'Indigenous peoples of South Asia'. *Daily Times* (Lahore), 22 December.

—— (2002b). 'Communal autonomy and the application of Islamic law'. *ISIM Newsletter* 10 (Leiden).

—— (2004). 'Turkish headscarves decision vindicated'. *Daily Times* (Lahore), 4 July.

Baumeister, A. T. (2000). *Liberalism and the 'Politics of Difference'*. Edinburgh: Edinburgh University Press.

Boyd, M. (2004). *Dispute Resolution in Family Law: Protecting Choice, Promoting Inclusion*.http://www.attorneygeneral.jus.gov.on.ca/english/about/pubs/boyd/. 29 March, 2005.

Brantenberg, T., J. Hansen and H. Minde eds. (1995). *Becoming Visible: Indigenous Politics and Self-Government.* Tromsø: University of Tromsø Centre for Sámi Studies.

Case of Leyla Sahin v. Turkey (2004). Application no. 44774/98, 29 June 2004. Strasbourg: European Court of Human Rights.

Chandhoke, N. (1999). *Beyond Secularism: The Rights of Religious Minorities*. New Delhi: Oxford University Press.

Crawford, J. ed. (1988). *The Rights of Peoples*. Oxford: Clarendon Press.

Doi, A. R. (1984). *Sharia: The Islamic Law*. London: Taha Publishers.

Etzioni, A. (1998). *The Essential Communitarian Reader*. New York/Oxford: Rowman & Littlefield.

Falk, R. (1988). 'A non-statist perspective: the rights of peoples (in particular indigenous peoples)' in Crawford ed.
Faruki, K. (1971). *The Evolution of Islamic Constitutional Theory and Practice.* Karachi: National Publishing House.
Gurr, T. R. and B. Harff (1994). *Ethnic Conflict in World Politics.* Boulder, Colo. and Oxford: Westview Press.
Gutmann, A. (1993). 'The challenge of multiculturalism in political ethics'. *Philosophy and Public Affairs* 22, No. 3.
Hammar, T., G. Brochmann, K. Tamas and T. Faist eds. (1997). *International Migration, Immobility and Development: Multidisciplinary Perspectives.* Oxford and New York: Berg.
Hobsbawm, E. (1990). *Nations and Nationalism since 1780.* Cambridge: Cambridge University Press.
—— (1997). 'The universalism of the Left' in Ishay ed.
Huntington, S. P. (1998). *The Clash of Civilizations and the Remaking of World Order.* London: Touchstone Books.
Hurst, L. (2004). 'Protest rises over Islamic law in Ontario'. *Ontario Star*, 8 June.
Hutchinson, J. (1994). 'Cultural nationalism and moral regeneration' in Hutchinson and Smith eds.
—— and A. D. Smith eds. (1994). *Nationalism.* Oxford/New York: Oxford University Press.
Ishay, M. R. ed. (1997). *The Human Rights Reader.* London/New York: Routledge.
Jiménez, M. (2003). 'Islamic law in civil disputes raises questions'. *Toronto Globe and Mail*, 11 December.
Krasner, S. D. and D. T. Froats (1998). 'Minority rights and the Wesphalian model' in Lee and Rothschild eds.
Kuper, L. (1982). *Genocide.* New Haven/London: Yale University Press.
Kymlicka, W. (1995). *Multicultural Citizenship: A Liberal Theory of Minority Rights.* Oxford: Clarendon Press.
Lee, D. A. and D. Rothchild eds. (1998). *The International Spread of Ethnic Conflict.* Princeton, NJ: Princeton University Press.
Lijphart, A. (1977). *Democracy in Plural Societies: A Comprehensive Exploration.* New Haven and London: Yale University Press.
Marshall, T. H. (1994). 'Citizenship and social class' in Turner and Hamilton eds.
Marty, M. E. and R. S. Appleby (1993). *Fundamentalisms and the State: Remaking Politics, Economics and Militancy.* Chicago: University of Chicago Press.
Marx, K. [1843]. 'On the Jewish Question' in Tucker ed.
Minde, H. (1995). 'The international movement of indigenous peoples: an historical perspective' in Brantenberg, Hansen and Minde eds.
Nandy, A. (1999). 'Coping with the politics of faiths and cultures: between secular state and ecumenical traditions in India' in Pfaff-Czarnecka *et al.* eds.
Naqvi, M. (1995) *Partition: The Real Story.* Delhi: Renaissance.
Nielsen, J. S. (1993) 'Emerging claims of Muslim populations in matters of family law in Europe'. University of Birmingham: CSIC Papers.

Pfaff-Czarnecka, J., D. Jajashingham-Senanayake, A. Nandy and E. T. Gomez eds. (1999). *Ethnic Futures: The State and Identity Politics in Asia*. New Delhi/Thousand Oaks/London: Sage Publications.

Phillips, A. and A. Rosas (1997). *Universal Minority Rights*. Turku/Åbo and London: Åbo Akademi University Institute for Human Rights.

Popkin, R. H. and A. Stroll (1995). *Philosophy Made Simple*. Oxford: Made Simple Books.

Rawls, J. (1971). *A Theory of Justice*. Cambridge, Mass.: Harvard University Press.

Rex, J. (1996). *Ethnic Minorities in the Modern Nation State: Working Papers in the Theory of Multi-Culturalism and Political Integration*. Basingstoke: Macmillan.

Robertson, G. (2002). *Crimes Against Humanity: The Struggle For Global Justice*. 2nd ed. London: Penguin.

Shue, H. (1980). *Basic Rights: Subsistence, Affluence and US Foreign Policy*. Princeton, N.J.: Princeton University Press.

Sieder, R. ed. (2002). *Multiculturalism in Latin America: Indigenous Rights, Diversity and Democracy*. New York: Palgrave Macmillan.

Tam, H. (1998). *Communitarianism: A New Agenda for Politics and Citizenship*. London: Routledge.

Toulmin, S. (1990). *Cosmopolis: The Hidden Agenda of Modernity*. Chicago: University of Chicago Press.

Tucker, R. C. ed. (1978). *The Marx-Engels Reader*. New York/London: W. W. Norton.

Turner, B. and P. Hamilton eds. (1994). *Citizenship: Critical Concepts, Vol. 2*. London: Routledge.

Walzer, M. (1983). *Spheres of Justice: A Defence of Pluralism and Equality*. Oxford: Martin Robertson.

Chapter Two

Group-Specific Rights as Political Practice

Ulf Mörkenstam

People who are sympathetic to minority rights and group-differentiated citizenship have reason to feel more than satisfied with recent theoretical developments. The question of minority rights has moved definitively to the forefront in political theory, where justice in terms of redistribution, impartiality and difference-blind principles no longer represents the only perspective or the prime focus of the debate. Indeed, it is not too far-fetched to claim that 'the defenders of minority rights have won the day', or at least that they have got rid of the burden of proof (Kymlicka 2001: 33). A similar development is discernible in political practice. Intellectual and political movements representing views and practices which differ from the dominant culture of the wider society have become, as Bhikhu Parekh argues, 'united in resisting the wider society's homogenizing and assimilationist thrust based on the belief that there is only one correct, true or normal way' to structure one's life (Parekh 2000: 1). In response to this struggle for recognition of identity and difference, better ways of accommodating cultural diversity have been sought in various countries, making this a major issue on governments' agenda and at the international level, as exemplified by the Council of Europe's Framework Convention on the Protection of National Minorities, and the European Charter for Regional or Minority Languages.

Yet despite these favorable developments, a severe tension persists between theory and practice. This turns, for instance, on the common critique of how to decide which groups are entitled to special rights, or to put it differently, on how to answer the charge that group-specific rights threaten the 'social glue' which holds citizens together (Barry 2001: 21). Furthermore, the focus on state-group relations tends to omit the effects of differentiated group rights on group-members themselves. Without attention to the relation between the group and the individuals within it, there is an obvious risk in some cases that such rights will reinforce 'some of the most hierarchical elements of a culture', leaving 'members of minority groups vulnerable to severe injustice within the group' (Shachar 2001: 3). In this chapter I will focus on another kind of tension between theory and practice, which appears due to the neglect of the constitutive character of politics. Though groups are the focus of the debate, constitutive ideas about them are almost absent. Collective identities appear as either timeless, or unaffected by historical change and political practice. This latter problem, which could be described as a major methodological flaw in theories of minority rights, is bound to have major implications for the normative debate.

In what follows, I distinguish three arguments in defence of minority rights, as part of my overall claim that group-specific rights as political practice have been inadequately examined in the contemporary theoretical debate. I then go on to analyze a specific case—Swedish Sami policy over more than a century—to show the importance of taking political practice into account. I argue that public policy actually constitutes collective identities (because group-specific rights are impossible to explain and justify without a distinct conception of the group itself), and that hierarchical power-relations are created and maintained in society through this process. Despite this critique, my discussion ends up with a defence of group-specific rights in which I try to take the constitutive character of politics seriously.

IN DEFENCE OF MINORITY RIGHTS

Today, the theoretical debate on minority rights hinges on a revaluation of the prospects for formulating a general will or interest in society, together with an acknowledgment that even the supposedly-neutral liberal state plays a role in confirming, constructing and indeed imposing national identity. As Will Kymlicka (1995: 108) puts it: 'Government decisions on languages, internal boundaries, public holidays, and state symbols unavoidably involve recognizing, accommodating, and supporting the needs and identities of particular ethnic and national groups. The state unavoidably promotes certain cultural identities, and thereby disadvantages others. Once we recognize this, we need to rethink the justice of minority-rights claims' (Kymlicka 1995: 108). On this view, culture is by no means to be treated comparably to religious belief, i.e. as a purely private affair, as opposed to a possible object of state action or support.

Yet this view has not eliminated theoretical arguments in favor of equal civil, political and social rights which tend to rule out rights-claims based on grounds of culture or the recognition of specific identities. Most commonly, opponents of minority rights take John Rawls' (1971, 1993) theory of justice as their starting-point. Rawls includes a mention of culture and identity, referring to 'natural' characteristics (culture, race and sex—seen by him as impossible to change by a person's own choice). On his view, if these affect a person's social position negatively in terms of equal concern and respect, justice demands compensation. However, Rawls leaves these characteristics aside, on the grounds that they make his principles of justice too complicated in practice. He adds that 'these inequalities are seldom, if ever, to the advantage of the less-favored, and therefore in a just society the smaller number of relevant positions should ordinarily suffice' (Rawls 1971: 99). From an individualistic standpoint, the equal political rights of citizens, equal opportunities, and the redistribution of basic social goods are held sufficient to protect minorities from possible injustice. This is the view expressed by, for instance, Susan Moller Okin (1999: 12) when she discusses the rights of women (as individuals) in male-dominated cultures claiming cultural rights:

> Suppose [. . .] that a culture endorses and facilitates the control of men over women in various ways [. . .] that there are fairly clear disparities in power between the sexes, such that the more powerful, male members are those who are generally in a position to determine and articulate the group's beliefs, practices, and interests. Under such conditions, group rights are potentially, and in many cases actually, antifeminist. They substantially limit the capacities of women and girls of that culture to live with human dignity equal to that of men and boys, and to live as freely-chosen lives as they can.

In my view, however, those who see minority rights-claims as excuses for repression in the name of culture miss one important point. Very few defenders of minority rights could be described as being outside a wider liberal framework, and they are surely committed to such ideals as the equal worth of all persons' interests, equal basic rights and liberties; in short, equal concern and respect for all persons. Hence the best way to understand this theoretical conflict is in terms of different interpretations of the abstract ideal of equality as specified by Rawls. Social goods like liberty, opportunities, income and wealth mean nothing without a social basis of self-respect—in Rawls' (1971: 440) words,

> a person's sense of his own value, his secure conviction that his conception of his good, his plan of life, is worth carrying out [. . .] Self-respect implies a confidence in one's ability, so far as it is within one's power, to fulfil one's intentions [. . .] Without it nothing may seem worth doing, or if some things have value for us, we lack the will to strive for them. All desire and activity becomes empty and vain, and we sink into apathy and cynicism. Therefore the parties

> [. . .] would wish to avoid at almost any cost the social conditions that undermine self-respect.

If the abstract ideal of equality inherently entails self-respect, it seems adequate to describe minority-groups' rights-claims, as Kymlicka does (2001: 23–32), as a defensive response to liberal nation-building. Self-respect is partly the cause and partly the outcome of a continuous struggle over values, where the goal is either to obtain the power to interpret a society's cultural and moral aims on its behalf, or at least to challenge its dominant norms and conceptions. Hence, the minority-rights debate is part of a fundamental struggle over the definition of politics as such. It is within this context that we can discern three distinct arguments—in my view, all within the liberal camp—in defence of minority rights: a 'liberal culturalist' one focusing on culture as a context of choice; a 'politics of recognition' focusing on identity; and a 'politics of difference' focusing on social power-relations.

Liberal Culturalism

The 'liberal culturalist' stand is developed most thoroughly by Kymlicka. According to him, self-respect in liberal democracies—a person's sense that his or her plan of life is worth carrying out—implies an independent choice of life-plan from various options provided by the societal culture in which people live; even more important, it is only within a culture that different options become meaningful (Kymlicka 1989: 162–204). The meaning of certain social practices, and belief in the value of these practices, directs people's choice. Without a cultural context, 'that is, a culture which provides its members with meaningful ways of life across the full range of human activities, including social, educational, religious, recreational, and economic life, encompassing both public and private spheres' (Kymlicka 1995: 76), the choice itself and individual autonomy become meaningless. Thus, the importance attached to a societal culture by 'liberal culturalists' is its function as context of choice—it enables and promotes individual freedom. Culture on this view has no value in itself, and specific values of importance to individuals have little or no normative significance. To protect specific values—a certain family structure, say, or religious practice—is to obstruct individuals' freedom and choice of life-plan.

This view of things, then, equates culture to a nation or a people sharing a language and/or specific territory. Cultural difference, which would justify special rights, is thus confined to two different minority groups—national minorities and ethnic groups—and the normative debate about minority rights is confined to cultural diversity and cultural rights (Kymlicka 1995: 10–19).

Ethnic groups differ conspicuously from national minorities, since they are not nations, and as constituted by immigrants they have no territorial belonging. The incorporation into a larger state has often been forced on national minorities, while cultural diversity in the case of ethnic groups arises from a voluntary choice on the part of individuals to leave their 'original' culture. Hence, in contrast to national minorities, ethnic groups cannot, according to Kymlicka, claim the right to live in 'their own' culture, i.e. self-government rights. They are expected to participate in and integrate into the dominant society and can legitimately demand the right to express their particularity without suffering discrimination, i.e. accommodation rights. Following this line of argument, the distinction between groups makes the moral legitimacy of different rights-claims dependent on the kind of group to which people belong, and different rights can legitimately be granted to different groups.

The Politics of Recognition

The 'liberal culturalist' conclusion that '[m]inority rights protect these cultural contexts of choice' (Kymlicka 2001: 47) is rather similar to the one reached by theorists emphasizing the importance of respect for identities. However, the normative argument for a 'politics of recognition' differs radically from the individualistic 'context-of-choice-argument', especially as put forward by Charles Taylor. He claims that the groundedness of individual identities is what makes moral and political choice possible: identities define what is important and what is not. The answer to the question: 'Who am I?' depends on where you stand and where you come from. It is the frame of horizon in which desire, taste, ideas and expectations are interpreted (Taylor 1989: 25–52). Since human identity is created dialogically, in response to others, dominant societal ideas and conceptions are important for individual identity-formation. Ideas and conceptions express values and constitute a moral framework:

> Frameworks provide the background, explicit or implicit, for our moral judgements, intuitions, or reactions [. . .] To articulate a framework is to explicate what makes sense of our moral responses. That is, when we try to spell out what it is that we presuppose when we judge that a certain form of life is truly worthwhile, or place our dignity in a certain achievement or status, or define our moral obligations in a certain manner, we find ourselves articulating inter alia what I have been calling here 'frameworks' (Taylor 1989: 26).

If a person's position, as defined by dominant ideas and conceptions, is marginal, then his or her identity will not be acknowledged, since these ideas and conceptions define the good in a way that he or she diverges from. Self-respect and self-esteem are bound up with respect for a person's culture. Hence, equal respect, equal opportunity and equality before the law need to be interpreted and defined in a culturally-sensitive manner. In this 'politics of recognition', the importance of a community's historical traditions and institutions, and the continuity of social practices, like a common language, are generally taken for granted, followed by the conclusion that minority rights which protect these traditions and institutions satisfy the need for recognition. Taylor expresses this view forcefully in his discussion of Quebec's constitutional status within Canada (Taylor 1994: 56–64). Within a culture or community, there are certain values that ought to be articulated as moral sources necessary for the formation of identities—and these values can be or are already defined within that same culture.

The Politics of Difference

In a similar vein, proponents of a 'politics of difference' focus on identities and dominant societal ideas and conceptions—but as institutional obstacles to self-development and autonomy. These limitations are interpreted as structural oppression, where social relations of power are expressed through collective identities that assign individuals a degree of agency. As Iris Young (1990: 41) puts it:

> Oppression in this sense is structural, rather than the result of a few people's choices or policies. Its causes are embedded in unquestioned norms, habits, and symbols, in the assumptions underlying institutional rules and the collective consequences of following those rules [. . .] In this extended structural sense oppression refers to the vast and deep injustices some groups suffer as a consequence of [the] often-unconscious assumptions and reactions of well-meaning people in ordinary interactions, media and cultural stereotypes, and structural features of bureaucratic hierarchies and market mechanisms—in short, the normal processes of everyday life.

Thus it is the systematic character of oppression in group-belonging, not the recognition of identities *per se*, that makes groups the primary focus of analysis. In fact, Young (2000: 87) describes 'identity politics' as potentially oppressive, entailing 'a logic of substance to conceptualize groups'. Within this logic a group 'is defined by a set of essential attributes that constitute its identity as a group.'

Young divides oppression into five categories: exploitation, marginalization, powerlessness, cultural imperialism and violence (1990: 48–74). The dominant societal conceptions are decisive in institutionalizing these different obstacles to self-respect, as they explain the prevailing political order and social relations among groups in terms of neutrality, necessity and impartiality. The first three categories of oppression are quite concrete, referring to relations of power caused by the social division of labor. Thus groups are constituted by the economic and material course of events. Oppression in terms of violence and cultural imperialism, on the other hand, presupposes a group membership based on the constitution of collective identities. For instance, group-related violence presupposes inequality between groups as to which experiences most to value within a society. Violence, thus, can be interpreted as a consequence of cultural imperialism structuring social relations, where the experiences of certain groups—like men in a patriarchal society, or whites in a racist one—are universalized as social norms. These groups dominate the formulation and interpretation of different societal conceptions, positing their position as neutral, i.e. as the general interest or will. In contrast, people who are exposed to cultural imperialism are constantly reminded of their group identity, singled out as deviant, and left with a limited capacity to influence dominant norms. A 'politics of difference' therefore implies equal opportunities of participation for social groups (Young 2000: 153). By means of group-specific rights, social relations of power may be challenged and dominant conceptions made transparent.

Although the normative starting-points differ in these arguments in defence of minority rights, the focus of the arguments is strikingly similar: in the context of liberal nation-building, collective identities and social relations matter. And in this defence, the authors all set out to answer three decisive questions:

(i) why should a certain group be treated differently from other citizens (i.e. have special rights)?
(ii) how should these groups be treated (i.e. through which measures)?
(iii) who should be treated differently (i.e. who can legitimately lay claims to certain rights)?

However, my brief reconstruction of the basic arguments also shows that *constitutive* ideas about groups are absent from the theoretical debate. Although group membership is considered important in the context of ensuring equal treatment for individuals, the notion of groups itself is insufficiently examined. Groups, in short, are taken for granted.

When the constitutive character of politics is neglected, three kinds of problem arise. First, the focus on culture and group-specific measures presupposes a definition of minority groups and their culture. Even though it is not too difficult to define a *societal* culture, it is quite a different thing to determine politically the 'authentic' culture of a specific minority group—the 'real' context of choice—without leaning on established definitions of that culture. Quite simply, minority politics are explained and justified by reference to a particular conception of the group, and simultaneously become partly responsible for its construction. Second, and as a direct consequence of this ahistorical perspective, minority politics tend to reify recognized and well-defined identities. Thus, non-recognized identities, which may on some views be part of that same culture, are not critically examined, and the possibility of the forced description of certain identities is overlooked. Third, heterogeneity within groups is overlooked. As Okin (1999: 12) puts it, defenders of minority rights 'tend to treat cultural groups as monoliths—to pay more attention to differences between and among groups than to differences within them'.

To correct the methodological flaw of current theories of minority rights, group-specific rights as institutionalized political practice must be taken seriously. A proper theory of minority rights must come to terms with political practice and the constitution of collective identities. This leads us to the question of how to understand the relationship between conceptions of the group and political practice. This analytical step, away from the purely-normative discussion, emphasises the importance of the public debate on minority issues, and the role of the state. The public construction of groups is decisive for answers to the questions: why? how? and for whom?

SOCIETAL CONCEPTIONS, POLITICAL PRACTICE AND GROUP-SPECIFIC RIGHTS

The sovereignty of the modern state is, according to Zygmunt Bauman (1991: 8), 'the power to define and to make definitions stick—everything that self-defines or eludes the power-assisted definition is subversive.' In his view, the state monopoly on violence outlined by, among others, Max Weber is not enough to maintain social and political order; instead, the ideas and conceptions that dominate in society are decisive in explaining and justifying that order. For a specific institutional order—like a system of group-specific rights—'to be taken for granted in its totality as a meaningful whole, it must be legitimated by "placement" in a symbolic universe. Other things being equal, however, this universe itself does not require further legitimation' (Berger and Luckmann 1991: 122).

Thus, an essential part of the process in which an institutional order and political actions gain legitimacy is the manner in which reality is depicted.

First, the prevailing political order is explained by reference to statements about reality. How the group is described is in this context crucial for the elaboration of public policy: for the problems formulated, for the suggested causes of the problems, and for how to address them. Second, political proposals are justified by giving 'practical circumstances' a normative value. For instance, self-determination for a minority group cannot be considered if its members are held to be incapable of handling their own affairs. Rather, this belief would justify a paternalistic and 'protective' policy. Knowledge of 'how things are' is therefore closely linked to 'how things ought to be' and 'what should be done'.

No less than in other policy-fields, public policy plays an important role in constituting legitimate conceptions of reality in minority issues. To quote Bauman again, it is the state that makes 'authoritative statements which arbitrate in controversies of opinions and which select those opinions which, having been selected, become correct and binding. The authority to arbitrate is in this case legitimized by superior (objective) knowledge' (1995: 4). A specific description of reality is officially authorized while others are rejected. The authorized description is institutionalized, either implicitly, underlying legislation, or explicitly expressed in law.

One way to understand how a conception of a minority group is institutionalized as a framework for political action is through the distinctions, categorizations and definitions by which reality is ordered. Linguistic distinctions are needed to determine what belongs to one field of politics and not to another, but are also important for the creation of categories that determine who is concerned by certain policies and why. Politics therefore necessarily classifies the surrounding world, creating sharp boundaries between insider/outsider, friend/enemy, us/them, and subject/object (Bauman 1991: 53–61). These boundaries can of course be a deliberate act in the political game to obtain political support, a symbolic struggle pursued 'by identifying as the enemy a group widely regarded as different and alien and therefore not sharing the human qualities of the people we know well' (Edelman 1975: 31). Nevertheless, these categorizations are most often not the result of conscious strategies, but primarily created when political actors try to solve concrete problems. When political action is explained and justified, distinct identities are constituted for the group concerned by each political issue. The state's power to define and to make the definitions stick by legislation results in a collective identity forced upon both individuals and the group.

In what follows, the relation between societal conceptions and minority rights, i.e. the consequences of the (necessary) constitution of collective identities in public debate, is illustrated by the case of Swedish Sami policy over more than a century. To quote one of the leading Swedish Sami politicians, Lars-Anders Baer (1982: 11), the Sami are an indigenous people living 'in their own land, Sámi-Aednan [Lapland]', yet also 'a people in four countries, the people and the land having been divided up over the course of history by the nations of Sweden, Norway, Finland and [Russia]. Despite this fact, we Sami consider ourselves one people and a cultural, linguistic, economic and political unit'. As citizens of four different countries, the Sami face different sets of legislation, and as a people they have both similar and different experiences of the dominant society's 'homogenizing and assimilationist thrust', as well as of policies striving to separate Sami from other members of society. It is quite common to distinguish Sami ethnicity by, for instance, attachment to language (there are several dialects, or languages), their traditional livelihoods according to their place of residence (foremost among these being reindeer herding and fishing), a common historical memory of an ancestral homeland and the traditional Sami religion. As a result, even the estimates of the Sami's numbers differ according to the sources used, and the way of defining who is a Sami differs between the four countries. The figures most often seen vary between 60,000 and 100,000 people, of which more than half reside in Norway. In Sweden the estimated number of Sami differs between 17,000 and 20,000 people.

My critique of the normative debate on minority rights has put public policy, such as official government reports and legislation, in focus. Consequently the political mobilization of the Sami, their resistance and struggle, is only noticeable in the margin, and the importance of the Sami struggle for political change is partly neglected. All such analytical approaches 'from above' run the risk of reifying a picture of the dominated group as mere objects in the hands of the dominating society, in contrast to their own struggle and experiences as autonomous political agents. However, I hope to counteract this marginalization of the group in the following analysis by my focus on how this marginalization has been explained and justified in public debate by the constitution of a specific Sami identity.

Swedish Sami Policy and the Constitution of a Sami Identity

The point of departure for my analysis of the institutional system of rights for the Swedish Sami people is the preparatory work of the first *Reindeer Grazing Act* of 1886 (Swedish Code of Statutes No. 38, 1886). This aimed mainly to regulate the relation between reindeer herders and the settled population, and was an attempt to separate spatially the different forms of activity pursued by each group. However, by this act common law was relinquished, to be replaced by special legislation, with immense consequences for the Sami, who irretrievably lost land ownership. By the same act, individual pasture rights were made into an exclusive communal right for Sami villages. The potential rights of the Sami as an indigenous people disappeared, and the prerequisites for Swedish Sami policy changed (see, for instance, Beach 1981; Korsmo 1992; Kvist 1992; Lewis 1998; Mörkenstam 2005; Sillanpää 1994).

The dominant view in Sweden at the end of the 19th century was that the interests of settled peoples and nomads necessarily came into conflict, ostensibly because of reindeer-herding practices, which failed to prevent the animals from damaging settlers' property. Thus, it was considered important to study how the Sami handled reindeer herding in order to highlight any 'bad' practices. With this formulation of the problem, the management of reindeer herding became a fundamental component in justifying differential treatment. Legislation was organized around a conception of the 'good' reindeer herder—in practice, the nomad. Reindeer herding could not, according to this approach, be successfully pursued to any greater extent, if the herder did not follow the reindeer on its wanderings. As a Royal Commission Report (1909: 18) put it, 'the herding of reindeer demands that the Lapp has a nomadic way of life'.

The dominant conception of Sami identity thus became evident, when the 'natural cause' of the 'underdeveloped' Sami culture was described in terms of civilization coming into conflict with reindeer herding. Civilization was claimed to be a worse enemy of the Sami than limited grazing areas. An official report on Sami schools is a typical example of this position. The school system needed to be reorganized, the argument went, partly as a consequence of the low quality of teaching, partly because the existing school contributed to 'weaning the Lapps' children away from the nomadic life and the herding of reindeer' (Royal Commission Report 1909: 17). The solution was to separate nomadic Sami children from other Sami, who were to be directed into the Swedish school system. Thus, Sami were nomads and should be treated differently by segregation, while others should be assimilated. Similarly, state expenditure for Sami education should only concern nomads, and 'other Lapps and Lappish children ought not to have other or greater demands than other Swedish citizens [. . .] only nomadic Lapps could make demands for support in their capacity as Lapp' (Government Bill No. 97 1913: 57).

In this way, as an unintended consequence of the regulation of reindeer herding, the Sami identity was simplified and narrowed down. Protection of the nomadic culture emerged as the sole and coherent foundation for Swedish Sami policy and for the Sami's different and, indeed, special treatment. Through this approach, the different and deviant was both constituted and given priority, and without this differentiation the grounds for special rights would fall away. The system of knowledge and belief that explained and justified a system of Sami rights could be visualized by a chain of analogies, as follows:

Sami—nomads—reindeer herders—good herding—nomadic culture—special rights (**segregation**)

The constitution of a collective Sami identity in the public debate, i.e. as the nomadic reindeer herder, explained and justified a narrow system of rights that focused on 'proper' reindeer herding—first and foremost, a specific Sami right to herd reindeer (as being '*the* Lappish occupation'), including a right to hunting, fishing and forestry on Crown land. Group-specific rights were legitimate if granted to nomads with the objective of solving conflicts with the settled population—thus ruling out a whole set of possible political options, like self-government or language rights. The possibility of formulating problems and questions based on other conceptions of Sami identity, for instance the living conditions of settled Sami, were also eliminated from public debate.

The necessary moment of classification in politics presupposes that a certain way of life—a specific identity—is emphasized or recognized, at the expense of other possible identities to which political priority may be given. In this context, non-nomads and non-reindeer-herders were excluded from the system of Sami rights. Furthermore, the chain of analogies pointed out that Sami identity was defined by way of the conception of the way of life of the Sami *man*. Reindeer herding was a male occupation and the herder was the yardstick for Sami identity and culture. Sami women were thereby made invisible, especially in legislation. Sami women and men were not granted equal legal status until the *Reindeer Farming Act* of 1971 (Swedish Code of Statutes No. 437, 1971: §1).

The Sami identity as thus constituted also established an opposition between being a Sami and being a Swede in terms of culture. It contained an explicitly-evaluative element and a comparison with the majority of citizens, who represented the societal norm. To the Sami identity 'unchangeable qualities' were attributed, such as the Sami 'nature', 'race' or 'culture', which defined the relationship between the Sami group and the dominant society in terms of the Sami's lesser value. The system of special rights thus segregated the Sami from the dominant society, to save them from being weaned from their traditional way of life, but at the same time excluded them from the national community. Thus a Sami stereotype was created and maintained, in a paternalistic policy which excluded them from mainstream political life. By establishing a specific conception of Sami identity, the state's policy acquired a built-in logic which influenced both the subsequent formulation of problems and the concrete measures taken to solve them.

The central problem in Swedish Sami politics in the 1920s was formulated as the need to regulate and limit the number of reindeer (Swedish Code of Statutes No. 895, 1919; Government Bill No. 201, 1919). One obvious solution, the argument went, was to limit the number of Sami with reindeer-herding rights, in order to restrict the application of the 'Lapp privilege', as it was now called (Parliamentary Commission of Inquiry No. 25 1927: 45). Enormous difficulties then arose in the legal definition of who could be granted these rights. The politically-constituted status of nomadic reindeer herder came into conflict with the effort to reduce the number of reindeer, since this reduction necessarily implied the view that the Sami group was not homogeneous. With Bauman (1991: 60), we can understand this in terms of the category 'stranger' emerging when those not part of the dominant societal conception of Sami identity could not be counted as (ordinary) Swedes: 'The stranger's unredeemable sin is [. . .] the incompatibility between his presence and other presences, fundamental to the world order: his simultaneous assault on several crucial oppositions instrumental in the incessant effort of ordering.' These strangers challenged the categorization that explained and justified special legislation, and the previous link between nomads and Sami rights was no longer self-explanatory. Consequently, new explanations and justifications for treating Sami differently from the majority population were needed.

To grant all Sami the right to herd reindeer, it was claimed, would be in opposition to public opinion. Thus, descent was ruled out as a criterion for granting Sami rights. Language as a criterion was also excluded, on the grounds that it was too broad; its application would not advance the chosen goal of limiting the number of reindeer. The implication was that it was most natural to exclude those whose parents had abandoned reindeer herding and chosen other occupations. As expressed in the *Reindeer Grazing Act* of 1928, the right to herd reindeer belonged to those of 'Lappish origin', if the father, mother or grandparents had been been reindeer herders by permanent occupation (Swedish Code of Statutes No. 309, 1928: §1). The discussion on the right to herd reindeer thus constituted two different categories of Sami in the public debate—herders and non-herders. This means, as far as public policy was concerned, that the question of who was considered a Sami was not the same as the question of whom to include in the system of special rights.

Decisive for making this distinction, and to explain and justify the exclusion of those who actually were defined as Sami, but still 'not quite', was the well-established notion of the 'true' Sami identity, represented more or less by the same chain of analogies we recognize from the previous period:

Sami—nomad—reindeer herder—good herding—nomadic culture—special rights (**segregation**)

The category of non-reindeer-herder was defined by what it was not, i.e. neither nomad nor Swede, and a chain of analogies was established based on negatives.

> Sami—non-reindeer-herder/non-settler—not-nomad/not-settled—bad reindeer herding/bad farming (**assimilation**)

Even if the *non*-reindeer-herders were now an explicit part of the debate for the first time, there were categories to explain and justify a rejection of their rights-claims. When the Sami difference was so obviously related to reindeer herding, group-specific rights were still not considered to have to reach beyond the Reindeer Grazing Acts. This 'category-split' (Ruong 1982: 181) implied, for instance, that the League of Nations programme for minority protection, where minorities should be given rights to keep their racial and national qualities and traditions, never became an important issue in the Swedish debate. The category of the non-reindeer-herder legitimized both the practice of excluding from the system of Sami rights those Sami not exercising this occupation, and the continued centrality of reindeer herding in the debate on group-specific rights. Furthermore, the category of the non-reindeer-herder confirmed the Sami's difference even beyond a nomadic way of life. Thus, the paramount distinction between Sami and Swedes was upheld and the Sami stereotype reified, which made a continued paternalistic and hierarchical policy possible.

During the first decades after the Second World War, this conception of the group was challenged by an apparent change in public policy as the socio-political context itself changed radically. Sweden had entered the modern era, the argument went, where intellectual enlightenment (including a new democratic outlook on minority groups) and technological advance had made traditional reindeer herding and, accordingly, traditional Sami policy obsolete. In addition, Sami Assembly meetings were institutionalized after the war and when the National Union of Swedish Sami (SSR) was constituted in 1950, the Sami had an organization—a 'pressure group', according to the Swedish state—that could represent Sami interests (see, for instance, Lantto 2000, 2003; Svensson 1976, 1997).

In the post-war era the main problem was formulated in terms of how reindeer herding, regarded as 'underdeveloped', could be rationalized in order to survive in competition with other occupations. Rationalization was considered necessary for survival, but hindered by 'a certain conservatism' on the part of the reindeer herders themselves, and 'the traditionalism that a peculiar occupation and way of life tend to bring' (Parliamentary Commission of Inquiry No. 16, 1968: 51). This traditionalism held back rationalization, and 'society' needed to intervene. Seen this way, reindeer herding appeared like any other economic activity, facing similar problems to any other occupation. Primarily, the solution was of course to reduce the number of people occupied in herding, and the individual Sami was basically seen as a labor-market problem. Hence, the rationalization of reindeer herding presupposed changed perceptions of Sami identity. The good reindeer herder was no longer considered to be the conscientious nomad, but rather one who was profitably employed (Parliamentary Commission of Inquiry No. 41, 1960: 78–81).

From a special-rights perspective, the 'normalization' of reindeer herders is troubling, because it could be taken to mean that the previous foundations for special rights had disappeared. Why, now, should the similar be treated differently? Parallel to the issue of rationalization, however, the minority position of the Sami was discussed. Sami culture became for the first time a separate issue in discussions of special legislation, and since culture as such, unlike reindeer herding, is not geographically limited, it can be shared by many—thus potentially challenging the existing system of rights. Still, the prerequisite for political measures in support of Sami culture was the existence of a coherent, 'normal' and 'true' culture, considered to be upheld by reindeer herders—the core of the culture. In statistical terms the herders were put forward as the norm, with non-herders as deviant and marginal. In accordance with this viewpoint it was the reindeer herders 'that should be built upon for measures supporting the Sami culture' (Parliamentary Commission of Inquiry No. 99, 1975: 131). Thereby, the question of culture as a challenge to traditional Swedish policy was undermined. Instead, this perspective actually strengthened the dominant conception of a necessary focus on economical and political support for reindeer herding, and reinforced the distinction between reindeer herders and other Sami.

From the perspective of group-specific rights, then, a new chain of analogies was constructed for the 'true' Sami identity:

> Reindeer herder—professional/businessman/profitability—Sami culture/language—special rights (**assimilated**)

Again, a corresponding chain of analogies in negative terms follows for those who are Sami, but not close to the 'true' identity. Quite clearly, hardly anything meriting special rights is encompassed in that conception:

> Non-reindeer-herder—Swedish way of life—marginal—non-Sami-speaking—no Sami culture (**Swede**)

Thus, despite a more democratic vocabulary, the 'rationalistic era' did not result in a revised system of special rights. Furthermore, the distinct boundary between Sami and Swedes was upheld when the traditional Sami way of life was considered to be obsolete and an actual obstacle to the Sami obtaining a socio-economic position equal to that of other citizens. When explicit race-biological and hierarchical cultural arguments could not be publicly expressed after the Second World War, hierarchical assumptions became expressed in neutral economic terms. Only by state intervention could modern methods of herding and a new, modern (Swedish) way of life be introduced. Paradoxically, Sami rights based on reindeer herding were still held to be legitimate, even as attempts were being made to induce the Sami to break away from those cultural traditions for which reindeer herding was considered the prerequisite.

Nevertheless, making Sami culture the basis of policy has the potential to challenge Swedish policy, if the question is posed of whether culture is more than reindeer herding and shared by more than a professional group. This question arose in the 1980s, when the major problem in Swedish Sami politics was formulated as an explicit question of Sami rights. One factor in turning the public debate in that direction was the Swedish Supreme Court judgement in the 'Taxed Mountains' case, in which several Sami villages and individuals in the province of Jämtland sued the Swedish state. They claimed 'full ownership rights to the property in dispute [. . .] located in taxed mountains' and to 'extended homesteads'. The Swedish state maintained 'that the State is the owner of the properties in dispute, and that only the special rights stated in the *Reindeer Farming Act* [of 1971] now belong to the Sami and the Sami villages' (Supreme Court Decision, in Jahreskog 1982: 148, 151). The court ruled that the state was the rightful owner of the Taxed Mountains. However, the court's ruling was claimed to clarify the legal rights of reindeer herding and was interpreted as strengthening the herders' legal position. The Sami were stated, in an official report of the time, to have 'a firmly-protected usufructuary right of a particular kind, based upon use and prescription from time immemorial' (Parliamentary Commission of Inquiry No. 41, 1989: 257).

A second factor was the increasing importance of the international debate on minority rights, which suggested a view of the Sami as both an indigenous people and a national minority in their own country. As a result, the Swedish authorities acknowledged their 'obligations to show respect for Sami culture and customs' and 'make room for the Sami to decide and influence' their vital conditions 'based on Sami values' (Parliamentary Commission of Inquiry No. 67, 1983: 134).

Overall, this point of view had a major impact on the well-established link to reindeer herding. In the public debate, policy on reindeer herding became an explicit policy for the protection of the Sami minority, the ultimate objective being to protect the Sami population's opportunities to maintain and develop its own cultural life (Parliamentary Commission of Inquiry No. 67, 1983: 135). But reindeer herding as the prerequisite for Sami culture was not only discussed in terms of its legal status. The legislation itself came under scrutiny for the first time, since it was explicitly acknowledged as having a divisive effect on the Sami as a group. As a prerequisite for Sami culture, it was emphasized that 'the right to herd reindeer is a collective right that belongs to all Sami in Sweden. Reindeer-herding rights should therefore not be lost in [the] third generation' (Parliamentary Commission of Inquiry 41, 1989: 264).

At the same time, Sami identity itself was redefined in terms of the sum of the group member's values and world-view. This change of official stance—linked to the discussion on international law—gave rise to proposals for different forms of Sami rights not related to reindeer herding, like language rights and a proposed constitutional change, which would acknowledge the Sami as an indigenous people (Parliamentary Commission of Inquiry No. 41, 1989: 126–128; Parliamentary Commission of Inquiry No. 91, 1990: 149). Thus, during the 1980s and 1990s, a new chain of analogies emerged as a basis for Sami rights, still dominant in the contemporary debate:

> Sami origin—Sami language—Sami culture—sentiment of belonging—indigenous people—national minority—special rights

This chain implies that Sami are not like other citizens, and consequently both explains and justifies a deviation from the ideal of equal treatment of all citizens. It also warrants commitments to international law and different kinds of affirmative action. The previous categories—reindeer herders, non-reindeer-herders and Swedes—are definitively abandoned, and the Sami are considered to be a heterogeneous group: both a national minority and an indigenous people.

This new conception, then, is of immense importance as it opens up the public debate on Sami rights. Sami identity can no longer justify a legislation based on distinctions *between* Sami, or a limited system of special rights based on reindeer herding. This becomes obvious in the discussion on ratifying the Council of Europe's conventions on the protection of national minorities and historical minority languages in the late 1990s (Parliamentary Commission of Inquiry No. 192 and 193, 1997; Government Bill No. 143, 1998/99). The conception of the Sami identity clearly indicates that the Sami self-evidently belong to those national minorities referred to by the conventions. Through Swedish accession to the conventions in 2000, the Sami language was publicly recognized, implying language rights at least to the level required by those documents. The dominant Sami identity also figures as explanation and justification, for the first time ever, in an official report leading to a proposal to ratify the 1989 International Labor Organization's Convention 169 (*Concerning Indigenous and Tribal Peoples in Independent Countries*). The ratification is, however, a long-term objective, and it is claimed that a number of investigations are needed—including one to resolve the controversial and long-standing issue of land ownership (Parliamentary Commission of Inquiry No. 25, 1999).

So far, however, the rights actually granted to the Sami do not fully correspond to this new conception of Sami identity, or the explicit policy objective to maintain and develop Sami culture by recognizing the Sami as a group with a certain amount of autonomy. As a matter of fact, most proposals on legislative change put forward in the public debate have not been enshrined in legislation (see, for instance, Government Bill No. 4, 1990/91: 32; Government Bill No. 32, 1992/93: 30, 102). A Sami Parliament was, however, established in 1993, institutionalizing for the first time a degree of cultural autonomy for the Sami as a group (Swedish Code of Statutes No. 1433, 1992). Nevertheless, the organization of this parliament corresponded to the traditional pattern of Swedish Sami policy, and its role as an 'impartial and objective' administrative authority was emphasized, at the expense of its status as an elected political body, and the parliament's field of action was very limited. It was, for instance, not granted a right of participation in decision-making, or veto rights concerning administrative decisions, or legal status as a body to which proposed legislative measures on Sami issues ought to be referred for consideration by other administrative bodies.

Thus, it seems as if the solutions proposed to reverse the Sami's inferior status in Swedish society are in many ways formulated on the basis of the same social relations and hierarchical viewpoint that originally constituted the problems. The most striking example of this lingering hierarchical worldview may be the case of Sami hunting and fishing rights. The inauguration of the Sami Parliament coincided with an encroachment on the exclusivity of Sami hunting and fishing rights on Crown land allocated judicially 'to the sole disposition of the Sami' (Beach 1995: 113). Ignoring the firm opposition of the Sami, the Swedish government claimed hunting and fishing rights parallel to that of the Sami, arguing that the state ought to have the freedom, for instance, to increase the number of hunting and fishing licences.

Thus, in political practice, Sami self-determination and cultural autonomy still seems far off, and a continued marginalization of the Sami in decision-making processes is possible.

NORMATIVE THEORY AND GROUP-SPECIFIC RIGHTS AS POLITICAL PRACTICE

The specific problems brought to the fore by my case study seem to undermine the very possibility of legally ensuring a social basis of self-respect for a group like the Sami. From an equality-oriented point of view, the connotations of group-specific rights as political practice are not clear. First, as we have seen, it is impossible to formulate a minority policy based on such rights without simultaneously constituting politically the group which is to be treated differently and protected by law. A certain conception of the group is institutionalized in and through legislation by, among other things, the definition of special rights and of who is entitled to them. Thus, the group is homogenized, and the collective identity attributed to it both explains and justifies the inclusion of some members of the group, and the exclusion of others from the system of special rights.

Second, the group is taken for granted in a specific historical-political context. The collective identity itself provides the starting-point for the articulation of problems, and is in fact often considered to be the source of those same problems. It is thereby provided with attributes that imply inherent limits to the range of political options. The dominant conception of the minority group functions as a node in the public debate. Highly-praised values—democracy, justice, freedom, equality, as well as race, nation, culture or a multicultural society—receive their meaning in relation to a distinct and comprehensive conception of the group. This supplies the answers as to *why* the policy should deviate from the ideal of equal treatment of citizens, but also as to *how* group-specific rights should be designed and *to whom* these rights should be granted.

Third, group-specific rights as institutionalized practice tend to confirm rather than challenge the social relations of power already existing in society, as the case study indicates. The constitution of well-demarcated categories in political life covers notions of good and bad, right and wrong, nature and culture, which reinforce and maintain the boundaries between categories. 'There are rational men, and then there are women; there are civilized men, and then there are wild and savage peoples [. . .] Difference here always means absolute otherness, the group marked as different has no common nature with the normal or neutral ones. The categorical opposition of groups essentializes them, repressing the differences within groups' (Young 1990: 170). By pointing out what should be treated as special, an evaluation is made of what is of higher or lesser value, and the idea of minority groups as different and inferior tends to provide the rationale behind different treatment. A system of group-specific rights that does not change the social relations of power thus runs the risk of being just another indication of the group's low status and value. As Murray Edelman remarks in his discussion of anti-discrimination laws (1988: 26), it 'legitimizes the view that is already widespread [. . .] More important, it contributes to [. . .] the public impression of them as inferior'.

Quite clearly, a theory of minority rights based on exceptions from an ideal of equal treatment of citizens cannot avoid categorization as a prerequisite for special rights. Group-specific rights therefore imply the constitution of identities, and, thus, a potentially oppressive element. In a multicultural society equal citizenship rights may, in a number of ways, be seen as the only possible solution to the problems that derive from the constituting aspect of politics. However, in the liberal ideal of self-respect and the possibility of realizing one's life-plan a contradiction is lodged, between the idea that citizens are of equal value and their potential for realizing their life-plans irrespective of group or cultural membership. This duality is apparent in the case of Swedish Sami policy and might be formulated in two ways. First, on a concrete level, the specific set of rights, liberties and a certain socio-economic standing conferred on all citizens by their citizenship is surely insufficient to ensure Sami self-respect. The Sami are in a permanent minority position, with a very limited capacity to influence the decision-making process. Second, and on a more abstract level, the ideal of equal treatment might end up in direct opposition to equality as self-respect, by transmuting itself into an ideal of assimilation. The assimilationist ideal, as described by Young (1995: 162),

> envisions a society where a person's social group-membership, physical attributes, genealogy, and so on, make no difference for their social position, the advantages or disadvantages that accrue to them, or how other people relate to them. Law and other rules of formal institutions will make no distinction among persons and will assume their moral and political equality. In a society which has realized this assimilationist ideal, people might retain certain elements of group identity [. . .] But such group affiliation would be completely voluntary, and purely a private matter. It would have no visible expression in the institutional structure of the society.

Turning the focus onto the social basis of self-respect as an essential part of the ideal of equality, special rights seem necessary to guarantee certain groups, such as the Sami, an equal standing in a modern welfare society like that in Sweden. If we return to the theories in defence of group-specific rights briefly mentioned earlier, the normative arguments put forward all seem to be of relevance in this context. A legally-defined sphere of action is needed to guarantee certain groups a cultural community in which meaningful choices of life-plans are possible; political autonomy is necessary to overcome the obstacles for self-development and self-determination inherent in social power relations; and the identity of minority groups is often marginalized in the wider dominant society, with their experience going unrecognized.

However, the way to resolve the situation for minority groups cannot consist solely—as the 'liberal culturalist' one does—of a defence of minority rights conceived of as protecting a societal culture without giving a privilege to certain values within it. That would be an illusory attempt to avoid explicit evaluation of the values, or way of life, to be protected. Nor can the solution consist of constructing political identities, as in a 'politics of recognition' or a 'politics of difference'. Rather, the main objective must be to open up ways to question *dominant* identities. Because groups are constituted politically, the limits to what may be asserted by whom, and in what way, must be in a permanent state of revaluation and flux. The 'definitive definition' is always oppressive. As Chandran Kukathas (1995: 234–235) argues—and my case study confirms—groups 'take their particular shape only because of certain historical circumstances or because particular political institutions prevail and not because they are a part of some natural order [. . .] group composition changes over time [and] most groups are not homogeneous at any given moment'. The group is ascribed certain characteristics in the public debate, which reifies identities and institutionalizes an ahistorical outlook, confusing social relations and pre-allotted attributes.

Taking politics seriously in the multicultural debate thus implies that the actual process of recognition through special rights must be the focal point in theories of minority rights, and an acceptance that group-specific rights as an institutionalized practice mirror the prevailing power relations within any society. Only through an awareness of the constitutive character of politics may group-specific rights steer clear of reproducing socially-dominant ideas and conceptions of the group, or appropriating new, oppressive identities. To keep publicly-constituted identities 'open'—i.e. essentially contestable—is thus necessary in order to ensure a space for challenge and change in those relations that feed on collective identity construction. The ideal of equal concern and respect must give 'more room for difference by calling attention to the contingent, relational character of established identities' (Connolly 1991: 33). I believe that this may be accomplished only through a 'fugitive', temporary or preliminary minority politics.

In using the term fugitive, I refer to Sheldon Wolin's (1996: 39) views on how the institutionalization of democracy simultaneously undermines it; thus democracy 'seems to be a moment rather than a form'. There are two components I find compelling in order to develop a 'fugitive' theory of minority rights: historicity and heterogeneity. Historicity means that established social relations of power and dominance have to be analyzed in historical perspective. By investigating in what fashion the identity to be recognized has been formed, neither groups nor cultures are taken as given in the light of certain notions pre-defining the value of specific cultures, traditions or practices. Heterogeneity, in turn, implies that there are no universal solutions in terms of special rights applicable to all groups, not even to all individuals defined as belonging to the same group. If the objective of minority politics is to guarantee individuals a social basis of self-respect and to subvert social power relations, it is essential to know from which perspective group-specific rights and recognition are formulated, and which values and identities are favored by the political act of legal recognition.

Hence, we should theoretically formulate specific procedures which include a momentum of continuous questioning and problematizing of established identities and the prevailing social power relations, rather than search for a full-fledged predetermined theory or system of rights. In this perspective the debate on group-specific rights can be interpreted as part of a wider project to 'expand the circle of democratic inclusion' (Benhabib 2002: x). The abstract ideal of equality requires an institutional redesign where minority groups are guaranteed a 'fair say' in the democratic procedure, and we have to find new answers to the question of how to include them. The strong normative concept of political inclusion inherent in some versions of deliberative democracy could function as a starting-point for such a project, as it underlines both equality and discursive openness. In Jürgen Habermas' well-known words: 'Only those norms can claim to be valid that meet (or could meet) with the approval of all affected in their capacity as participants in a practical discourse'.

The key issue here is to construct institutional arrangements that counteract external and internal exclusion. This exclusion may take the form either of the actual debarring of minority groups from public debates and decision-making processes, or the functioning of the terms of discourse themselves in an excluding way. This requires a process of deliberation in minority politics not only characterized by 'the same chances to initiate speech acts, to question, to interrogate, and to open debate', but also a process which ensures minority groups the right 'to question the assigned topics of conversation' and 'to initiate reflexive arguments about the very rules of the discourse procedure' (Benhabib 1996: 70).

The objective of constructing these kinds of procedures cannot be to find a common ground, or common values, i.e. to reach consensus on societal norms and aims; rather, these procedures should be considered a way to enhance the legitimate sphere of political action for marginalized groups. However, the groups or identities represented in a deliberative model characterized by discursive openness are constituted in political practice. Thus, they are a result of the social relations of power, and cannot be taken for granted. Democratic equality and specific procedures cannot eliminate the question of power. To increase the scope of legitimate political action, however, is a way to answer one of the main questions in democratic politics: 'not how to eliminate power but how to constitute forms of power more compatible with democratic values' (Mouffe 2000: 100).

To conclude my argument here, theories of minority rights must be much more concerned with the question of the power to define and, even more important, with the relation between the power to define and the field of possible political options, meaning legitimate political action. To create such a theory, capable of dealing with the constitutive character of politics, is in my opinion to bridge the gap between theory and practice. However, this calls for a much more elaborate theoretical discussion on group-specific rights, and a rethinking in political practice of the relationship between the dominant majority society and dominated minority groups.

[The author would like to thank Ishtiaq Ahmed, Kjell Engelbrekt, Virinder S. Kalra, Peter Lomas and Jorge Solares for many thoughtful comments on an earlier version of this chapter. All quotations from Swedish government reports and legislation are translated by the author.]

REFERENCES

Baer, L.-A. (1982). 'The Sami: an indigenous people in their own land' in Jahreskog ed.

Barry, B. (2001). *Culture and Equality*. New York: Columbia University Press.

Bauman, Z. (1991). *Modernity and Ambivalence*. Cambridge: Polity Press.

—— (1995). *Legislators and Interpreters: On Modernity, Postmodernity and Intellectuals*. Cambridge: Polity Press.

Beach, H. (1981). *Reindeer-Herd Management in Transition: the Case of Tourpon Saameby in Northern Sweden*. Stockholm: Almqvist & Wiksell.

—— (1995). 'The new Swedish Sámi policy—a dismal failure: concerning the Swedish Government's proposition 1992/93:32' in Gayim and Myntti eds.

Benhabib, S. ed. (1996). *Democracy and Difference: Contesting the Boundaries of the Political*. Princeton: Princeton University Press.

Berger, P. and T. Luckmann (1991). *The Social Construction of Reality: A Treatise in the Sociology of Knowledge*. London: Penguin.

Cohen, J., M. Howard and M. Nussbaum (1999). *Is Multiculturalism Bad for Women?* Princeton: Princeton University Press.

Connolly, W. E. (1991). *Identity/Difference: Democratic Negotiations of Political Paradox*. Ithaca: Cornell University Press.

Edelman, M. (1975). 'Symbolism in politics' in Lindberg *et al*. eds.

—— (1988). *Constructing the Political Spectacle*. Chicago: University of Chicago Press.

Gayim, E. and K. Myntti eds. (1995). *Indigenous and Tribal Peoples' Rights: 1993 and After*. Rovaniemi: University of Lapland.

Gutmann, A. ed. (1994). *Multiculturalism: Examining the Politics of Recognition*. Princeton: Princeton University Press.

Jahreskog, B. ed. (1982). *The Sami National Minority in Sweden.* Stockholm: Almqvist & Wiksell.

Korsmo, F. L. (1992). *Empowerment or Termination? Native Rights and Resource Regimes in Alaska and Swedish Lapland.* Albuquerque: University of New Mexico.

Kukathas, C. (1995). 'Are there any cultural rights?', in Kymlicka ed.

Kvist, R. (1992). 'Swedish Saami policy, 1550–1990', *Readings in Saami History, Culture and Language III*. Umeå: Umeå University.

Kymlicka, W. (1989). *Liberalism, Community and Culture.* Oxford: Oxford University Press.

—— (1995). *Multicultural Citizenship: A Liberal Theory of Minority Rights*. Oxford: Clarendon Press.

—— ed. (1995). *The Rights of Minority Cultures*. Oxford: Oxford University Press.

—— (2001). *Politics in the Vernacular: Nationalism, Multiculturalism, and Citizenship.* Oxford: Oxford University Press.

Lantto, P. (2000). *Tiden börjar på nytt: en analys av samernas etnopolitiska mobilisering i Sverige 1900–1950.* Umeå University: Department of Historical Studies.

—— (2003). *Att göra sin stämma hörd: Svenska Samernas Riksförbund, samerörelsen och svensk samepolitik 1950–1962.* Umeå: Kulturgräns norr.

Lewis, D. (1998). *Indigenous Rights Claims in Welfare Capitalist Society: Recognition and Implementation. The Case of the Sami People in Norway, Sweden and Finland.* Rovaniemi: University of Lapland Arctic Centre.

Lindberg, L. N., R. Alford, C. Crouch and C. Offe eds. (1975). *Stress and Contradiction in Modern Capitalism*. London: D. C. Heath.

Mörkenstam, U. (forthcoming). 'Indigenous peoples and the right to self-determination: the case of the Swedish Sami people'.

Mouffe, C. (2000). *The Democratic Paradox*. London: Verso.

Okin, S. M. (1999). 'Is multiculturalism bad for women?' in Cohen *et al*. eds.

Parekh, B. (2000). *Rethinking Multiculturalism.* Cambridge, Mass.: Harvard University Press.

Rawls, J. (1971). *A Theory of Justice.* Cambridge, Mass.: Harvard University Press.

—— (1993). *Political Liberalism.* New York: Columbia University Press.

Royal Commission Report (1909). *Förslag till omorganisation af lappskolväsendet.* Stockholm.

Ruong, I. *Samerna i historien och nutiden* (Stockholm: Bonnier, 1982).

Shachar, A. (2001). *Multicultural Jurisdictions: Cultural Differences and Women's Rights.* Cambridge: Cambridge University Press.

Sillanpää, L. (1994). *Political and Administrative Responses to Sami Self-Determination*. Helsinki: Societas Scientiarum Fennica.

Svensson, T. G. (1976). *Ethnicity and Mobilization in Sami Politics.* Stockholm: Stockholm University Socialantropologiska institutionen.

—— (1997). *The Sámi and Their Land: The Sámi vs. the Swedish Crown. A Study of the Legal Struggle for Improved Land Rights: the Taxed Mountains Case*. Oslo: Novus.

Taylor, C. (1989). *The Sources of the Self.* Cambridge: Cambridge University Press.
—— (1994). 'The politics of recognition' in Gutmann ed.
Wolin, S. (1996). 'Fugitive democracy' in Benhabib ed.
Young, I. M. (1990). *Justice and the Politics of Difference.* Princeton: Princeton University Press.
—— (1995). 'Together in difference: transforming the logic of group political conflict' in Kymlicka ed.
—— (2000). *Inclusion and Democracy.* Oxford: Oxford University Press.

Chapter Three

The Muslim Presence in Sweden

Jan Hjärpe

The presence of Muslims in Sweden is a rather new phenomenon in what was previously a more homogeneous country. In debates on this subject, a certain rhetoric has developed, in which earlier relations between Scandinavia and the Muslim world play a certain role. Among the signs of early contacts is the large number of coins from the Viking era that have been found in the soil of the Nordic countries. The coins are mainly Arab coins from the Abbasid period, but some originate from other parts of the Muslim world. Another symbol of these early relations is the runic inscriptions on Viking-era tombstones and menhirs which explicitly mention 'Särkland', the land of the Saracens (Jansson 1997: 63ff). To these can be added accounts of barbaric Vikings by Arab authors, especially that of the Abbasid diplomat Ibn Fadlan (Hjärpe 1998: 65–70; Wikander 1978: 63–70).

In reality the Viking era was a short parenthesis, but for Muslim immigrants and their children the archaeological evidence of these early relations has played a part in their integration into Swedish society, for the history of the contacts is arguably older than the history of the Swedish state as a political and administrative entity. A series of exhibitions in the mid-1980s has been of importance in this respect, especially one in the Museum of National Antiquities in Stockholm (*Islam, Konst och Kultur* 1985).

In the Middle Ages the European North came under the dominance of the Catholic Church, which was centred on the Mediterranean region. When the Scandinavian countries began to crystallize as political entities, they were on the periphery of Mediterranean culture, and direct contacts with the Muslim world became rarer. Scandinavians' participation in the Crusades was minimal, restricted to a few persons from the upper classes (Wennerholm 2002). This too has a certain political significance, in a climate in which Islamist movements describe European colonialism, and the present US hegemony, as 'crusades', especially since the occupation of Iraq in 2003 (Hjärpe 1997a: 115–122). The fact that the Reformation of the 16th century can be regarded as the emancipation of the Northern part of Europe from the dominance of the South should also be stressed. It was during this period that the Scandinavian countries became political, economical and cultural entities in their own right. For Northern Europe this meant the development of princely states or monarchies with close links between the seat of political power, administrative structures, and the national church, but independent of the Pope and the Catholic church as an international entity. The most appropriate term for this new state-church relation is Erastianism, a quasi-identity between nation, state, and the national church with the monarch as its head.

The Swedish state in the 17th and 18th centuries covered a considerably larger area than the present one, including the Finland of today, parts of Russia, the states of the Eastern Baltic coast, and parts of northern Germany. There were many ethnic groups and languages. Thus, the national marker had to be something other than language, and this was religion (in the event, Lutheranism). This was the time of the 'Westphalian' system of confessional princely states (*cuius regio eius religio*: religious and political affiliations went hand-in-hand). As the political purpose of religious affiliation was to establish a certain social homogeneity associated with loyalty to the monarch, the practice of the state religion was a civic duty—not necessarily synonymous, therefore, with personal belief. There was an obligation on citizens to participate in religious services and rituals, but simultaneously a prohibition against manifestations of excessive religious zeal. The so-called Conventicle Act (*Konventikelplakatet*) in force in Sweden from 1726 to 1858 prohibited assemblies for worship which were not controlled by the legal authorities. Similarly, loyalty to the official religion and its (controlled) practice was a general condition for employment, especially in all posts of any importance in the state. When a very limited immigration of Jews was permitted in the late 18th century, the formulation of the decision was that 'those of the Jewish nation' could be permitted to settle—under very severe restrictions (Valentin 1964: 52–55). When the conditions were changed in 1838, the formulation referred to 'Swedes of the Mosaic creed' (Valentin 1964: 77). Here we can see a remarkable change in the concept of religion, from a national marker to a question of belief. What was the driving force behind this change?

The beginning of the 19th century brought a significant reduction in the political role of religious affiliation. The most important cause of this was probably the change in the country's actual size. Sweden had already lost the eastern Baltic regions to Russia, and Finland was conquered by Russia in 1809.

The north German provinces had likewise departed from Swedish dominion. From then on the borders of the Swedish state almost completely coincided with linguistic ones. With the exception of very small Sámi- and Finnish-speaking minorities, almost every citizen spoke some dialect of Swedish. Thus, the Swedish language came to constitute the national marker, and the idea of a specific Swedish ethnicity became connected with the idea of the state and its political basis. Consequently, the need for confessional unity and conformity progressively declined. The Conventicle Act was abolished, a number of 'dissenter laws' became part of established legislation and the idea of personal religious freedom was raised more frequently in debate. The schools remained confessional, and confessional conditions were retained for special posts in the state, including government ministers, primary-school teachers and, rather curiously, midwives (they were required to be confirmed members of the Lutheran church, as they had to be schooled to perform the baptism of a child if there was a risk that he or she might die.)

The secularization process continued, and gradually these confessional conditions disappeared as they lost relevance. An important change came in 1951, when new legislation came into force. Until then all Swedish citizens had had to belong to a religious denomination recognized by the state. With the new law, however, this condition for citizenship was abolished. One could be a citizen with all personal rights and duties, and with full legal rights, without being affiliated to any religion or religious body. All legislation was made secular, including personal law. The new law can be seen as the application of the definition of religious freedom in the UN Universal Declaration of Human Rights of 1948, especially Article 18 (Hjärpe 1997b). This was a significant change, replacing the concept of a person's religious affiliation as a legal status in society with that of personal belief. Simultaneously, the official registration of religious affiliation ceased. (Thus, we cannot obtain statistics on it with the same accuracy as on other aspects of social and political life in Sweden.) When the remnants of a state church system were abolished entirely in the year 2000, the secularization of the state and the differentiation between religion (as a private matter) and citizenship was established as a fundamental principle. All confessional conditions for official posts or legal status disappeared.

During the long period of the confessional state (17th to mid-20th century) relations with the Muslim world were not entirely severed. In the 18th century Russian expansion aimed at reaching both the Baltic and the Black Sea stimulated Swedish diplomacy towards new overseas contacts. Indeed, during the entire 18th century there was a military alliance between the Ottoman Empire and the Swedish state governed from Stockholm. Likewise, this was a time of commercial treaties with North Africa. Learned Swedes began to take an interest in scientific and scholarly expeditions to far-flung lands. Upper-class tourism became fashionable in the 19th century, and skilled workers from Scandinavia migrated to Ottoman Turkey and North Africa. This is also the period of the first Swedish translations of the Qur'an and of works by learned orientalists (Hjärpe 1999a: 35–46).

The Scandinavian countries in the 19th and early 20th centuries were also rather homogeneous entities, but this was to change (Hjärpe 1994: 18–28). Secularization brought a different political role for religion compared with its earlier function, when religious affiliation had been a national marker and the ideological foundation of the state, with the established church as a tool in the administration of the state (Hjärpe 1999b: 111–120). In those earlier times, religion had served to add legitimacy to central government power, but this practice was now supplanted by the idea of the popular mandate.

These processes, from the early 19th century on, coincided with the technological development of modernity, in the shape of industrialization and urbanization, and later the creation of the welfare state, under which citizenship became not simply a status but a very substantial asset. It made the individual citizen part of the welfare system without any confessional preconditions, in a nation in which religious communities played only a very limited socio-economic role. Indeed, the very concept of Sweden, from the 1960s on, was very often expressed in a common language of civil rights and welfare—as 'the Swedish model'.

IMMIGRATION AND THE WELFARE STATE

All this is important for our understanding of the context for the immigration into Sweden of persons with another religious affiliation. The development of the modern welfare society coincided, in fact, with the beginning of a Muslim presence in Sweden. An official census in the early 1930s (the very last census of religious belonging performed) indicated that this presence amounted to fewer than 15 persons. The first conceivable group, although still very small in number (less than 100), was the Tatars who came from Finland (and Estonia) in the wake of the Second World War, some as refugees, others as migrant workers. (Tatars had originally settled in Finland when it was still part of Tsarist Russia). Their activities, as an association formed in Stockholm in 1949, included Islamic religious education and religious services (Soukkan 1985: 84–119; Otterbeck 1998: 145–153). In the beginning the aim of the association was to maintain a specific ethnic identity. Later, as a result of the immigration of manpower of other ethnic descent, which soon outnumbered the Tatars, it developed into a more specifically religious community, the Islamic Congregation of Sweden (*Islam Församlingen i Sverige*). This also meant changes in outlook.

The development of the Swedish welfare state was possible due to the economic affluence of the 1950s, which came about through industrialization and the fact that Sweden had not been directly involved in the Second World War. There was a substantial need for industrial manpower, and the Muslim immigrants of the 1960s and early 1970s consisted mainly of so-called guest workers, who were not only welcomed but actively recruited in Yugoslavia (to be precise, in Bosnia) and in Turkey. Their integration was relatively easy, and the question of any separate religious status was simply not on the agenda. Here the change came about through the more numerous immigration of the 1980s and 90s, which consisted almost entirely of refugees from political oppression, war and natural disaster. This in itself constituted a problem. The immigration had not come in answer to a need for labor; thus it became a burden on a society where there was already a comparatively-high level of unemployment, and public opinion began to turn in favor of a change in immigration policy. Almost inevitably, the new immigrants became marginalized in Swedish society, and the marks of this were (and still are) attributed to differences in culture or religion, as shown by letters to newspapers and opinion polls (Hvidfelt 1998). Also contributing to Islam's bad press during this recent period were the conflicts in the Muslim world, the connections between certain Islamist movements and violent actions, and the open justification for the violence in the rhetoric of those movements. The public found it difficult to distinguish between their particular arguments and the (various kinds of) Islam of immigrant Muslims in Sweden.

Since religious affiliation is no longer registered in Sweden, there is no official census of this status, and all the numbers presented as statistics are more or less qualified guesswork. Already the fact that the numbers are dependent on how religious affiliation is defined (activity, membership in organizations, actual practice, ethnicity or names) results in huge differences. Figures varying from 60,000 to 300,000 are quoted for the number of Muslims in Sweden (Sander 1997). This statistical uncertainty is also a consequence of Swedish democracy, in which the registration of a person's religious affiliation has come to be regarded as an infringement of individual freedom. Citizenship, the argument goes, should not be graded. Religious belonging has no legal consequences and a religious hierarchy has no recognized jurisdiction over the members of its community. As a consequence, religious affiliation often comes low in public discussions of norms and identities (compared with a person's professional status, for instance, or family situation). Attempts to produce more elaborate statistics are of very limited value, as it is very difficult to judge the strength and scope of religious attachment (or the lack of it).

At most, we can see an increase in religious attendance in the wake of disasters (as in the great fire in Gothenburg in 1998, where more than 60 young people, mostly of immigrant descent, died). There is also very often a difference between formal membership of a religious community and the more or less informal group within which individuals practice religious rituals.

Moreover, the welfare state influences the actual function of religious communities, insofar as it provides all citizens with basic security. Protection of life and property, health care, education and political rights are extended regardless of group belonging, family means, or affiliation to a religion or other specific cultural group. The citizen exists and has his/her being within the framework of state legislation, assuming that it is actually implemented. This means, for example, that people marry the spouse of their choice. Moreover, as the state guarantees children's security and support, stability in family relationships is not fore-ordained. State pensions mean that individuals are not dependent on their children in old age, or on relatives in general, or a religious/cultural community, for survival and a decent standard of living.

All this leaves very little appeal for the idea of a separate legal status in Sweden based on religious affiliation (Hjärpe 1997b: 52–69). For Muslims, in fact, it becomes conceivable to interpret the country's welfare system and secular legislation as being in harmony with (even as an expression of) true Islam. This proved to be a common argument in discussions on the role of religion and the state, not only in the 1960s and 1970s, but also in the early 2000s, among Muslim intellectuals and professionals in Sweden. The secular welfare system and contemporary legislation were found to be much more 'Islamic' than either the actual systems found in the Muslim world or the ideas propounded by Islamist groups; more expressive of the mental associations of *adl* (justice) for many of the new citizens.

There are a number of organized religious communities in Swedish society: churches, denominations, sects, cults and religious organizations. However, the individual is free to choose whether or not to participate in any of these. Moreover, a religious community and its leadership have no recognized jurisdiction over the members. Its spokesmen and -women can give advice and express opinions, but they cannot give orders. Members are free to leave the community at will. One consequence is that the concept of religion as an order of society, or connected with a special legal status, fits in awkwardly with the functional structure of Swedish society. Religion can still be regarded as a comprehensive system of living, but only for the individual and by personal choice. It is difficult to apply a more collectivist concept of religion in practice—as has been seen, for instance, in attempts to establish Islamic schools (Gerle 1999). Naturally, this concept of religion as unrelated to legal status can seem very strange to someone with a traditional Islamic approach, like that of *fiqh*, a rule system that is collectively applicable in society. Only within a certain enclavization is such a concept relevant, and in the suburbs there have been certain tendencies to such an enclavization, but to a rather limited extent and only among certain ethnic groups, such as Somalis (cf. Johnsdotter 2002: 35–46).

The Muslim refugees who entered Sweden in the 1980s and 90s evidently did not come from countries which could in any way be described as welfare states. On the contrary, these people had previously been dependent, as individuals, on other sources of help than the state for their needs. We can label this tribalism: the dependence on family, clan, tribe, religious community. In societies characterized by this kind of dependence we can assume that the tribal norms (loyalty to family, clan and religious community) are stronger than all other norms. As a rule, these immigrants have not abandoned their religious affiliations (one exception is Iranian refugees where one often finds an anti-religious attitude); but the notions both of family and religion have become problematic for them in the new Swedish environment. The actual role and functions of family, clan and religious community are not the same as in the old environment. A frequently-observed phenomenon is that of tension between new immigrants and earlier, well-integrated minority groups.

For the individual Muslim immigrant, the new environment is felt in a variety of ways. Non-believers, for instance, no longer need to pay lip service to any religious affiliation, because this has nothing to do with their personal legal status any longer. Similarly, the function of religion as a mark of ethnicity becomes successively less important; in any case, as becomes evident, there are many different ethnicities and social strata represented among immigrants with the same nominal religious affiliation. Customs and habits, clothes and rituals, which in the previous environment had the function of showing that someone was 'like everybody else' now have the opposite effect of showing that he or she is different. A distinction is routinely made between customs and religious belief. A common culture for all, regardless of ethnic descent, increasingly comes to mean the Swedish language, educational background and citizenship. For children in school the tools of communication become Swedish, English—and the Internet.

The functioning structures of a society with a strong official sector and administration decide the conditions and framework of Muslim institutions, at both local and national levels. The result is that different Muslim groups organize themselves in conformity with a distinctly-Swedish institutionalized tradition, which ceases to correspond with organizational structures in Muslim countries. For instance, several different Muslim umbrella organizations operate on the national level and display different tendencies, including a special Bosnian Muslim organization (Svanberg and Westerlund 1999: 14–139).

There are practical reasons for this: to apply a concept of religion regarded primarily as an order of society or a system of jurisdiction would result in institutions unacceptable to Swedish integration policy, and hence ineligible for government economic support. Not surprisingly, the concept of *fiqh* (jurisprudence as part of religion) becomes supplanted by the notion of personal moral values. An early example of this is the very revealing interview with the imam Faruk Celebi in Stockholm in 1985 (Richert, Unge and Wagner 1985: 195–199). As statistics on the frequency of participation in Friday prayers show, the majority of Muslims in Sweden tend not to practice their religion very diligently. On the other hand, aspects of Islam stressing personal religious experience and engagement, such as *tasawwuf* (mysticism), appear to have been promoted through the *Tablighi* and Süleymaniye movements. There are also, as noted above, Muslim immigrants who have come to reject their religion entirely.

Muslim immigrants in Sweden come from very different ethnic, social and educational backgrounds. Thus, it becomes necessary to distinguish between Muslim identity and ethnic identity, and between Islam and the norms, habits and customs of one's traditional environment that were once regarded as Islamic and taken for granted. Personal frames of reference have changed, resulting in new interpretations of religion, quite obvious among young persons who have grown up in Sweden (an example among many is a small book which young Muslims in Malmö published in 2003 (M'Rad & Kopilovic 2003). 'Swedish' forms of Islam have emerged, polarizing groups and individuals not simply over differing opinions, but also over integration into Swedish society and the secular state. An interesting part of this is the increasing role of women in Muslim communities and their leadership and services, this again especially in the younger generation.

An illustrative example here is Jonas Otterbeck's analysis of the magazine *Salaam*. He examined the changes in its contents, layout, editorial policy, and literary style, and its relation to international trends, including in the Islamic world, during the entire period of its publication, which has now ceased (Otterbeck, 2000a and 2000b). This research is of interest in several ways. The organization to which *Salaam* was connected, the Islamic Information Association (*Islamiska informationsföreningen*), has an evident relationship to the Islamic Foundation in Leicester with its typical Maududi background and personnel, and its ideological links to the Pakistani Jamaat-i Islami. However, Otterbeck's study charts successive changes in the magazine's outlook, and in the personal relations between its writers (involving some conflicts and changes in staff), from a 'Maududist' Islamist stance to a tendency to stress religion as a personal engagement and include Sufism within the realm of accepted Islam. Also part of this evolution was a stress on the importance of ecology and environmental protection, a theme very much in tune with debates in Sweden at the time (Ouis 1999: 196–216). There are Muslims (nominal or believing) as members in all the parties now represented in the parliament, but there is a tendency for committed Muslims to have a preference for the Green Party.

This growing confidence has also meant a decreased dependence, for the *Islamiska informationsföreningen*, on material from abroad. In turn, this implies a process of growing Muslim integration into Swedish society, and an understanding that in order to be taken seriously in public debates, one must concentrate on concrete questions, whether they concern issues of special interest to Muslims (mosque-building, schools, promoting a new Qur'an translation) or problems of society as a whole. The idea of the Muslim community as a separate body, and of Islam as a system totally alien to Western values, thus fades into the background. Equally, it has become increasingly clear that Muslims in Sweden do not constitute one single community, but display different tendencies and interests, which are likely to persist and be accepted as legitimate variations of Islam. There is a new generation, born and educated in the state school system, and with frames of reference differing from those who came as migrants. Sweden has a very high density of personal computers, and the young generation has learnt to use them at school. It is interesting to follow the rather candid debate between young Muslims of different trends on the Internet, which clearly shows that the feeling of belonging to an identifiable group, and the actual networks of contacts themselves, are no longer restricted to a geographical neighborhood (Stenberg 1999: 128).

A field where the question of belonging comes into focus is that of education. The Swedish school system has a rather low degree of acceptance of independent schools. They are few in number, and the curricula and functioning of the existing ones are controlled by the authorities. They have to comply with a number of conditions, including on the norms and values they convey to their pupils. All schools, for example, even private ones, must conform to principles of gender equality, democracy and democratic values, and anti-racism, and must promote the idea of human rights (as defined by international declarations and conventions) regardless of religious identification. This means that the question of confessional schools, be it Christian or Muslim, is a very tricky and controversial one: these schools are regarded by many people in Sweden as contravening the ideal of an integrated society. The fear is that they could be instrumental in creating separate communities, that is, a segregated society. There are some functioning Muslim schools in Sweden; others have been set up but closed after a certain time (Johansson 1999: 175–194). The whole question of confessional schools, with special regard to the Muslim ones, has been analyzed by Elisabeth Gerle (1999). As she clearly shows, the debate on separate Islamic schools exposes the tensions between differing values and norms in Swedish society, and the ambiguous character of the idea of multiculturalism. What values and ideas can be accepted or tolerated in such a society? In fact, a very small proportion of Muslims in Sweden make use of or promote confessional schools for their children; most of them simply express an interest in giving their children the education that would provide them with the best professional opportunities in future. Nevertheless, the issue has triggered a wider debate on the role of religion in society, and shown up as problematic the rather restricted approach to this question which long held sway in Swedish national policy. Is religion really an entirely private matter, as these long-held assumptions imply?

A SEPARATE COMMUNITY?

In recent times the Christian Democratic Party (*Kristdemokraterna*) in Sweden has had a stronger position in the electorate than at any time in its history (up to 10% of electoral votes). Owing to the balance of forces in parliament, it has been able to engineer a programmatic change in the school system's directives.

In the previous educational plan (dating from 1980) it was stated that 'the school . . . has to develop such qualities among pupils as can support and strengthen the principles of democracy, tolerance, co-operation and equal rights between human beings.' This formulation, which enjoyed considerable support among teachers and in public opinion, was replaced after 1995 with the following rather peculiar formula: '[Pupils shall be educated] in accordance with the ethic that has been administered by Christian tradition and Western humanism.' That said, this change has not yet had any discernible effect on actual school curricula. Nor has it found very much support among teachers, or been advanced as an argument for separate schools. The leading personalities in the Christian Democratic Party deny that the formula should in any way be regarded as directed against Islam—a denial that has not, however, convinced everybody.

We should also note that the Swedish welfare system came under considerable pressure during the economic crisis of the 1980s and 1990s. Without question, social and economic conditions for certain strata in society worsened, and segregational trends became apparent. A high percentage of immigrants in the suburbs of the larger cities are unemployed, and the performance of schoolchildren in these areas has deteriorated. There has been an increased incidence of family problems, ethnic tensions, gang warfare and crime. In a much-noticed book on Islam in Europe written at this time (and translated into Arabic and Turkish), the Swedish diplomat Ingmar Karlsson pointed to the dangers of this situation (Karlsson 1994). As he argues, marginalized young people, weak in language competence, education and employment skills, constitute a potential recruitment base not only for organized crime but also for politico-religious extremism.

So far, however, there appears to be very little engagement, among Swedish Muslims, with religious extremism or even with a non-violent political Islam. The mosques promote other spheres of activity. Criminal or semi-criminal gangs and ethnic tensions have been in evidence, as well as very concrete problems of disaffection and violence, including 'honour' killings. But these problems appear to have less to do with religious affiliation than with tensions between the norms and concepts of the secular welfare state and those of patriarchal tribal societies with a system of extended families and clientism, sometimes combined with what might be called Mediterranean concepts of sexual honour, in which male authority dominates and conditions female sexual norms (Koctürk 1991: 125ff, 191ff, Wikan 2003: 59–83).

Interest has been expressed, in some quarters, in the question of a judicially-separate status for Muslims, which would entail the application to them of separate personal law (*ahwâl shakhsiyya*). In Sweden both family law and the law of inheritance are as secularized as any other part of national legislation. In 1999, however, some heat developed in public discussions on these matters. Mahmoud Aldebe, a spokesman for the Islamic Co-operation Council (*Islamiska samarbetsrådet*), an umbrella organization for some of the officially-recognized Muslim communities, argued in an interview that *sharia* rules should be allowed to apply, among Muslims, in matters pertaining to family and inheritance (*Svenska Dagbladet* 17 September 1999). Aldebe asserted that freedom in this area for Muslims was as important as the freedom to build mosques. The newspaper *Dagen* in particular (connected with the Pentecostals and other evangelical groups) took up the question in a rather polemical way, and a debate ensued in the media in both Sweden and Denmark, provoking some strong reactions.

The question is a particular instance of the wider one of how to define religious freedom. As noted above, the legal definition of religious identification or affiliation was changed in 1951 in Sweden. Up till then every citizen had had to belong to a religious community recognized by the state. After 1951, religious affiliation was no longer registered and had no relevance whatever in judicial matters; the same laws applied, in principle, to everyone. A person could go without any religious identification and the authorities had no right to demand a declaration of such status. Religious freedom thus meant freedom of belief, freedom of worship and freedom of practice (insofar as participation itself was a manifestation of individual free choice). Religious leaders (however defined) ceased to have any jurisdiction over members of their communities, and religious laws had no validity before the courts. The very few exceptions to these principles that have in fact occurred have all had to do with people choosing to emigrate back to countries where personal law is dictated by religious affiliation. Thus, a *collective* freedom of religion, or a freedom for religious communities, was definitively replaced in 1950–51 by the concept of individual religious freedom.

Aldebe's proposal was therefore inherently against the spirit of the Swedish legal system. If any part of it, such as the part referring to family law, were to be applied, this would require the reintroduction of registered religious affiliation—a practice which has come to be regarded as an infringement of individual freedom. The idea of citizenship itself would have to be qualified by confessional identification, leading to distinctions between citizens of different religious affiliations. The definitions of religion and religious freedom would change back from being individual to being collective. Such ideas are totally alien to how citizenship is conceived in Swedish society today.

Some kind of counselling, however, on confessional matters is not inconceivable. Thus, '*sharia* boards' exist to give advice to Muslim believers who seek it—but without exercising any jurisdictional power. A parallel here is the Canon Law courts within the Catholic Church in Sweden. When the idea of *sharia* courts was again put forward (on a local television station), there were protests, including from Muslim intellectuals, writers, professionals, and members of political parties. A Muslim MP had already, at the beginning of the televised discussion, reacted very negatively to Aldebe's idea, and she later protested in a radio interview at what she regarded as defunct patriarchalist concepts which, moreover, lacked any Islamic legitimacy. Protests from Muslim intellectuals, academics, and members of political parties focused on the danger of segregation inherent in the idea of legally-recognized religious affiliation, and refuted the claim of specific conservative religious leaders to speak for all Muslims in Sweden.

There have been some signs of official interest in the debate, as the government initiated in the mid-1990s a project to study 'Euro-Islam' under the Ministry of Foreign Affairs and the Swedish Institute (a semi-official body connected to the Ministry). The stated field of interest was relations between European and Islamic cultures and the position of Muslims in Europe. A conference was organized in Stockholm in June 1995 (Swedish Institute: 1995). Among secular Muslims in Sweden the reaction was to criticize the fact that only religiously-committed people from Islamic organizations in Sweden represented the Muslim presence in the country. There was also criticism from those who preferred a policy of isolating political Islamists and Islamist groups, including the Iranian regime, which was represented at the conference. Opinions were polarized in the Swedish political debate. There was a second conference in Jordan in June 1996, organized in co-operation with the Jordanian government (Swedish Institute: 1996). Within the so-called Barcelona Process of the European Union, the Swedish government promised to engage in Euro-Mediterranean co-operation with special regard to culture and cultural manifestations. A workshop (mainly for diplomats) was arranged in Stockholm in April 1998, called 'Dialogue between Cultures and Civilizations' (Swedish Foreign Ministry 1999: 63). Government energies in these directions have, however, waned of late, and the government of Prime Minister Göran Persson has followed a more cautious policy than that of his predecessor, Ingvar Carlsson.

One may also note the publication in 1998, with government support, of a new Swedish Qur'an interpretation by the retired Swedish diplomat and Muslim convert Mohammed Knut Bernström, *Koranens budskap* ('The Message of the Qur'an'). This new work is very different in character from earlier versions, produced by Swedish orientalists from strictly linguistic and historical premises. The most influential of these, published in 1917 and still in print, was the work of K. V. Zetterstéen, Professor of Semitic Languages at Uppsala University. His aim was to present a translation of a historical text, the Arabic Qur'an, as a religious document from the Hijaz region of Arabia in the time of the Prophet, the 7th century AD. In his new approach, Bernström sought to present the Qur'an not only as a historical document but also as a normative text, a document with consequences for Muslims living in Sweden today. His translation is a huge work, comprising the text of the Qur'an, a paraphrasing translation and, as footnotes, a Swedish revised version of Muhammad Asad's Qur'an commentary. The translation-interpretation has been scrutinized by a group working with the consent of al-Azhar University in Cairo, which means that in the Islamic world it has a kind of official recognition. More important is the reception of the translation in Muslim circles in Sweden, which has generally been very positive. There are several reasons for this. The literary style of the translation is of a high quality, the translator is himself a believer and practicing Muslim and, as a retired ambassador, he has a high status in Swedish society. Government support for the publication, and its appearance from a renowned publishing house, have also helped it to obtain wide acceptance.

CONCLUSION

For the 'new Swedes' of immigrant background, the religious affiliation becomes only one among many identities (ethnic, professional or social), and not necessarily the most important for each individual. It is often, in practice, seen as a purely private matter, or even dispensable with no legal consequences. One characteristic of religion today, especially in a developed and prosperous society, is availability. Through new means of communication such as television, video and audio cassettes, and satellite channels, the individual can choose from many alternatives. Especially for the younger generation, religion on the Internet is a very concrete attraction, which removes its link to a local community or traditional leaders. Tradition itself, therefore, and thereby the religious affiliation and what it should imply, has lost its self-evidence. Even if the religious affiliation is retained, and its importance is stressed, people are aware of the existence and availability of alternatives. The secular aspects of religious affiliation become weaker, too, as the welfare society takes over the traditional function of the religious community as a social and economic security network.

For the believer, religion retains its role as a source of comfort and reassurance when individuals encounter difficulties in their lives. We can also see some examples of revitalization: religious rites and customs that were not in use in the country of origin obtain new functions in the new society, and an active reinterpretation of the religious tradition becomes very evident. The influence of religion perceived through the electronic media has diminished the role and power of traditional hierarchies and of local communities, especially where the younger generation is concerned. The religious identity is much less related to an ethnic identity, and 'Swedish' forms (and interpretations) of Islam are developing.

REFERENCES

Alwall, J. (1998). *Muslim Rights and Plights: The Religious Liberty Situation of a Minority in Sweden*. Lund: Lund University Press.

Berg, M. and V. Trépagny eds. (1999). *I Andra Länder: Historiska Perspektiv på Svensk Förmedling av det Främmande*. Lund: Historiska Media.

Bernström, M. K. trans. (1998). [*The Qur'an*]. *Koranens budskap i svensk tolkning av Mohammed Knut Bernström med kommentarer av Muhammad Asad*. Stockholm: Proprius.

Berqvist, J. (1999). 'Gröna svar på gröna frågor: Muslimskt miljöengagemang' in *Svensk Religionshistorisk Årsskrift*, 196–216.

Bexell, G. and D.-E. Andersson eds. (2002). *Universal Ethics: Perspectives and Proposals from Scandinavian Scholars*. The Hague: Martinus Nijhoff.

Brune, Y. ed. (1998). *Mörk Magi i Vita Medier: Svensk Nyhetsjournalistik om Invandrare, Flyktingar och Rasism*. Stockholm: Carlssons.

Dassetto F. ed. (2000). *Paroles d'Islam: Individus, Sociétés et Discours dans l'Islam Européen Contemporain*. Paris: Maisonneuve & Larose.

Forsgren, T. and M. Peterson eds. (1997). *Cultural Crossroads in Europe*. Stockholm: Forskningsrådsnämnden.

Fry, D. P. and K. Björkqvist eds. (1997). *Cultural Variation in Conflict Resolution: Alternatives to Violence*. Mahwah, NJ: Lawrence Erlbaum.

Gerle, E. (1999). *Mångkulturalism—för vem?* Nora: Nya Doxa.

Halldén, P. (2001). *Islamisk Predikan på Ljudkassett: En Studie i Retorik och Fonogramologi*. Lund Studies in History of Religions 13.

Hjärpe, J. (1994). 'Meeting with Islam' in *Meeting Foreign Cultures.*

—— (1997a). 'Historiography and Islamic vocabulary in war and peace: a memento for conflict resolution in the Muslim world' in Fry and Björkqvist eds.

—— (1997b). 'Some problems in the meeting between European and Islamic legal traditions: examples from the human rights discussion' in Forsgren and Peterson eds.

—— (1998). 'Islam and Scandinavia: the problem of religious influence' in Piltz ed.

—— (1999a). 'Det svenska studiet av islam' in Berg and Trépagny eds.

—— (1999b). 'Revolution in religion: from medievalism to modernity and globalization' in Therborn ed.

—— (2002). 'Religious affiliation as a problem for universal ethics' in Bexell and Andersson eds.

—— (2002). 'Political Islam and Sweden: integration and deterrence' in Karam ed.

—— (forthcoming). 'Islamic legitimation of democracy and human rights: trends and tendencies'.

Hvidtfelt, H. (1998). 'Den muslimska faran: om mediebilden av islam' in Brune ed.

Jansson, B. F. (1997). *Runes in Sweden.* Värnamo: Gidlunds.

Johansson, B. (1999). 'Islamiska friskolor: lyckad integration eller hot mot mångfalden?' in Svanberg and Westerlund eds.

Johnsdotter, S. (2002). *Created by God: How Somalis in Swedish Exile Reassess the Practice of Female Circumcision*. Lund Monographs in Social Anthropology 10. Lund: Department of Sociology, Lund University.

Junefelt, K. and M. Peterson eds. (1998). *Cultural Encounters in East Central Europe*. Stockholm: Forskningsrådsnämnden.

Karam, A. ed. (2004). *Transnational Political Islam: Religion, Ideology and Power.* London: Pluto Press.

Karlsson, I. (1994). *Islam och Europa: Samlevnad eller Konfrontation?* Stockholm: Wahlström & Widstrand.

Karlsson, P. (1999). 'Islam tar plats: moskéer och deras funktion' in Svanberg and Westerlund eds.

Koctürk-Runefors, T. (1991). *En fråga om heder: Turkiska kvinnor hemma och utomlands.* Stockholm: Tiden.

Meeting Foreign Cultures (1994). Scripta Minora Regiae Societatis Humanorum Litterarum Lundensis. Stockholm: Almqvist & Wiksell.

M'Rad, S. and S. Kopilovic (2003). *muslimer.nu: Islam & muslimer bortom nyhetsrubrikerna.* Malmö: Ideum Europa.

Otterbeck, J. (1998). 'The Baltic Tatars—the first Muslim group in modern Sweden' in Junefelt and Peterson eds.

—— (2000a). *Islam på svenska: tidskriften Salaam och islams globalisering.* Lund Studies in History of Religions 11. Lund: Department of the History of Religions, Lund University.

—— (2000b). 'Local Islamic universalism: analyses of an Islamic journal in Sweden' in Dassetto ed.

Ouis, P. (1999). 'Islamisk ekoteologi: en ny grön rörelse?' in Svanberg and Westerlund eds.

Piltz, E. ed. (1998). *Byzantium and Islam in Scandinavia. Acts of a Symposium at Uppsala University, June 15–16 1996.* Jonsered: Paul Åströms Förlag.

Richert, A., S. Unge, and U. Wagner eds. (1985). *Islam: Religion, Kultur.* Stockholm: Samhälle.

Sander, Å. (1997). 'To what extent is the Swedish Muslim religious?' in Vertovec and Peach eds.

Soukkan, T. (1985). 'Ett tatariskt lokalsamhälle i Sverige: en minoritetsgrupp i ett brett tidsperspektiv'. Swedish Research Institute in Istanbul *Meddelanden* No. 10, 1985.

Stenberg, L. (1999). *Muslim i Sverige: lära och liv.* Stockholm: Bilda Förlag.

Svanberg, I. and D. Westerlund eds. (1999) *Blågul islam: Muslimer i Sverige.* Nora: Nya Doxa.

Swedish Foreign Ministry (1999). Report Ds 1999:63: *Tradition och Förnyelse: En Studie av Nordafrika och Mellanöstern.* Stockholm.

Swedish Institute (1995). *Euro-Islam Report.* Stockholm, 15–17 June 1995.

Swedish Institute (1996). *The Second Conference on Euro-Islam: Relations between the Muslim World and Europe.* Mafraq, Jordan, 10–13 June 1996.

Therborn, G. ed. (1999). *Globalization and Modernities: Experiences and Perspectives of Europe and Latin America.* Stockholm: Forskningsrådsnämnden.

Valentin, H. (1964). *Judarna i Sverige.* Stockholm: Bonniers.

Vertovec, S. and C. Peach eds. (1997). *Islam in Europe: The Politics of Religion and Community.* London: Macmillan.

Wennerholm, O. (2002). *Korsriddaren i Forshem och Tempelriddarorden.* Fjärås: Carse.

Wikan, U. (2003). *For aerens skyld: Fadime til ettertanke.* Oslo: Universitetsforlaget.

Wikander, S. (1978). *Araber vikingar väringar.* Norrtälje: Svenska Humanistiska Förbundet.

Chapter Four

Group-Rights Theory Meets Balkan Secessionism

Kjell Engelbrekt

For the past decade, intergovernmental organizations in Europe and beyond have been striving to limit ethnic violence in the Balkans. A flurry of European and US diplomatic activities aimed at halting the wars of former Yugoslavia culminated in the Dayton Agreement of 1995. In addition, the European Union (EU) has funnelled large sums of economic aid into south-eastern Europe (except for Serbia, which was subject to United Nations sanctions). Then in the spring of 1999, the armed forces of a group of NATO member-states launched a large-scale operation, for the first time in the alliance's history, to thwart ethnic cleansing in the Serbian province of Kosovo. Two years later the United States government and the EU combined their diplomatic leverage to compel the majority Slavs and ethnic Albanians to renegotiate the constitutional makeup of the Republic of Macedonia.

A key element of these international efforts has been to persuade political leaderships in south-eastern European states to accept the notion of minority-group or collective rights. Partly with the problems of the Balkans in mind, Europe's entire minority-rights regime was significantly bolstered in the 1990s. In 1991 the Conference on Security and Co-operation in Europe (CSCE) agreed on an ambitious declaration which paved the way for a new office of High Commissioner on National Minorities (established in 1993 in Prague). In 1992 the Council of Europe adopted a European Charter for Regional and Minority Languages. Three years later that organization concluded a vague but binding Framework Convention on the Protection of National Minorities. The European human-rights regime was further extended through the adoption of certain provisions in the EU's Amsterdam Treaty, which went into force in 1999, and a new human-rights catalogue endorsed at the EU's Nice Summit of December 2000.

These and other documents were all brought to the attention of governments in south-eastern Europe. Membership of the Council of Europe was made contingent on acceptance of its legal instruments, in particular the 1950 European Convention on Human Rights. The new High Commissioner on National Minorities began to figure as the chief European diplomat on questions of minorities and group-related legislation. By way of membership negotiations, the EU acquired considerable influence, in the second half of the 1990s, over the handling of minority issues in Balkan countries. For its part, NATO made accession to the alliance conditional on these countries' resolution of outstanding disputes with their neighbors and their adoption of high standards of minority legislation (Asmus 2002).

The satisfaction of minority-group claims implies the institution of long-term arrangements in favor of communities who feel they share an ethnic, religious, cultural, linguistic or other social heritage, one which warrants special political provisions (extending, at the most formal level, to the state). Will Kymlicka (1995: 6–7) has famously distinguished between three categories of such claims, aiming at, in turn,

self-government rights (the delegation of actual powers to national minorities, perhaps through some form of federalism),
polyethnic rights (financial support and legal protection for certain practices associated with particular ethnic or religious groups), and
special representation rights (guaranteed seats for ethnic or national communities within the central institutions of the state).

In my conclusion, I shall return to Kymlicka's group-rights theory in an attempt to assess the relevance of each analytical category in the context of south-eastern Europe. But I want to begin by discussing the history of nationalism in that region, and then turn to novel developments in minority protection. I will use the second half of the chapter to analyze a critical case with regard to group-rights theory, namely the Republic of Macedonia. The conditions in Macedonia pose a major challenge because of the rapid deterioration in ethnic relations there and the scale of the commitment by outside parties required to halt the process. It is a suitable test of that commitment, for the EU and the USA had clearly accumulated considerable experience from previous post-Yugoslav wars, and the dangers of inaction were well known. In other words, their diplomats and officials had had plenty of time to work out the basic design of a political and legal solution for the Balkan context.

NATIONALIST PROJECTS IN SOUTH-EASTERN EUROPE

In several respects south-eastern Europe (perhaps even Central and Eastern Europe in general) represents inhospitable territory for minority-group rights (Kymlicka 2001a: 61–70). The Ottoman Empire, which for nearly five centuries dominated the region, rested on well-defined practices. Muslims, Jews and Orthodox Christians typically played complementary roles in the economy and everyday life of Ottoman society, so that ethnic diversity was perpetuated and reinforced only insofar as it overlapped with religious differences. On the other hand Muslims, with few exceptions, were granted a higher status, expressed through their exemption from the poll tax (*cizye*) paid by Christians and Jews, and their exclusive right to hold public office in the Ottoman Empire and carry arms (Lewis 1961: 331). Though the *Tanzimat* reforms of 1839 made Christians and Jews formally equal to Muslims, in practice widespread discrimination against non-Muslims remained (Shaw 1991: 75–78, 129–169).

Beyond these restrictions, there was acceptance of religious differences, secured by pervasive imperial legislation and, for the most part, protected public practices. As a congregation associated with the Holy Scriptures, the Orthodox Christians of south-eastern Europe were represented by the Patriarch of Constantinople at the Ottoman court. The same applied to Jews, whose prime advocate was the Grand Rabbi. Smaller groups of Christians and Jews, and indeed non-mainstream Muslim sects, could in addition ask the Sublime Porte for permission to set up a self-governing religious community (*vakf*) that would be answerable not to local administrators but directly to their own religious authorities in the imperial capital.

Thus, as in most historical empires, the Ottoman rulers relied on a high level of social stratification, in particular a religious-ethnic hierarchy, among their subjects (Friedman 1998: 233–250 and 1994: 42–66). Together with demands from non-Muslim intellectuals for modernization and industrialization, the call for destruction of this religious-ethnic hierarchy was a major factor in the 19th-century movement toward independence of the Balkan lands. The notion of religious-ethnic hierarchy, and by association that of group rights, was largely rejected and replaced by the west European model of a homogeneous nation-state.

The local awareness of group distinctions and of the injustice engendered by hierarchy was often enhanced by nationalistic historians, who were eager to portray the movement toward independence as an heroic struggle (Kitromilides 1990: 23–66). It subsided somewhat in areas where the former landlords and elites abandoned their estates and positions within the Ottoman administration, paving the way for the social ascent of ambitious non-Muslims.

In many instances, however, the project to build a homogeneous nation-state, with a modern economy and a body politic loyal to central government, was carried out with assimilationist zeal, coupled with insensitivity to the fate of minority communities.

In the eastern Balkans, the emergent political order tended to be dominated by the traditionally-rural Orthodox Christian population, and in the ex-Habsburg territories of the west by Catholic Slovenes and Croats. There was a more delicate balance in the central portion of the Peninsula. In what today are Bosnia-Herzegovina, the Republic of Macedonia, and the Serbian province of Kosovo, Orthodox Christians faced a life together with Muslim Bosniaks and Albanians, who had occupied a higher rung on the ethno-social ladder of the Ottoman Empire. Within this society, the Slav-speaking Bosniaks fared much better than many Muslim Albanians in that they could retain a certain social standing (helped by their common language). Further east, where the Ottomans were not ejected until 1913, the Albanians became unjustly associated with resistance to independence. Ever since, Slav Macedonians have tended along with Serbs and Greeks to regard the Albanian community as backward opponents of modernization, indeed of civilization itself. This view, however, is over-simple. The Albanian component of the Ottoman Empire was regarded as comparatively loyal to the Sultan, as reflected in the elevated status of Muslim Albanians. Equally, the emergence of Albanian nationalist, modernizing ideals predates the Slav-dominated campaign for a Macedonian state. Albanian national ideals were for the first time proclaimed by intellectuals in 1878, when they founded the League of Prizren. Also, many nationalist Albanians were Christians.

Under Communist rule, the competitive character of Balkan nationalist projects was played down, out of the fear of escalating mutual recriminations and territorial claims still dormant in folk memory. The success of this strategy may be due to a degree of genuine collective or internationalist solidarity promoted by the Communist parties. Yugoslavia, with World War II atrocities fresh in people's minds, is a case in point, even if nationalist sentiments had found partial expression in the idea of a broader South Slavic nation embracing Serbs, Croats and Slovenes (Denitch 1994: 30–36; Connor 1984, ch. 6). At any rate, ideologically-motivated suppression of nationalist rhetoric in Bulgaria, Romania and, initially at least, Albania did appear to have a substantial effect in the aftermath of the war.

It was not long, however, before the 'bent twig' of nationalist identity began to swing back (Berlin, cited in Gardels 1991). As long as totalitarianism retained its grip on Communist-run societies, the reassertion of national goals mainly assumed the expression of foreign-policy initiatives not approved by the Soviet Union. First of all, there was a serious disagreement between the

Yugoslav and Soviet regimes in 1948, mainly over ideology but also over independence of action and the Yugoslavs' attitude toward their Soviet-satellite neighbors (Micunovic 1980). As a consequence, there was a sharp clash in Albanian-Yugoslav relations which effectively ended all ties for many years to come. The next shoe to drop was Romania, where the Ceaucescu regime, in April 1964, refused to subordinate national needs to pan-socialist planning objectives. In the following years it gradually disentangled itself from commitments in the Soviet bloc.

In the next phase, Communist rulers in some countries of south-eastern Europe tried to enhance their legitimacy by resorting to nationalist rhetoric. Ceaucescu in Romania was a pioneer in this regard, partially revamping the theology of Marxist-Leninism to fit his aggressive brand of Balkan nationalism. In the late 1960s he replaced the working class with the socialist nation as the avant-garde of historical development and world progress (Verdery 1991: 116–21). Other Communist leaders followed suit. In 1981 a megalomaniac performance was put on to celebrate the 1300–year anniversary of the founding of the Bulgarian state, which subtly hinted at a longer lineage than Russia's (Crampton 1997: 204).

Meanwhile in Yugoslavia, the politics of nationhood and ethnicity had been hijacked by the anti-Communist movement. In Croatia and Kosovo overt nationalism resurfaced in the early 1970s. In 1974 Josip Broz Tito, a Croat who had been the chief architect of a federal Yugoslavia, tried to address the issue by revising the constitution into a looser framework which would allow greater autonomy to the republican chapters of the Yugoslav Communist party. The outcome, however, was an eight-sided political game in which the Serbs, though the largest community in the federation, had only one vote against those of five other republics and two autonomous provinces (Cohen 1992: 51–55). Tito's death in 1980, after thirty-five years of rule, signalled the beginning of a painful process in which the South Slavic state gradually unravelled into its component parts. The federation no longer had an ultimate arbiter; there was little co-ordination of economic policy; and pressures were growing for further decentralization of power. Finally, the 1981 Albanian rebellion in Kosovo deeply undermined the notion of a unitary Yugoslavia, while reviving Serb nationalism (Ramet 1992).

These developments suggest that nationalist projects in the Balkans had never been abandoned or discredited during the period of Communist rule. They had simply had to compete with other politically-approved goals, such as the attainment of industrial quotas of production or an egalitarian social framework. There had also been many constraints on the expression of political ideas, and obstacles to mobilization among those who differed from the official government line. As Soviet-sponsored international Communism began to disintegrate in the late 1980s and early 90s, the nationalist twig lashed back with a vengeance. It did so violently in Yugoslavia, where Slovenes and Croats were soon seeking a reasonable exit strategy from the ailing federation. Not unexpectedly, the final blow came at the congress of the Communist party, the one organization that had kept the federation together for almost half a century. On 23 January 1990 the Slovene delegation walked out of the Fourteenth Congress, formally pulling out of the party twelve days later. Later that year independence was proclaimed in Slovenia, Croatia and Bosnia-Herzegovina. In January 1991, on the orders of Serbian President Slobodan Milosevic, the federal Yugoslav army invaded first Slovenia and Croatia, and then Bosnia, in an attempt to block the drive toward full sovereignty in those countries (Ramet chs. 12 and 13; Cohen chs. 6–7; Glenny 1992; Woodward 1995).

The situation in Romania, Bulgaria, and Albania was more mixed (Ortakovski 2000). Tensions re-emerged in the 1990s between the large Hungarian minority in Transylvania and the government authorities, dominated by the majority Romanians. One of the largest political forces, the Greater Romania Party, was (and remains) fervently anti-Hungarian as well as anti-Roma, though the presidency and cabinet have so far been only marginally influenced by its stance. In Bulgaria, the Communist party conducted a harsh assimilation campaign in the late 1980's against the country's ethnic Turks and Bulgarian-speaking Muslims, forcing them to adopt Bulgarian-sounding names and banning a wide range of Islamic customs and rituals. Since the end of communism the Turkish and Roma communities have been much better treated, while more subtle forms of discrimination clearly linger. Finally, Albania has largely been a rallying point of Albanian nationalism among the Albanians of Kosovo and of the Republic of Macedonia. On the other hand, the long-standing rivalry between Albania's Gegs and Tosks cannot be ignored; it is widely perceived as a key factor behind the large-scale unrest of 1997, when arms deposits were raided in many parts of the country. (Many of the weapons ended up in Kosovo, facilitating the establishment of the Kosovo Liberation Army.)

In the Balkan political legacy, then, minority rights yet again tend to be subservient to the realization of the most cherished long-term goal of larger political communities—that of a monolithic nation-state bringing together citizens who share the whole range of ethnic and cultural attributes. Some governments in the region, it is true, are content to promote the majority culture with or without this long-term objective. Others have shown themselves prepared to apply methods of assimilation ranging from subtle discrimination to population displacements and the ethnic cleansing of minorities in pursuit of their ends.

THE POST-COMMUNIST MINORITY RIGHTS REVOLUTION

The fall of the Berlin Wall and the demise of Communist rule in Europe rekindled many of the hopes first raised by the Helsinki process of the mid-1970s. The democratic transformations of the early 1990s then went a long way towards fleshing out, in national legislation and (to a lesser extent) state practices, the human-rights principles in the so-called 'third basket' of the Helsinki commitments. The European human-rights regime, formally agreed under CSCE auspices in the Finnish capital in 1975, finally began to take hold on the continent as a whole.

The CSCE Paris summit of November 1990 recognized the need to improve protection for national minorities. Apart from reaching consensus on the Paris Charter, which included certain novel formulations regarding minority protection, the CSCE decided to convene a meeting of experts on such matters in July 1991. At its next summit in Helsinki, the CSCE went on to create the office of the High Commissioner on National Minorities as part of its conflict-prevention mechanism. At the subsequent Budapest summit of 1994, it reinvented itself as the Organization on Security and Co-operation in Europe, to affirm its own key place in the continent's new 'security architecture'.

As a pan-European forum, the OSCE chiefly remained a champion of individual political and human rights. Typically, minority issues were dealt with under the somewhat inconspicuous heading of the 'human dimension of security'. The Organization's Istanbul Declaration of 1999 acknowledged the protection of minority rights as an important goal, though only as part of the rights of individual citizens. In article 15 of the Declaration, the formula is to guarantee rights 'to persons belonging to a national minority'; in other words it is individuals, rather than groups, who are endowed with rights, and governments should try and accommodate these within the framework of existing states.

The newly-created High Commissioner on National Minorities, on the other hand, formulated a series of recommendations and suggestions in the fields of education, employment, home and justice affairs that in part, at least, underwrite a group approach to minority rights. One example concerns polyethnic rights to tertiary education in minority languages in Romania, Albania and the Republic of Macedonia. Another is the HCNM's clear endorsement of opportunities for minority groups to express their ethnic, cultural and linguistic identities.

As for the Council of Europe, its original engagement with the Balkan region was similarly derived from an individualistic conception of human and minority rights. There is no reference to collective rights in the 1950 European Convention on Human Rights, and the principle of minority protection may only be inferred from those of freedom of thought, association, and expression, and of non-discrimination 'on ground of national and social origin'. In the 1990s, however, the Council moved closer to a group conception of minority rights, through its European Charter for Regional and Minority Languages (1992) and its Framework Convention for the Protection of National Minorities (1995). Both clearly support polyethnic rights, urging governments to ensure the advancement of minority customs, language-instruction, and culture, and to abstain from 'politics aimed at assimilation' (Framework Convention, article 5).

The same can be said for the most important European institution, the EU, which indirectly acknowledged minority-group rights in its diplomatic efforts to prevent the outbreak of the Yugoslav wars of secession and, later, to mitigate their effects. In elaborating a plan for the warring parties in Bosnia-Herzegovina in particular, British diplomat David Owen and his US colleague Cyrus Vance proposed a new constitution and state structure that would accommodate the rights of ethnic groups as well as individuals. The Vance-Owen plan implied polyethnic rights as well as rights to community representation and self-government (Owen 1995: 94–159). With developments in the Balkans fresh in their minds, the EU decision-makers appeared anxious to stress the importance of minority questions when offering, in 1993, the possibility of EU membership to the countries of Central and Eastern Europe. The so-called Copenhagen criteria started out with a provision that candidate countries acquire 'stability of institutions guaranteeing democracy, the rule of law, and respect for and protection of minorities'.

The same line was followed by ad hoc institutions, such as the Contact Group bringing together the initiatives of the major European NATO powers, the United States and Russia in the context of the war in Bosnia-Herzegovina. The subsequently-established Stability Pact for South Eastern Europe, agreed on 30 July 1999, affirmed the commitment of the signatory states 'towards preserving the multinational and multiethnic diversity of countries in the region'. In the Sarajevo Summit Declaration, representatives of twenty-five countries pledged to protect established ethnic, cultural and linguistic identities and rights in accordance with relevant international mechanisms and conventions. The signatory-governments were first criticized for not being as forthcoming in committing money as they had promised, but by early 2002 almost all of the original 244 projects had been launched to the tune of €2.4bn. Further investments have been made to enhance regional infrastructure, develop free trade and a well-functioning energy market, and address a range of humanitarian issues.

Things would obviously have been much simpler if Western countries and their partners had elaborated a more cohesive approach to the problem of group rights in the European and Balkan contexts. There seem to be at least three important obstacles to this. First, there is the multitude of international organizations which consider it part of their mandate to cater for minority protection and are therefore reluctant to embark on a joint effort to establish a common conceptualization. Second, there is a constant tendency in minority-rights politics, as in most policy-making, for matters of principle to be subordinated to election cycles. Third, in many of the European countries (mainly EU ones) where norm-creation in human rights has been pioneered, contrasting ideas persist of what constitutes a minority and what level of protection, privileges and rights to representation and self-rule a minority should enjoy. The Framework Convention for the Protection of National Minorities itself contains no definition of 'national minority', because it was 'impossible to arrive at a definition capable of mustering the general support of all Council of Europe member states' (Framework Convention 1995: 13).

MINORITY PROTECTION: FROM INDIVIDUAL TO GROUP RIGHTS

Among the various forms of minority-rights protection in existence or being set up in south-eastern Europe, we can identify two patterns. One is that of an unwieldy patchwork of political and legal arrangements for minority groups, produced by historical circumstance and by pressure from international and European organizations over the past few years. Proposals, recommendations and outright power leverage abound in this area of policy-making. Many organizations, including NGOs, obviously regard it as their primary objective to elaborate and campaign for their own solutions to problems involving minorities.

The second pattern is an overall direction of change toward the enhancement of minority-group rights in general. In many ways this is the more interesting pattern, as it shows a slowly-evolving radicalism in relation to minority issues. While the European Convention on Human Rights and the CSCE's 'third basket' opened the gates for a European revolution in *individual* rights, the perceived need to deal with the minority problems of post-Communist countries appears to have pushed open the doors with regard to collective rights. Because the latter represent a field in which sovereignty (and thus the principle of non-intervention) went largely unchallenged during the Cold War, the turnaround now is much more noticeable. Not even the atmosphere of post-9/11, which in some respects reinforces a status quo approach to international affairs, seems to have undermined minority-rights radicalism.

A handful of examples, subtle as well as blatant, will show how international intervention in the cause of minority protection is now commonplace. Among the subtle ones is the fact that European Commission annually urges the Bulgarian authorities to clarify what is meant by the country's constitutional ban on political parties of an ethnic, racial or religious character. (This ban may well be inspired by a desire, on the part of the majority Slav community in Bulgaria, to declare illegal at some time in the future the party which represents the country's ethnic Turkish and Muslim minority.) Regarding Romania, the Commission has criticized the authorities' repeated failure to protect their largest minority, the Roma (European Commission, Enlargement Directorate-General, *Progress Report 2000*: 22, 24). The same report complained that university education in the Hungarian language was nonexistent in Romania, while acknowledging that new legal measures had made it a theoretical possibility (cf. Weber 1998: 199–322).

When it comes to contemporary Serbia, international actors long preferred a carrot, but have more recently pulled out a stick. Overall, a relatively permissive attitude was shown towards Serbia and Montenegro after the electoral defeat and downfall of Serbian President Milosevic in 2000. This is probably due to the tremendous contrast in dealings with the new government in Belgrade. Milosevic consistently resisted criticism of his regime's treatment of minorities. On taking power, President Vladimir Kostunica and Prime Minister Zoran Djindjic were much more co-operative. The latter jeopardized his political career and, indeed, his life by delivering Milosevic to the International Tribunal on Former Yugoslavia in The Hague; many believe this act prompted his assassination in March 2003. (Milosevic was handed over in direct connection with a US decision to make the disbursement of American aid dependent on Belgrade's full co-operation with the tribunal.)

Perhaps expectedly, the truly blatant examples of external pressure to conform to the notion of group rights are available in those parts of former Yugoslavia where nominal sovereignty counts for little in the aftermath of the wars of separation. This applies to Bosnia-Herzegovina in particular (Woodward 2000: 252–300). In accordance with the Dayton Agreement a total of sixteen international human-rights treaties were incorporated in full into the Constitution of Bosnia-Herzegovina. In fact, even the 1995 Framework Convention for the Protection of National Minorities, which is not legally binding on the signatory member states of the Council of Europe, was included as Annex 1 and then made obligatory. These treaties are to be applied before any other national or local law or regulation. As pointed out by one commentator, only three of the sixteen UN-related human-rights treaties have actually been ratified in the USA, let alone granted a status above domestic legislation there (Chandler 1999: 91–92).

More important, the entire structure of government envisaged for Bosnia-Herzegovina by the Dayton Agreement was founded on the group-rights principle of special representation. The presidency consists of three members, one from each of the largest ethnic communities (Bosniaks, Croats and Serbs). The same goes for the office of Prime Minister and for cabinet members, each of whom has to work alongside deputies from the other two community populations. Analogous quotas are valid for the upper chamber of parliament, whereas a third of the representatives to the lower chamber are elected in Republika Srpska and the rest in the Bosnian-Croat federation, the two constituent components of Bosnia-Herzegovina. The country now sports thirteen prime ministers and four levels of government for some four million inhabitants (Ourdan 2002).

The obvious aim behind these arrangements, to compel politicians and citizens from the different communities to work together and forge multi-ethnic partners and organizations, has so far miserably failed (Breitenstein 2004; Engelbrekt 2004). In the daily politics of many areas in Bosnia-Herzegovina, a recurring practice is still to sideline and snub members of the other main communities. In fact, Western governments have had to lean heavily on Sarajevo as well as the administration of the Republika Srpska to repeal additional privileges that apply exclusively to Bosniaks, Croats or Serbs. Finally, at the Bonn Peace Implementation Summit in December 1997, the Office of High Representative of the UN to Bosnia-Herzegovina was given powers to dismiss any local official for non-implementation of the Dayton Accords.

Even so, the institutionalization of a system of community representation, coupled with far-reaching delegation of authority to city and regional councils, has produced a re-politicization of ethnic differentiation in some parts of Bosnia-Herzegovina. In municipalities with a sizeable majority and a recent experience of conflicts and atrocities, the other two groups are marginalized in politics and local administration. The new powers granted to the UN representatives at the Bonn Summit have helped temporarily to suppress this trend in Mostar, Brcko and Sarajevo. In Brcko, for instance, the UN intervened to annul the September 1997 municipal election results and appoint an ethnically more-balanced city council. Nevertheless, ethnicization of politics in Bosnia-Herzegovina remains a deeply-ingrained obstacle to democracy. There are still no multi-ethnic parties with wide appeal (Chandler 1999: 84–87, 111). In fact, nationalist parties made additional gains in parliamentary elections in October 2002.

Today, international support for the notion of minority-group rights in the sense of special representation is no longer as strong and unqualified as in 1995 when it comes to Bosnia-Herzegovina. Although implementation of the Framework Convention for the Protection of National Minorities and the European Charter for Regional and Minority Languages remains a priority, some Council of Europe bodies have now taken stock of local experience and concrete dilemmas. Still a champion of group rights in Bosnia-Herzegovina in terms of polyethnic rights, the Venice Commission of legal experts has begun to advise against the widespread practice of appointing ranking officials on the basis of ethnicity, as this 'would increase the conflict with the democratic principle'. So far, the Commission suggests, the practice of granting special rights to self-representation has tended to 'cement the antagonism between the various groups instead of inducing them to co-operate' (Council of Europe 2001).

This acknowledgment that minority-group rights (here, in the form of special representation) cannot compensate for the absence of democratic experience, or offset the outright hostility between communities, should probably be welcomed. Still, if this policy were to be extended to other countries in the region, it might actually contravene the sole form of group rights that for historical reasons appears acceptable there. Polyethnic rights—the idea that the state should help to sustain and promote minority-culture ethnicity—is not a popular concept in the Balkans, despite (or perhaps precisely because of) the fact that it was widely practiced in Titoist Yugoslavia. Even more sharply rejected is the notion of extending self-government to minorities. Indeed, the latter is a prospect abhorred by many in the Balkans, not least by those who lived through the disintegration of post-1974 Yugoslavia. In fact, people who hold this event to have been a historical mistake tend to regard the decentralization allowed in the revised Yugoslav constitution of 1974 as the first step towards disaster and war.

A CRITICAL CASE: ETHNIC TENSIONS IN MACEDONIA

Regular observers of events in south-eastern Europe were not surprised by the outbreak of political violence along ethnic lines in the former Yugoslav Republic of Macedonia in early 2001. Even without the locally-high unemployment, or the violent rivalry between arms and drugs traffickers, the politics of nationhood and ethnicity is a powerful explanation for the widespread hostilities. This was a country harboring communities with competing national projects, and an ethnic hierarchy turned upside down. Slav Macedonians in particular in Albanian-majority areas feared the prospect of domination by that community in what during the Communist era was a 'Slav' state. (The 1994 census found that 'Slav' Macedonians made up 66.6% of the population, 'Albanians' 22.7%, 'Turks' 4.0%, 'Roma' 2.2% and 'Serbs' 2%. The number of Albanians may now be understated due to illegal immigration in recent years). (Tosheva 1997: 51). Similar ethnic resentment was a prime motive behind ethnic Serb violence in eastern Croatia and parts of Bosnia in the early 1990s.

Slav Macedonian identity in its present shape is in fact of rather recent date (Kofos 1990: 103–141; Poulton 1995). Less than a century ago, a Swedish writer referred to the majority population of Macedonia as 'flour from which one can bake any cake one would want, as soon as the citizenship question has been settled' (Kjellén 1916, 51–52). Even by then, however, the Macedonian Slavs had begun to be affected by the virulent nationalism sweeping other Balkan countries. Such sentiments predictably deepened during the wars of independence against the Ottomans in the early 20th century. The evolving national doctrine held that in order to be Macedonian one needed to be a Slav-speaking Orthodox Christian. Thus, Muslim Albanians and other groups living in the same territory were progressively marginalized (Perry 1997: 226–281).

Under Communist Yugoslavia, tensions between Slavs and Albanians in Macedonia were subdued by a combination of federative arrangements and socialist ideology. While the Slav majority had to settle for the primarily-cultural project of developing a national language and literature within the Yugoslav framework, many in the Albanian minority saw the Socialist Republic of Albania as a stepping-stone toward the loftier goal of Greater Albania. This delicate balance, which Tito had pragmatically provided for, was maintained as long as the broader Yugoslav federation was still in place—helped, of course, by the principles of Communist solidarity nominally binding Yugoslavia and the Albanian Republic.

With the break-up of Yugoslavia, however, and the establishment of a sovereign state of Slav Macedonians, based on 19th-century assimilationist notions which favored the majority culture, this balance was upset. In the Balkans more broadly, there was concern that the regional equilibrium would be affected. Most neighboring countries were able to successfully deal with such anxieties, including Bulgaria, which recognized the state but not the national community (all being regarded as Bulgarians). Paradoxically, the country with the most impressive democratic and economic record, Greece, was the most profoundly affected, rejecting the right of the former Yugoslav republic to use the name 'Macedonia', which was perceived as inherently Greek (Kofos 1999).

In the early 1990s, the Republic of Macedonia unambiguously came into existence as a state for, and dominated by, the Slav majority. Several passages in the constitution served to underline this fact. For instance, the Slavic language was the sole official language of the Republic. Its use was expressly protected by the constitution, while other languages were permitted in local self-government 'where there is a considerable number of inhabitants belonging to a[nother] nationality'. Furthermore, one article of the constitution established 'the right to create schools and charitable organizations under the Macedonian Orthodox Church and other religious communities', which again failed to acknowledge the existence of a large Islamic community in the country. In terms of primary and secondary education, the constitution allowed for instruction in languages other than Slav Macedonian, though it did not specify Albanian and made the former mandatory for all pupils (Articles 7, 19, and 45). Until recently, instruction in Albanian in institutions of tertiary education was prohibited.

Such provisions of the Macedonian constitution institutionalized the longstanding cleavage between Slavs and Albanians, and simultaneously reflected the entrenched antagonism between them. Since the creation of the independent Macedonian Republic in 1992, spokesmen for the Albanian minority have repeatedly warned that the asymmetry of the constitution would not be tolerated indefinitely (Perry 1997: 240–41). Signs of confrontation between the populations have been increasingly frequent in recent years. The fear of violence escalated on both sides in connection with the war in neighboring Kosovo, a conflict which led many Slav Macedonians to side with the Serb cause and oppose self-determination for the Kosovar Albanians. The sense of mutual insecurity did not disappear with the stationing of Nordic and US forces, through the UNPREDEP initiative, on Macedonia's physical border with Kosovo. In any case these troops were soon withdrawn following a cynical Chinese vote in the UN Security Council (intended merely to express displeasure at the decision of the Macedonian government, in its desperate search for outside investment, to establish diplomatic ties with Taiwan).

Slav-Albanian tensions were subsequently heightened by the Western intervention that brought open military conflict to an end in Kosovo. One example of growing distrust was the fervently anti-Albanian elements of the presidential election in November 1999, where the socialist candidate Tito Petkovski repeatedly charged the Albanians with systematic violations of the election procedure and falsification of the results (*Neue Zürcher Zeitung* 20 & 29 November 1999).

Deliberating Group Rights During Armed Insurrection

Attacks on the town of Tetovo in March 2001 by Albanian Macedonian rebels, reportedly augmented by Kosovo Liberation Army veterans, threw the conflict into an acute phase. For several weeks snipers held this northern town of the landlocked republic in terror. At one point, the rebels started calling themselves the National Liberation Army (NLA). They demanded a new

Macedonian constitution, better civil rights for Albanians, and international mediation in the dispute with the government. While claiming that they did not seek the destruction of the Republic, they insisted that the government's neglect of their grievances justified their armed insurrection. The name they adopted, however, inevitably suggested an association with the Kosovo Liberation Army, organizationally and in terms of objectives. This is one reason why many Macedonian Slavs were sceptical that the rebels' stated goals regarding the constitution and the status of the Albanian language represented their true agenda.

Initially, international institutions and Western governments sided fully with the Skopje government. Few did so more unambiguously than NATO. A press release issued on 21 March stated:

> NATO is absolutely committed in its support of the government in Skopje as it faces the challenge of extremist groups, whose violent activities we totally condemn. We reject any attempt at the forcible changing of borders. We stand fully behind the sovereignty, stability, and the territorial integrity of the former Yugoslav Republic of Macedonia.

This statement was followed by others to the same effect, stressing the solidarity of European and US officials with the Macedonian government. Throughout April and May, there was no let-up in this tough line. Even if the language no longer followed the lead of Skopje, which continued to brand the rebels as terrorists, the NLA was considered a non-political force, as shown in the joint NATO-EU communiqué of 30 May:

> Ministers reaffirmed that the international community will work only with the legitimate political representatives and not with armed extremists or their representatives. There can be no place at the table for those who have taken up arms against this democratic government.

In the next joint NATO-EU communiqué, however, issued on 5 July, Western politicians dramatically changed tack. While still referring to the rebels as armed Albanian extremists, the text no longer included the standard condemnation of their actions. On the contrary, the decision of both rebels and government forces to agree to a cease-fire was now warmly welcomed. Even more noteworthy, far from demanding that the rebels end their insurgency, the statement went on to say that 'there can be no military solution to the present conflict' and called on 'all parties to respect fully these cease-fire declarations and to act with utmost discipline and restraint'.

This about-turn by NATO and the EU irritated the government of Lyubcho Georgievski, leader of the nationalist VMRO party, and enraged many Macedonian Slavs. On 26 June the government consented to a NATO proposal to strike a deal with a large group of rebels, surrounded near the village of Aracinovo, and allow them to retreat in an orderly convoy. That same night the Macedonian parliament was stormed by thousands of angry protesters who urged the political establishment to abandon its acceptance of recommendations from the West (Fidanovski 2001). The sense of a breaking-point having been reached in Slav-Albanian relations enveloped people who had previously been favoring the search for a peaceful solution to the insurrection. In mid-July even the formerly-moderate head of the Orthodox Macedonian Church, Patriarch Stefan, publicly expressed scepticism at the feasibility of peace (Latifi 2001).

Increasingly, European and UN institutions began demanding that Skopje yield to ethnic Albanian human-rights demands, including those for group rights. Two negotiators were appointed, US envoy James Pardew and François Léotard for the EU. Looking for a compromise acceptable to the Albanian rebels and the Slav-dominated cabinet, they set out to formulate a settlement based on reciprocal actions by the rebels and the Macedonian government, namely disarmament of the Albanian insurgents in return for substantial changes in the Republic's laws. At this point the armed rebels were clearly treated as a legitimate party to the conflict, though contacts with them were made through ethnic Albanian parties represented in the legislature.

This increasingly-symmetrical diplomatic approach provoked frustration among Macedonian Slavs, who argued that armed insurrection was being rewarded by the international mediation, which was pressing hard for concessions on both sides. (The EU was threatening to withhold an aid package worth $77 if the Macedonian government rejected the agreement.) (Carrol 2001). After renewed fighting in northern Macedonia, Premier Georgievski vented his anger at Western proposals that seemed further-reaching than most Slavs had anticipated:

> The offer by Mr. Pardew and M. Léotard represents a serious interference in the interior affairs of the country and they de facto mean federalization of Macedonia. [. . .] Their text is brutal and with their cowboy style they are trying to break the institutions of the country. (Ordanoski 2001).

Eventually, however, Georgievski gave up his resistance to the peace deal. The agreement signed at Lake Ohrid on 15 August 2001 included provisions for the 'de-ethnification' of the constitution through the replacement of a key reference to 'the Macedonian people' (implying the Slav community) with 'the citizens of the Republic of Macedonia', an amendment that conforms with a liberal, individualistic conception of rights (Nanevska 2001). At the same time, the agreement raised the standing of Albanian to an official language, to be used where that ethnic community numbered above 20% of the population, and by the same token increased the number of official documents to be made available in Albanian. It also provided for an increase in Albanian membership of the police, to 25% from the current level of 5%, and for partial devolution of power from the central to the municipal level. Finally, it envisaged amnesty for the rebels.

Needless to say, the last two provisions were at once hotly contested among the Macedonian public and political establishment. Among Slavs, some sympathy remained for the goals of the Albanian rebels (though much of this had evaporated during the conflict of the last six months). But the majority of the public strongly rejected the idea that a political compromise could be reached as a result of an armed insurrection. Many contested the political legitimacy apparently granted to the NLA by the channelling of its demands through top-level EU and US mediators, and resented the generous amnesty it received in March 2002 (Carrol 2002). These developments implied that NLA commanders would be in a position to seek public office, or membership of the reformed police force. Indeed, according to the Lake Ohrid agreement and an amnesty law subsequently passed by parliament, only those persons subject to indictments for war crimes or crimes against humanity in connection with events in 2001 were to be barred from public office (*Neue Zürcher Zeitung* 8 March 2002).

Perhaps the most controversial changes were to Macedonian provisions regarding the balance between central government and municipalities. The partial devolution of power was only briefly outlined in the peace accords, and was supposed to follow a revision of current legislation on local administration and territorial division of municipalities. When finally adopted on 24 January 2002, the reforms hardly qualified as 'federalization' of the Republic—a label used by some of the agreement's fiercest critics (*Neue Zürcher Zeitung* 25 January 2002). However, they expressly envisaged the devolution of education, cultural and home affairs to reinforced municipal authorities (Pampur 2001). And under the new provisions Albanian-majority local authorities would be able to fly a red flag with the double-headed eagle, like that of Albania proper, alongside that of the Macedonian Republic.

The Lake Ohrid agreement and the ensuing legislative reforms were hailed internationally as diplomatic feats. They helped to ensure the cultural rights of Albanians, for instance through placing the administration of primary schools in the hands of local authorities. At the same time, they avoided full-blown 'federalization' along ethnic lines, by maintaining the centralization of key institutions. Only time will tell of their stabilizing effects in Macedonia. It should be noted that the majority of politicians who originally signed the

Lake Ohrid agreement later expressed their regret at doing so. (One exception was President Boris Trajkovski, who died tragically in a plane crash in February 2004.) In the medium term, awarding tax-collecting powers to local government is a major concession to radical Albanians that might be used to undermine central-government authority.

SUMMING UP: INCONGRUITIES AND INCOMPATIBILITIES

Group rights are perceived, debated and applied differently in different parts of the world. Even in a relatively small region like Europe, there are distinct variations. In Belgium, for instance, they already operate extensively, whereas the idea of such provisions has met considerable resistance in France and Germany (Brubaker 1992; Soysal 1994; Martinelli 1997: 287–301).

The difference is sharper still between the theoretical conceptions of an analyst like Kymlicka and those prevalent in post-Communist south-eastern Europe. Whereas individualistic conceptions of human rights have long been at variance with state practice in the Balkans, group-rights theory seems to clash in principle with the nationalist projects of recent times. (In this context one could include Greece, albeit a long-standing member of the Council of Europe, the OSCE and EU.) By and large the peoples of the Balkans share the project of a nation-state bearing the identity of major cultural and linguistic communities, with borders that coincide with distinct populations. To remedy the putative imperfections left behind by history, especially Ottoman history, the ideal of the nation-state in the Balkans has been coupled to an assimilationist ethos. Given the patchwork of ethnic and cultural identities on the ground, such an ideal has unavoidably proven divisive in practice.

In the 1990s, the human-rights revolution that followed on the end of Communist rule in Eastern Europe did not spread naturally to the Balkans, and the efforts of external actors to encourage this spread had mixed results. The introduction of the idea of group rights may very well have helped sensitize Balkan governments to some of the problems faced by minorities. Those governments may also have begun to realize that previous policies of assimilation or marginalization are unlikely to work in an internationalized world with high-speed communications, literate and vocal minority activists, and an array of international bodies and non-governmental organizations monitoring developments.

At the same time, one may fairly ask whether the heavy-handed approach often adopted by external actors, as described earlier in this chapter, can produce the desired results. The Council of Europe, the OSCE and the EU have repeatedly made various forms of aid or institutional membership conditional on an individual country's human-rights performance. Yet it is not always clear whether conditions in even 'established' Western societies match up to those demanded of governments in post-Communist countries, as shown by the candid Council of Europe reports on national practices in combatting racism. Kymlicka himself has been profoundly critical of the activities of some international organizations, especially the OSCE (Kymlicka 2001a: 371–387). At the same time, he is supportive of a tough stance by international actors against illiberal tendencies in former Communist countries and does not, as a matter of principle, object to the imposing of conditions on aid (Kymlicka 2001a: 370).

In Kymlicka's understanding of group rights, a minority community can seek political provisions within the state in terms of three types of claims. It has been noted above that polyethnic rights, through financial support and legal protection for practices associated with ethnic or religious groups, are commonplace though unpopular in south-eastern Europe. In the assimilationist vein, many people would prefer not to subsidize, as it were, the preservation of the culture, customs and language of minorities. As described above, their active opposition would typically concern self-government rights in the sense of delegation of substantive powers to national minorities or the creation of federalist arrangements. Such rights imply the relinquishing of power on the part of the majority population, and clash directly with aspirations of consolidating the nation and the state.

Turning to what Kymlicka calls special representation rights, the picture is more complex. On the one hand, the provision of guaranteed seats for ethnic and national communities within states represents a controversial form of group rights, widely applied in Titoist Yugoslavia and in part of the present constitutional set-up of Bosnia-Herzegovina (in accordance with the Dayton Agreement). On the other hand, special representation rights seem to find an echo in historical practice in the Balkan region, in the long lineage of 'ombudsman' roles traditionally assumed by religious leaders and later by influential merchants. In former Yugoslavia, opinion surveys show that such representation, with symbolic overtones, continues to be more acceptable than either federalist arrangements or polyethnic rights (Magnusson 2001).

Two tentative conclusions therefore flow from this analysis of group rights and their application in south-eastern Europe. The first is that one might want to seriously consider a retreat to the classic liberal position, aiming to bolster individual rights in the region, instead of 'reintroducing' group ones (admittedly of a different kind from those of the Ottoman era, and under more democratic conditions). Despite many problems in putting them into practice, the rights of individuals are disputed by few. All constitutions in the region include an extensive rights catalogue, based primarily, like their counterparts in the West, on an individualistic understanding of human rights (in some countries, for instance Bulgaria, a couple of duties have been included as well).

If the classic liberal position is more readily accepted in south-eastern Europe, Kymlicka would be leading us onto the wrong path in arguing that individual human rights need to be supplemented by collective minority rights (Kymlicka 1995: 6). First of all, this approach relies on an *a priori* distinction between ethnicity and nationality, with only the latter having a legitimate claim to sovereignty. In a sense, this is the bone of contention between the Slav majority in Macedonia, who tend to treat Albanians as an ethnic minority, and the latter, who say they form a nationality by virtue of their share of the population or through their association with a neighboring society (in the Republic of Albania). So this distinction would raise the stakes even higher for the communities engaged in confrontation.

In his more recent *Politics in the Vernacular*, Kymlicka momentarily retreats to a non-normative, almost fatalistic defense of group rights, saying that 'the horse is out of the barn. It is now too late to put minority rights back into the box of merely discretionary politics and pragmatic compromises' (Kymlicka 2001b: 8). He further discards the argument that individual rights might provide a better approach in the Balkan context, saying that liberals typically become 'passive spectators in the struggles between majority and minority nationalists' (Kymlicka 2001b: 273). However, this assertion is simplistic, ignoring the fact that in south-eastern Europe, non-implementation of rights is more often the problem than existing legal provisions.

Second, Kymlicka's group rights are obviously based on an assumption of benign or in some sense civilized relations between the groups involved. His liberal (and logical) argument that autonomy and federalism should be created for minorities presupposes an optimistic scenario where the majority and minority communities gradually grow to understand each other's viewpoints. Consequently, Kymlicka seems not to reckon with the theoretical possibility that group rights could be counterproductive if the basic loyalty to a common state is lacking. The only exception to this stance occurs in a chapter in his edited volume with Opalski from 2001, in which he briefly addresses this problem (Kymlicka 2001a: 387–393). Here he appears to acknowledge that the expansion of group rights in the face of virulent secessionism has the potential temporarily to heighten conflict between minority and majority populations (Kymlicka 2001b: 92). But he goes no further. In the next stage it would seem feasible that armed struggle could erupt over the issue of secession and effectively undermine any optimistic scenario. Unfortunately, it is typically only when the conflict turns malignant that outsiders are finally invited, or drawn, in to try and mitigate or resolve it.

One might also disagree with Kymlicka's underlying assumption in placing the onus of responsibility exclusively on the state and the majority population, as when he writes that the existence of 'secessionist movements suggests that contemporary states have not developed effective means for accommodating national minorities' (Kymlicka 2001b: 92). According to an alternative view, secessionism is not simply the result of rationally summing up injustices done to the minority, but is also related to nationalist ideology and political culture. In the case of the Republic of Macedonia, secessionism is quite common among ethnic Albanians despite the fact that this minority is represented in parliament and the ruling cabinet. For instance, one of the most intractable disputes between Macedonian Slavs and Albanians has arisen over the demand for tertiary education organized by Albanians, and taught in Albanian, in the largest town of that community, Tetovo. It is difficult to see how the satisfaction of this demand—or indeed its rejection—could cause an injustice grave enough to risk triggering civil war, but the dispute should probably be regarded through the lenses of Albanian, and Slav Macedonian, nationalism and the aspirations linked to their ideology.

A further reservation to be noted here concerns the universalistic ambitions of Kymlicka's reasoning. It is clear that in his own view he remains sensitive to local circumstances and pragmatically regards, for instance, the establishment of territorial autonomy for minorities as merely 'a tool among many for promoting ethnocultural justice' (Kymlicka 2001a: 362–363). What emerges from the analysis of Balkan cases, however, is the overwhelming significance of unique political and historical settings—a point also made by Parekh (2000: 9). Although two sets of constitutional and legal arrangements may seem identical when observed from the outside, the circumstances in which they were made and remain upheld are never exactly the same, nor is the meaning of such circumstances necessarily the same to local political actors. As I have suggested, even in adjacent areas such as Macedonia, Kosovo and Bosnia, the prerequisites for ethnic co-existence were quite different before violence erupted in recent times. Whereas antagonism and deep distrust was widespread in Kosovo, the vast majority of the inhabitants of Bosnia-Herzegovina had never considered *not* living together in the same neighborhood or village (in fact, in Sarajevo children and teenagers were often completely unaware of ethnic distinctions). In Macedonia, the population found itself, in the early 1990s, somewhere between these extremes.

Due to several such factors, I have cited the Republic of Macedonia as a critical test-case for group-rights theory. One reason is the acuteness of the crisis in 2001, which seemed to warrant rapid and decisive intervention from outside. A second is the considerable degree of such intervention that actually occurred. A third is the demonstrably-limited local affinity for the common whole which this intervention was intended to promote. Most of the Slav majority, for instance, remain opposed to any Republic of Macedonia not bearing the definitive stamp of their culture. Simultaneously, a large segment of the minority Albanian population feel only a limited loyalty to a state that separates them from their ethnic kin in neighboring Albania and Kosovo. In this predicament the diplomatic intervention of international organizations and European governments, accompanied by conditional assistance, amounts in my view to the imposition of group-rights arrangements in a fragile state. In early 2002, the Slav-dominated legislature passed the controversial local-government bill—but this, one should note, was an explicit precondition for a Western donor conference to take place (*Nova Makedonia* 8 February 2002). Meanwhile, an uneasy and unstable situation persists in the country.

The critical case of Macedonia thus reveals at least one important weakness of group-rights theory. Against Kymlicka's universalism, recognition of the uniqueness of local circumstances has to be taken one step further, and brought to bear on at least some forms of group rights. Just as a country's constitution is the result of a specific set of historical factors, any agreement thrashed out between groups of different self-identification will inevitably be contingent on various idiosyncratic conditions. And while there may be reasons generally to endorse those internationally-promoted polyethnic rights that aim to sustain and develop a culture, language or any other property of a minority community, and to overcome discrimination against people on the grounds of such properties, the same universalism may not automatically apply to the two other categories of group rights.

This is because the rights to community representation and self-rule refer to relations and arrangements of power, including power over another community. The stakes are consequently much higher when it comes to special representation and self-government, and this fact conceals considerable potential for ethnic mobilization and confrontation. Due to the higher stakes and greater potential for violent conflict, such arrangements are much more likely to remain stable if they constitute the outcome of a negotiated settlement between the parties concerned. (As far as I can see, Kymlicka pays practically no attention to the process by which a liberal pluralist framework is set up). In this context the single most important component of such negotiations is mutual trust. Not necessarily trust toward another community (as the lack of this trust is often precisely what makes a rearrangement of power relations crucial for a continuation of peaceful co-existence), but a sense of mutual trust at least that the joint project on which one is poised to embark is seriously intended.

Strong sentiments of secessionism effectively undercut this latter kind of trust. Put differently, a viable deal on minority-group rights involving elements of community representation and self-government is unlikely to be forged where there are strong secessionist sentiments on even one side of the table. Negotiations conducted under the direct threat of secessionism cannot produce a stable legal and political framework for the simple reason that many people will not take them seriously. Secessionism means that the exit strategy always remains a live option.

Finally, I fear there is precious little that outside parties can do, in situations like that prevailing in Macedonia, to facilitate an agreement in which group rights, in Kymlicka's second (self-government) or third (special representation) sense, will constitute a vital component. With luck, many people's lack of faith in the negotiating process will prove temporary, and a renewed sense of trust will be vested in the negotiated outcome. The chances of success may be improved by the robust and long-term physical presence of a third party, civilian and military. Still, the assistance rendered by an assertive external party—whether a single influential government, or a collective of states such as NATO or the EU—is no guarantee of a solution, still less of one sustainable in the long term. By raising false hopes or confusing the real issues at stake, it might even serve to weaken, rather than strengthen, the process of finding a durable settlement.

REFERENCES

Asmus, R. D. (2002). *Opening NATO's Door: How the Alliance Remade itself for the New Era.* New York: Columbia University Press.

Blinkhorn, M. and T. Veremis eds. (1990). *Modern Greece: Nationalism and Nationality*. Athens: ELIAMEP.

Breitenstein, A. (2004). 'Draussen vor Europas Tür'. *Neue Zürcher Zeitung*, 26 November.

Brubaker, R. (1992). *Citizenship and Nationhood in France and Germany*. Cambridge, MA: Harvard University Press.

Carrol, R. (2001). 'Macedonians furious as West imposes cease-fire'. *Guardian Weekly*, 28 June-4 July.

—— (2002). 'Albanian rebels bask in sun and sense of glory'. *Guardian Weekly*, 23–29 August.

Chandler, D. (1999). *Bosnia: Faking Democracy after Dayton*. London: Pluto Press.

Cohen, L. J. (1992). *Broken Bonds: The Disintegration of Yugoslavia*. Boulder, CO: Westview Press.

Connor, W. (1984). *The National Question in Marxist-Leninist Theory and Strategy*. Princeton, NJ: Princeton University Press.

Constitution of the Republic of Macedonia. Available in English at www.izbori98.gov.mk/English/html/constitution.html

Council of Europe (1995). *Framework Convention for the Protection of National Minorities, and Explanations*. Strasbourg.

—— (2001). 'Opinion on the implications of Partial Decision III of the Constitutional Court of Bosnia and Herzegovina in Case U5/98 on the issue of the "Constituent Peoples" '. Strasbourg, 12 March.

Crampton, R. J. (1997). *A Concise History of Bulgaria*. Cambridge: Cambridge University Press.

Dawisha, K. and B. Parrot eds. (1997). *Politics, Power, and the Struggle for Democracy in Southeast-Europe*. Cambridge: Cambridge University Press.

Denitch, B. (1994). *Ethnic Nationalism: The Tragic Death of Yugoslavia*. Minneapolis: University of Minnesota Press.

Engelbrekt, K. (2004). 'Back to basics? International engagement and recurring conflict in south-eastern Europe'. *Global Review of Ethnopolitics* 3, Nos. 3–4 (March/June).

European Commission (2000). *Progress Report 2000*. Brussels: Enlargement Directorate-General.

Fidanovski, Z. (2001). 'Makedonija pred proglasuvane voena sostojba'. *Makedonija Denes*, 5 July.

Friedman, J. (1994). *Cultural Identity and Global Process*. London: Sage.

—— (1998). 'Transnationalization, socio-political disorder, and ethnification as expressions of declining global hegemony'. *International Political Science Review* 19, No. 3.

Gardels, N. (1991). 'Two concepts of nationalism: an interview with Isaiah Berlin'. *New York Review of Books*, 21 November.

Glenny, M. (1992). *The Fall of Yugoslavia: The Third Balkan War*. London: Penguin.

Kitromilides, P. (1990). ' "Imagined Communities" ' and the origins of the national question in the Balkans' in Blinkhorn and Veremis eds.

Kjellén, R. (1916). *Die politischen Probleme des Weltkrieges*. Leipzig and Berlin: B.G. Teubner.

Kofos, E. (1990). 'National heritage and national identity in nineteenth- and twentieth-century Macedonia' in Blinkhorn and Veremis eds.

—— (2001). 'Greece's Macedonian adventure: the controversy over FYROM's independence and recognition' in Van Coufoudakis and Gerolymatos eds.

Kranz, J. ed. (1998). *Law and Practice of Central European Countries in the Field of National Minorities Protection after 1989*. Warsaw: Center for International Relations.

Krasner, S. D. ed. (2000). *Problematic Sovereignty: Contested Rules and Political Possibilities*. New York: Columbia University Press.

Kymlicka, W. (1995) *Multicultural Citizenship: A Liberal Theory of Minority Rights*. Oxford: Oxford University Press.

—— (2001a) 'Western political theory and ethnic relations in Eastern Europe' and 'Reply and conclusion' in Kymlicka and Opalski eds.

—— (2001b) *Politics in the Vernacular: Nationalism, Multiculturalism, and Citizenship*. Oxford: Oxford University Press.

—— and M. Opalski eds. (2001). *Can Liberalism be Exported? Western Political Theory and Ethnic Relations in Eastern Europe*. Oxford: Oxford University Press.

Latifi, V. (2001). 'Religious strife fuels Macedonian conflict'. BCR 262, 12 July.

Lewis, B. (1961). *The Emergence of Modern Turkey.* Oxford: Oxford University Press.

Magnusson, K. (2001). 'Distant neighbors: perceptions of Self and Other in Bosnia, Croatia and Serbia'. Paper presented at the Annual Convention of the Association for the Study of Nationalities, 5–7 April.

Martinelli, M. (1997). 'The dilemma of separation versus union: the new dynamic of nationalist politics in Belgium' in Wicker ed.

Micunovic, V. (1980). *Moscow Diary*. London: Chatto & Windus.

Nanevska, S. (2001). 'Start za pomiruvaneto'. *Puls*, 14 August.

Ordanoski, S. (2001). 'Skopje talks survive PM setback'. BCR 364, 20 July.

Ortakovski, V. (2000). *Minorities in the Balkans*. Ardsley, NY: Transnational Publishers.

Ourdan, R. (2002). 'En Bosnie, le Britannique Paddy Ashdown se impose en véritable chef d'Etat'. *Le Monde*, 29 May.

Owen, D. (1995). *Balkan Odyssey*. London: Gollancz.

Pampur, R. (2001). 'Kakva lokalna administratsija?'. *Puls,* 31 August.

Parekh, B. (2000). *Rethinking Multiculturalism: Cultural Diversity and Political Theory*. Basingstoke: Macmillan.

Perry, D. M. (1997). 'The Republic of Macedonia: finding its way' in Dawisha and Parrot eds.

Poulton, H. (1995). *Who Are the Macedonians?* London: Hurst.

Ramet, S. P. (1992). *Nationalism and Federalism in Yugoslavia 1962–1991*. Bloomington, Ind.: Indiana University Press.

Shaw, S. J. (1991). *The Jews of the Ottoman Empire and the Turkish Republic*. London: Macmillan.

Soysal, Y. N. (1994). *Limits of Citizenship: Migrants and Postnational Membership in Europe*. Chicago: University of Chicago Press.

Tosheva, M. (1997). *Etnicheskite grupi vo Makedonija: Istoricheski kontekst*. University of Skopje: Filosofski fakultet.

Van Coufoudakis, H. J. P. and A. Gerolymatos eds. (1999). *Greece and the New Balkans: Challenges and Opportunities*. New York: Pella.

Verdery, K. (1991). *National Ideology under Socialism: Identity and Cultural Politics in Ceaucescu's Romania*. Berkeley, CA: University of California Press.

Weber, R. (1998). 'The protection of national minorities in Romania: a matter of political will and wisdom' in Kranz ed.

Wicker, H.-R. ed. (1997). *Rethinking Nationalism and Ethnicity*. Oxford: Berg.

Woodward, S. L. (1995). *Balkan Tragedy: Chaos and Dissolution after the Cold War*. Washington, DC: The Brookings Institution.

—— (2000). 'Compromised sovereignty to create sovereignty: is Dayton Bosnia a futile exercise or an emerging model?' in Krasner ed.

Chapter Five

Crisis in the Identity Politics of Turkey

Sahin Alpay

Identity problems and conflicts have occupied the centre-stage of Turkish politics since the early 1980s. Mass movements of population, increasing urbanization, and globalization have given rise to serious challenges to the country's official identity policies. While economic globalization has made it increasingly difficult to combine development with catering for the needs of the poor, socio-economic dislocation has instilled a search for greater certainty and security in threatened individuals and communities. Globalization in Turkey, as elsewhere in the world, has contributed to cultural fragmentation and to widening demands for the recognition of local and traditional culture.

The main aim of the Turkish Republic's identity policies since its founding years has been the creation, out of the Ottoman legacy of a multi-ethnic and multi-religious population, of a uniform and homogeneous nation speaking the Turkish language and adhering to Turkish culture, including the officially-sanctioned and promoted Sunni-Hanafi Islam. The main challenges to these policies have come from the largest ethnic and religious minorities, the Kurds and Alevis, and from Islamist movements. More recently, the problem has arisen of making the official policies compatible with membership, real or aspired-to, of various European-based intergovernmental organizations.

Turkey was declared a candidate for EU membership at the Helsinki summit of the European Council in December 1999. Opening membership negotiations with the EU was conditional on the fulfillment, in Turkey, of the 'Copenhagen Political Criteria' of 'stability of institutions guaranteeing democracy, the rule of law, human rights and respect for and protection of minorities.' But the country's identity policies have also come into conflict with the rules and norms of the Council of Europe, the OSCE, and even

NATO, where Turkish membership goes back to the organization's early years. Similarly, the decisions of the European Court of Human Rights, whose compulsory jurisdiction was recognized by Turkey in 1991, have often come into conflict with laws and regulations which not only denied citizens freedom to express their religious, ethnic and cultural identity, but also curtailed their basic freedoms.

In my view, therefore, Turkey's identity policies are in crisis, being increasingly challenged by popular opposition and unrest, which endangers domestic peace and integrity while seriously conflicting with repeated official claims to belong to the family of Western liberal democracies. In what follows I begin with an account of the evolution of these policies, and the unfolding of the principal challenges they have encountered during the past two decades. I then address, in the context of the minority-group rights vs. individual-citizenship rights debate, the question of how the crisis in those policies can be resolved, and suggest the kind of reforms that are necessary to ensure social unity and strengthened democracy in Turkey.

THE OTTOMAN LEGACY

The Republic of Turkey was founded in 1923 on the ruins of the Ottoman Empire. The Ottoman legacy has played a very important role in the shaping of modern Turkey, despite the efforts of the Republican regime to break completely with its past.

The multi-ethnic, multi-religious Ottoman Empire's identity policies were based on the *millet* system, which made religious community the prime focus of identity for the Empire's subjects. The sultans based the legitimacy of their rule on Islam, yet the Ottoman state was not a theocracy in the strict meaning of the term, a state governed by a Muslim clergy according to the *sharia*, or holy law of Islam. Not only were the Muslim *ulema* totally subservient to the ruler's authority; Ottoman lands were governed by both religious and secular law—the *kanun*, or laws enacted by the sovereign sultans.

Ottoman rulers did not seek to Islamicize the peoples under their rule, since they lacked the means to fully integrate and unify their subjects. Thus, in the classical age of the Empire the various ethnic and religious groups, with their greatly differing cultures, lived side by side. The *millet* system meant that the various non-Muslim groups were organized around their respective religious institutions and autonomous in their internal affairs. The Ottoman state did identify itself with Islam, but not with the Turks, the founding ethnic element of the Empire. The concept of the 'Turk' was in fact alien to the Ottoman elites who saw themselves as Osmanli rather than Turk (which to them implied the uneducated peasants of Anatolia). To join the Ottoman bureaucracy one had to be a Muslim and speak Ottoman Turkish, but the ruling elite was mostly composed of *devsirme*, or converts from various Christian minorities.

The *millet* system began gradually to disintegrate in the 18th century, providing a greatly favorable environment for the spread of the new European ideology of nationalism in the 19th century. Among the Christian communities the various churches became the primary disseminators of nationalism. Nationalism was later also to spread among Muslim-majority peoples such as Albanians, Arabs, Turks and finally the Kurds (Poulton 1997: 33–49). Countering the onslaught of nationalism and avoiding the dissolution of the Empire thus became the primary concern of the Ottoman elite. Ottomanism, Islamism and Turkism were then the three competing answers put forward by various thinkers to the question of 'How to save the Ottoman state?'

Beginning with Sultan Mahmud II (1808–38), Ottoman rulers tried first to promote an Ottoman identity for all their subjects, and to create an Ottoman nation on a territorial basis. They declared that all Ottoman citizens, irrespective of their ethnic or religious origin, possessed equal rights. Ottomanism failed, however, partly because of the swift spread of nationalism and partly because of suspicion among Christian subjects of the Empire that the policy was a cover for continued Muslim supremacy.

As the various Balkan possessions of the Empire were lost, Sultan Abdülhamit II, who came to power in 1876, launched a policy of Islamism aimed at preserving the unity of all Muslim subjects under the Ottoman state and stressing the role of the Sultan as Caliph (the traditional religious leader of the Muslim world), a title which Ottoman sultans had borne since the 16th century. But Islamism, like Ottomanism, proved unable to avert the disintegration of the Empire. The Ottoman elites of the late 19th and early 20th centuries then turned towards Turkish ethnic nationalism. This ideology, influenced by German notions of race-based nationalism, was propagated primarily by Turkic émigrés from Russia, and most prominently by Yusuf Akcura (Zürcher 2004: 129).

The contradictory programmes of Ottomanism, Islamism and pan-Turkism, seeking in turn territorial, religious and ethnic bases for Ottoman citizens' identity, created much confusion and ambivalence in the minds of Ottoman elites themselves in the final decades of the Empire. The 'Young Turk' opposition which organized itself around the Committee of Union and Progress to topple Abdülhamit in 1908 increasingly embraced Turkism. There were, however, competing versions of this ideology. In contrast to Yusuf Akcura's pan-Turkism, which sought to unify all Turks, including the Turkic peoples of Russia, under Ottoman rule, Ziya Gökalp argued in favor of a Turkish-Muslim cultural nationalism (Poulton 1997: 76–81). This version was to dominate the period of rule by the Union and Progress Party (*Ittihat ve Terakki Firkasi*, or ITF) between 1908 and 1919, and by the Republican People's Party (*Cumhuriyet Halk Firkasi*, or CHF) under Mustafa Kemal's leadership from 1919 to 1925.

Young Turk governments led the Ottoman Empire into the First World War on the side of Germany. When the war was lost the Ottoman state was faced with total dismemberment. The Young Turks, however, used the rallying-call of Islam to unite the Muslim population of Anatolia and Thrace in a war of resistance, primarily against the invading Greek army. Mustafa Kemal Pasha (later Atatürk) who led the Turkish nationalist forces, was able to enlist the support of the Kurds, the most numerous Muslim people after the Turks, by promising them some form of autonomy upon victory (Mango 1999: 6–7; Zürcher 2004: 170.)

A NATION FOR THE STATE

The definition of national identity in the formative period of the modern Turkish Republic was based on a combination of territorial and religious components. The War of Independence was fought not in the name of the Turkish people but in the name of the 'Muslim people of Anatolia and Rumeli [Thrace]'. The compulsory population-exchange with Greece agreed in the Lausanne Treaty of 1923 was based on the principle of religious adherence. Broadly speaking, the Muslims of Greece were exchanged for the Greek Orthodox of Anatolia, with the sole exceptions of the Muslims of western Thrace and the Greek Orthodox of Istanbul. Under the Republic, no minorities were recognized other than the Christian and Jewish ones mentioned in the Lausanne Treaty, who were granted special group rights, including the right to practice their religion freely, to establish private schools and provide education in their own language, and to settle family or private issues in accordance with their own customs. Non-Muslim minorities other than those mentioned in the Treaty, however, were granted no minority status or any group rights. This situation still obtains today.

Article 88 of the first Constitution of the Republic of Turkey, adopted in 1924, stated that 'the people of Turkey regardless of their religion and race are, in terms of citizenship, Turkish'. The clause 'regardless of their religion and race' was later dropped, but the principle persisted in the 1961 and 1982 constitutions and reflects a territorial, or civic, conception of Turkish national identity. The implementation of identity policy under the Republic has, however, been quite different (Kirisci 2000: 1–2). Following the Kurdish revolt led by the Nakshibendi Sheikh Said in 1925, the Law of Maintenance of Order was enacted. This was the beginning not only of the authoritarian single-party rule of Kemalists, but also the end to all promises of autonomy for the Kurds. After the suppression of the Sheikh Said uprising, which had both an anti-secular and an ethnic basis, the Kemalist leadership gradually turned towards a policy of Turkification of the various ethnic groups in the population in order to create a uniform and homogeneous nation. In this context the teaching and even the public use of Kurdish was prohibited (Zürcher 2004: 170).

With the development of the 'Turkish History' thesis, and its linguistic counterpart, the 'Sun-Language' Thesis, in the 1930s, the foundation was laid for modern Turkey's identity policies. Official policies turned increasingly away from Gökalp's Turkish-Muslim cultural nationalism towards Akcura's ethnic and secular nationalism. History was rewritten to define the War of Independence as a Turkish War of Independence. Any expression of the existence of Muslim peoples of other ethnic origin (Kurds, Circassians, Arabs, or others) was silenced. The Turkish language was declared the most important language in the world, and the Turkish race the motor of history. The Ottoman Empire, by contrast, was characterized as the most retrograde period in Turkish history, and its experience was said to be alien and non-Turkish (Poulton 1997: 87–114).

From the early 1930s onwards the influence of racist nationalism in Germany and Italy began to be felt in Turkey. Following the suppression of the Kurdish revolt led by Sheikh Said, Prime Minister Ismet Inönü declared: 'The revolution fanned by foreign intrigue in our Eastern provinces has lasted for five years, but today it loses half its strength. Only the Turkish nation is entitled to claim ethnic and national rights in this country. No other element has any such right'. Minister of Justice Bozkurt observed: 'I believe that the Turk must be the only lord, the only master of this country. Those who are not of pure Turkish stock can have only one right in this country, the right to be servants and slaves' (Poulton 1997: 120).

As Kirisci puts it, the Settlement Law of 1934 was 'designed as a tool for constructing a homogeneous sense of national identity based on the precepts of modernism and secularism'. In the words of a deputy who participated in the parliamentary debate, the law's basic aim was to create 'a country which would speak one single language, and which would think and feel alike', so that 'the Turkish state would no longer have to suspect the Turkishness of any Turk' (Kirisci 2000: 5).

SECULARISM *ALLA TURCA*

The Republic's policy towards Islam also underwent a radical change in the latter half of the 1920s. In the formative period of the republic (1919–22) the

Kemalist leadership, as we have seen above, used Islam to mobilize the people of Anatolia and Thrace against the Greek invasion, while Islam was also used to define who constituted the new nation under construction.

The Kemalist regime, however, soon abandoned this policy. It set out a series of reforms aimed at relegating Islam to the private sphere and putting religion under strict state control. The Grand National Assembly (which had abolished the Sultanate in 1922, and declared Turkey a Republic in 1923) voted in 1924 to abolish the Caliphate, the Ministry of Religious Affairs and Trusts, religious schools and the *sharia* courts. A new centralized secular educational system was established with the Unification of Education Law in 1924. The regime outlawed the Sufi religious brotherhoods (*tarikat*), which it regarded as potential centres of fanatical religious opposition, and closed all of their lodges and sanctuaries in 1925. New civil and criminal laws based on Swiss and Italian codes respectively were passed, and the European calendar was adopted in 1926. The alphabet was changed from Arabic to Latin in 1928.

In the same year, the statement 'The religion of the Turkish State is Islam' was removed from the Constitution, and in 1937 an amendment declared that the Turkish Republic was a secular state. Turkish secularism, called *laiklik* (from the French *laïc*), did not, however, mean the separation of state and religion. Rather, it meant that all the various interpretations of Islam other than the orthodox official (Sunni-Hanafi) version were to be suppressed, including both those favored by the *tarikat* and the heterodox beliefs of the Alevi community, which mixed elements of Shia Islam with the shamanism of Central Asian Turks and pre-Muslim Anatolian beliefs. The Directorate of Religious Affairs (*Diyanet Isleri Baskanligi*, hereafter referred to as the *Diyanet*), which replaced the Ottoman Ministry of Religious Affairs, was set up to put religious activity under state supervision and control (Shankland 1999: 15–87, Tarhanli 1993: 15–22).

Turkish secularism cannot be properly understood without reference to Young Turk and Kemalist attitudes toward religion in general and Islam in particular. The Young Turks and Kemalists were greatly inspired by Auguste Comte and his followers' positivist philosophy. According to the more radical secularists among the Young Turk-Kemalist elites, Islam was among the main reasons for the backwardness of Ottoman-Turkish society. In order for the country to progress, religious thinking had gradually to be replaced by rational, scientific thinking. As Andrew Davison puts it, the Kemalist view was that 'religious superstition held the nation back . . . Developing citizens with a positivist rationality was an explicit goal of *laiklik* policies' (Davison 1998: 164–165). Although Islam was, according to Mustafa Kemal, 'the most rational and natural of religions', those who wanted to use religion for political ends, the religious reactionaries (*irtica*), constituted a great danger which had to be suppressed by all means. It was therefore deemed necessary to put religion under strict state control. An effective way of doing this was the promotion of the Sunni-Hanafi version of Islam, which tended to accord legitimacy to whoever was in power, while all the mystical and heterodox forms of Islam were outlawed.

The prominent historian of modern Turkey, Erik J. Zürcher, argues that

> the Kemalist reforms of 1924 . . . can all be seen as logical conclusions to the Ottoman secularization process. Where the Kemalists really did go a lot further than their predecessors was in the banning of the religious orders and the closing down of shrines in 1925, and in wholesale introduction of European family law in 1926. These measures were radically new because they meant that the state now interfered with Islamic institutions unconnected to the state and with the personal relationships between the citizens to an unprecedented degree. This not only concerned institutions and legislation but the 'way of life' of ordinary citizens (2001: 5).

Turkish-style secularism, to repeat, does not regard all faiths as equal under the Republic, but favors one among them. All citizens, irrespective of faith, are required to support financially the *Diyanet* institution through general taxation. The *Diyanet* has developed a country-wide administrative structure with a share in public expenditure roughly equal to that of the Ministry of Education. Its central office in Ankara strictly oversees subordinate offices in each sub-province. Imams (prayer leaders) who administer the mosques under its supervision are not allowed to make their own interpretations of Islam; even the content of their weekly sermons is decided in Ankara.

EVOLUTION OF IDENTITY POLICIES

The identity policies of the Turkish Republic have undergone a certain evolution while retaining the basic principles established in the late 1920s and early 1930s. This evolution after the crucial year of 1925 can be divided into three main periods.

In the first, lasting for most of the period of single-party rule (1925–46), Turks' national identity was defined almost exclusively in terms of race and language, with special emphasis on their Central Asian roots. According to the 'Turkish History Thesis' of the 1930s, even the Kurds—in reality, an ethnically-distinct people with an Indo-European language—are of Turkic origin; they are ascribed common origins with Turks in Central Asia, living as they all did in their inaccessible mountains (thus the use of the expression 'Mountain Turks' to refer to them); and are said to have lost through the ages their 'mother tongue' (i.e. Turkish) in favor of a 'dialect' that is 'a mixture of old Turkish, Persian, Arabic and Armenian' (Poulton 1997: 87–109).

Etienne Copeaux, in his analysis of history books used in Turkish secondary schools, distinguishes a second stage in the evolution of official identity policies which roughly opens with the introduction of multi-party politics in the late 1940s. According to Copeaux, a 'humanistic' approach dominated in the teaching of history in this period which lasted well into the late 1970s. The books of this period, while not substantially deviating from the nationalist canon of the 'History Thesis', allowed much greater space to the history of the West, and contained a perspective of history that stressed, rather than their Central Asian origins, the Turks' history as an Anatolian and Mediterranean people (Copeaux 1998: 54–56.)

A reaction developed, however, to this approach, culminating in the late 1970s in an ideological movement identified as the 'Turkish-Islamic Synthesis' (hereafter referred as TIS) which emphasized both the Central Asian and Muslim legacies of the Turks. According to the proponents of TIS, Islam is superior to Turkish culture, and it would have been impossible for the latter to survive without the former. Turkish culture, on the other hand, has both protected and strengthened Islam (Poulton 1997: 179–187).

The proponents of TIS who organized themselves around the association of *Aydinlar Ocagi* approved of Kemalist policies that instilled confidence in the Turkish identity, but they were extremely critical of the 'humanists', whom they accused of spreading Westernist, even Marxist ideas: 'Humanism is a game played by the West on Turkey. Humanists are those who want to destroy our national culture. Communism has not been able to eliminate Turkishness, but humanism may well be more detrimental to the Turks . . . Humanists are those who want to trace our lineage and culture to ancient Rome and the Greeks . . . They deny us our own history, and force upon us the reading of Western history. Turkish youth is being brought up reading about Roman and Greek civilizations' (Copeaux 1998: 58–59).

A third phase in the evolution of Turkey's identity policies opened when TIS was adopted as the semi-official ideology of the Turkish state by the military regime that was established following the military intervention of 12 September 1980. This regime put to an end to the violent political conflict raging between extreme leftist and rightist groups in the country. While suppressing political Islam, it actively promoted the *Diyanet* version of Islam for the purpose of fighting the divisive effects of communism and (Kurdish) separatism. As Hakan Yavuz puts it:

> Through the Islamization of society, the coup leaders sought to engineer a new form of depoliticized Turkish-Islamic culture that would reunify society, and in

> order to attain this goal they issued a national culture report. This report . . . was based on the TIS whose bedrock was the family, the mosque, and the military barracks. These three institutional pillars were expected to produce a disciplined, unified and well-ordered organic society, and a powerful, united and harmonious state. The military government obviously preferred to employ religious sentiment and traditional allegiances, rather than the principles of participatory democracy, to achieve political stability and national unity. Through the TIS, it aimed to identify the state and the nation as one *cemaat* [community] modelled after the concept of *umma* [religious community] (Yavuz 1997: 68).

The Constitution of 1982 adopted under military rule made religious instruction (in official, *Diyanet* Islam) compulsory in primary and secondary schools. The budget of the *Diyanet*, the number of mosques built each year and the number and graduates of *Imam-Hatip* (prayer leader and preacher) schools greatly increased throughout the 1980s and even after the return to civilian rule in 1983. *Imam-Hatip* schools, originally set up to train religious functionaries, increasingly evolved into an alternative educational system.

The measures decided on in February 1997 by the National Security Council (the powerful organ combining Turkish military and civilian leaders) against the spread of 'religious reaction', and the resignation under military threat in June of the coalition government led by Necmettin Erbakan (the leader of the Islamist Welfare Party), may be said to have brought the end of TIS as the semi-official basis of identity policies in Turkey.

The effort to create a uniform and homogeneous Turkish nation speaking Turkish, adhering to Turkish culture and professing the official, *Diyanet* religion of Sunni-Hanafi Islam has been largely, if not entirely, successful. The Muslim, Alevi and Kurdish challenges of the 1980s and 90s prove the point. Paradoxically, increased modernization and secularization have brought a growing demand for a public role for Islam, while enhanced opportunities for upward social mobility have given way to a stronger assertion of the Muslim identity on the part of the newly-educated and urbanized sections of society. The vast majority of Alevis, despite official denials of their religious identity, have retained their adherence to their sect. Various Muslim ethnic groups have been successfully assimilated into the 'imagined' Turkish nation, but with the major exception of the Kurds. While an estimated majority of Kurds who migrated to the more developed and predominantly Turkish-speaking regions of western Turkey were assimilated and integrated there, those who remained in the predominantly Kurdish-speaking eastern and south-eastern regions of the country retained their attachment to Kurdish identity. Increased modernization and secularization contributed to the rise of ethnic Kurdish nationalism—the last of the nationalisms of the Ottoman subject peoples—and an armed separatist insurgency in the early 1980s.

The Islamist Challenge

It may be argued that like its nation-building project, the secularist project of Kemalism has on the whole been successful, insofar as recent surveys indicate that an overwhelming majority of Turkey's population embrace both Islam and secularism (Carkoglu-Toprak 2000: 70–79). This does not, however, mean either that there is no opposition to the state's secularist policies or that religion is not an important factor in people's lives.

The earliest and arguably strongest challenge to the official identity policies of Kemalist secular nationalism has come from the Islamists, who claim to represent the suppressed Muslim identity of the country. Led by Necmettin Erbakan, and first organized in the National Order Party (*Milli Nizam Partisi*, MNP), founded in 1969, they openly questioned the secularist policies of the Republic, and opposed policies of relegating religion to the private sphere. The MNP emphasized Islam as the real cultural basis and binding cement of the people of Turkey, and complained of moral degeneration (the increased use of alcohol, gambling and prostitution) which they said was the result of a turning-away from Islamic values and of imitating Western cultural patterns.

The Constitutional Court shut down the MNP in 1971 for engaging in activities against the secularist principles of the Republic. A series of parties which replaced the MNP have all shared the same fate. The National Salvation Party (*Milli Selamet Partisi*—MSP, 1973–80), the Welfare Party (*Refah Partisi*—RP, 1983–98), and the Virtue Party (*Fazilet Partisi*—FP, 1998–2001) were all banned, the first by a military court and the latter two by the Constitutional Court, on the grounds that they were engaging in activities against the principle of secularism.

Popular support for the Islamist movement reached its peak when the RP garnered about a fifth of the national vote in the local elections of 1994 and parliamentary elections of 1995—up from a mere 7% of the vote in the national elections of 1987. The RP became the senior partner in the coalition government formed in July 1996, but was forced to withdraw under the pressure of the military in June 1997.

A multiplicity of socio-economic and cultural factors explain the electoral success of the RP (Önis 1997: 746–49). These include its positions on identity and justice which appealed to the discontented masses, especially the urban poor. It also offered a framework for increased participation by new Muslim cultural and business elites. Its message of 'Muslim unity' appealed even to Kurds in east and south-east Turkey, many of whom adhered to their Muslim identity to the extent of disapproving of secular Kurdish nationalism. The RP projected its opposition to official secularism through demands for a lifting of the ban on wearing the headscarf, permission for prayer spaces in public buildings, and adjustments of working hours in public offices to accommodate Friday prayers. Some RP mayors took measures towards segregating the sexes in public transport, censorship on erotic art, and the prohibition of alcohol consumption in restaurants.

RP spokesmen also demanded that the concept of secularism, or *laiklik*, be given a clear definition in the constitution such that it would provide for a separation of state and religion on the American model. It remained, however, unclear whether the kind of secularism the RP demanded would guarantee equal treatment of all faiths. The most radical idea advocated by the Islamist movement came in the mid-1990s when Erbakan said that the RP, when in power, would introduce 'the greatest freedom for all citizens including the freedom to choose the legal system he or she desired to adhere to', based on a 'plurality of legal systems'. This idea, originally advanced by an Islamist intellectual (Bulac 1998: 176–78), foresaw a recognition of group rights which would allow various religious groups to implement religious rules in the sphere of personal and family law, in a system similar to that of India where there is no common-to-all Civil Code. The proposal never actually became a part of RP's official party programme, but was one of the reasons for the decision by the Constitutional Court to ban the RP (a decision upheld by the European Court of Human Rights).

In more recent times the Islamist movement in Turkey has gone through a remarkable ideological transformation towards increasingly moderate positions. The fourth party of the movement, the Virtue Party, founded in May 1998, declared the promotion of democracy, human rights and political liberties to be its primary goal. The leader of the party, Recai Kutan, a former close aide of Erbakan (who had been banned from politics for five years), remarked that their past experience had demonstrated that freedom and democracy came first and nothing could be achieved without them. The Constitutional Court nonetheless banned the FP in June 2001 for forming a 'centre of activity against the principle of secularism,' the main evidence being its opposition to the headscarf ban.

The Virtue Party's two factions then organized into two separate parties. The 'traditionalist' faction, controlled from behind the scenes by Erbakan, founded the Felicity Party (*Saadet Partisi*—SP) in July 2001. The 'renewalist' faction, led by the former mayor of Istanbul, Recep Tayyip Erdogan, established the Justice and Development Party (*Adalet ve Kalkinma Partisi*—AKP) the following month. The AKP adopted perhaps the most liberal political programme in the country's history of multi-party politics and defined itself as Conservative-Democratic. Erdogan, declaring the exploitation of religion for political purposes to be over, emphasized the AKP's commitment to secularism and its rejection of nationalism based on race, region or religion.

In the elections of November 2002 Erdogan was barred from running for a seat in parliament on the grounds of his conviction in 1997 for reading a poem that incited religious hatred. The AKP nonetheless managed to win 34% of the popular vote and two-thirds of the seats in parliament. After constitutional and legal amendments had cleared the way, Erdogan was elected to parliament in a by-election in March 2003 and assumed the premiership.

The transformation in the Islamists' approach has been portrayed, by the elites who support official secularism, as *takiye*—a tactic to deceive the public about their real intentions. Others, however, see in it proof of the moderating effects of the democratic process. Some former Islamists have declared 'the end of political Islam', implicitly admitting that the lessons of the Islamic revolution in Iran have demonstrated the importance of basic rights and freedoms for all (Bulac 1999: 40).

The Headscarf Controversy

The ideological transformation of the AKP is unlikely, however, to remove the controversy around the headscarf ban from Turkey's political agenda. The prohibition on the wearing of headscarves by women in government offices and on university campuses remains the most important issue of the debate over secularism in Turkey at the turn of the 21st century.

Until the late 1960s, there seemed to be a general consensus that the principles of secularism required the prohibition of Islamic attire in public offices and on university grounds, although there were no legal provisions to that effect. The de facto ban began to be challenged by Islamist groups in the 1970s. The first outright prohibition of the headscarf was enacted by the Council of Higher Education (*YÖK*) in 1982 during military rule. The regulation has since stayed in place with alternating periods of strict and softened implementation (Özdalga 1998: 39–49).

Opposition to the headscarf ban was the reason for the outlawing of the Virtue Party by the Constitutional Court in June 2001. The first headscarved parliamentarian, Ms. Merve Kavakci, was elected to parliament in April 1999. She was, however, booed and stopped from taking the oath in parliament by radical secularists, and eventually stripped of both her parliamentary membership and citizenship when it was found she had acquired US citizenship without informing the Turkish authorities, as required by law.

The ban is rigorously implemented, but the AKP government seems unlikely to antagonize the state authorities over this issue, though it remains committed to lifting the ban when a consensus can be reached. The demand, moreover, for the lifting of the ban is widely popular (Carkoglu-Toprak 2000: 68–70). Both Islamists and liberals oppose it as a gross violation of the freedom of religious expression, as open discrimination against women and a denial, in practice, of the right to education of girls from conservative or religious families. The secularist establishment, on the other hand, resolutely supports the ban on the grounds that wearing the headscarf is a political gesture against the principle of secularism and, implicitly, in favor of an Islamic state. The ban is also defended on the grounds that the headscarf imposes restrictions on women's liberties, and that it can lead to unequal treatment by differentiating them from others. In a highly controversial decision, the European Court of Human Rights upheld the ban in 2004, on the following grounds: "In a country like Turkey, where the great majority of the population belong to a particular religion, measures taken in universities to prevent certain fundamentalist religious movements from exerting pressure on students who do not practice that religion or on those who belong to another religion may be justified" (Leyla Sahin vs. Turkey, 29 June 2004).

The Alevi Revival

Rigid secularism in Turkey has also been challenged by the Alevis, the largest religious minority in the country. Official statistics affirming that the population is 99% Muslim conceal the vast diversity of Islam in Turkey. There are three main groups. The Sunni majority is divided into those who adhere to the Sunni-Hanafi creed supported and promoted by the *Diyanet*, and those who belong to the various religious brotherhoods and communities of Sufi or 'folk' Islam. The Alevi minority, on the other hand, practices a heterodox form of Islam, as described above.

Alevis are estimated at 12–13m, or about 15%, of Turkey's population, though some estimates put them at a much higher proportion. There are no official statistics to help us here, because censuses since 1965 have not given any information on the religious or ethnic composition of the population. Academic studies, however, identify no less than 47 ethnic and religious groups of different sizes (Andrews 1989). Alevis are divided not only according to different interpretations of Alevi belief, but also along ethnic lines. The majority are of Turkish ethnic origin, while 25–30% belong to the Kurdish minority (Shankland 1999: 137).

The founding of the republic of Turkey was welcomed by the Alevis as a whole, who saw the new Republican regime as a liberator from Ottoman oppression and a guarantee against religious persecution by the Sunni majority. They approved of the Republican interpretation of Turkish history, and the construction of a nation based on Turkish heritage. Many among them claim to represent authentic Turkish Islam, arguing that Sunni Islam was introduced later. The secularist republican regime, in its understanding of modernity as uniformity, while not actively trying to assimilate Alevis into the Sunni majority, denied their existence as a distinct group until as late as the 1990s. Meanwhile, the Sunni *ulema* (theologians) and Islamist intellectuals of the Republican period treated the Alevis with much the same contempt as in Ottoman times, describing them as heretics and enemies of Islam, and making regular allegations of promiscuity and incest against them. Alevis, while largely left alone to practice their religion in rural areas, were often forced to hide their identity and pose as Sunnis when they migrated to the towns and cities. It may in fact be argued that the discovery by the Alevis of their distinct religious and ethnic identity began with their mass migration to the towns and cities of Turkey and, later, of the Federal Republic of Germany.

During the 1960s and 70s, the Alevis were an important source of support for the various leftist and Marxist groupings, and the Alevi religious identity (like the Kurdish ethnic identity) was in a way hidden behind the universalist identity of socialism. From the late 1980s on, however, a process of rediscovery of the Alevi identity began. A great number of books and periodicals were published on or around this theme, and community-based Alevi associations were established (Camuroglu 1998: 79).

According to Reha Camuroglu, a leading researcher on Alevi issues, several factors explain this revival. With the collapse of communism and dissolution of the Soviet Union, 'socialism, which in the previous two decades had an indisputable authority as an ideological alternative for the young and middle generations of Alevis, lost its former importance'. The rise of political Islam awakened their 'defensive instinct', while the rise of the Kurdish identity forced them to make practical choices. Faced with the rise of Islamism they supported official secularism; faced with Kurdish nationalism they sought unity around a common religious identity (Camuroglu 1998: 81–82).

From the early 1990s onwards the Alevis began openly to demand their basic rights, in the form of the free practice of their religious rituals, an end to legal and social discrimination, the right to organize as a distinct confessional community, and state funding for their religious and cultural activities. The first explicit expression of the Alevi revival was the petition signed by 22 Alevi associations in 1992 asking the government to reform the *Diyanet* to include their representatives, and to provide support for their cultural and religious activities since they, like all other Turkish citizens, helped pay the *Diyanet*'s budget (Poulton 1997: 256).

Faruk Bilici makes the following comment on the position of the *Diyanet*:

> Instead of declaring openly . . . that Alevism is incompatible with Islam, they have attempted to assimilate it by adopting one of the three following courses. One method is to regard Alevism as a type of folklore or sub-culture . . . thus denying it any significance on the theological level . . . As opposed to those who say that the Alevis should be represented in the Directorate . . . they prefer to re-

> gard Alevism as a mere sect or religious order and oppose its representation on the grounds that the Directorate is superior to all sects and religious orders . . . Finally they assume the position of a referee sifting the good Alevis from the bad on the grounds that Alevism is being used as a tool by atheists, materialists, Marxists, Christians and Jews. The Alevis in general, however, have little respect for this body, and the dialogue initiated by the Directorate . . . in 1992 to discuss these topics proved abortive in face of a severely-hostile reaction on the part of broad sections of the Alevi community (Bilici 1998: 60).

Meanwhile, the efforts of the Cem Vakfi, a foundation supported by upper-class Alevis, 'to re-orientate the Alevi religion towards the state in such a way that it becomes perceived as a . . . legitimate, moderate form of Islam that should be recognized by the Republic' have met with widespread disapproval among Alevis, who 'simply do not like the state at all, and wish to have nothing to do with it in any form', arguing that 'the state is the instrument of oppressive Islam as much as it ever was before' (Shankland 1999: 162–63).

The attitude of the state authorities towards the Alevis since the early 1990s has been ambivalent. Consideration of the movement as a counterweight for political Islam may partly explain the increased tolerance at central-government level of the expression of Alevi identity. Since the mid-1990s Alevis have been freely opening their religious centres, or *cemevi*, in the larger cities. Leading politicians pay visits to the town of Hacibektas, where a yearly Alevi festival is held. Even some public funds have even been allocated to support Alevi cultural activities. The ambivalence of the Turkish authorities is perhaps best exemplified by the fact that while an Ankara court decided to close down the Cultural Association of the Federation of Alevi-Bektashi Institutions for promoting a sectarian belief and religious separatism, the state budget for the year 2002 provided 149 billion Turkish liras (about $80,000) in public funding for Alevi foundations and associations (*Radikal* 18 February 2002.)

The Resurgence of the Kurds

As in the case of Turkey's largest religious minority, the Alevis, there are no official statistics for the size of Turkey's largest ethnic minority, the Kurds. Most academic observers estimate their size at about 20% of the population of Turkey, or 13–14m. Speaking various dialects of Kurdish, an Indo-European language, the Kurdish peoples are spread over four countries of the Middle East (Turkey, Syria, Iraq, and Iran), and amount to some 25m in all, making Turkey the country with the largest Kurdish minority.

The Kurds of Turkey are generally believed to be concentrated in the east and south-east of the country (though some recent estimates claim that at least half of them live in the western regions). About 25–30% are Alevis, while the majority belong to the more orthodox *Shafii* sect of Sunni Islam. The Alevi Kurds speak mostly the *Zaza* dialect of their language, while the Sunnis speak *Kurmanci*.

The assimilationist policies of the Republic have been largely successful with regard to the Kurds. A significant share of the Kurdish population is believed to be fully assimilated into the dominant Turkish identity, while a considerable number of Kurds who are conscious of their Kurdish identity nevertheless speak no Kurdish. There are many mixed marriages between Kurds and Turks who share the same religion. The question of who is a Kurd in Turkey is therefore a complicated one; many Kurds and Turks have multiple identities. Persons in the same family can perceive themselves as Kurdish or Turkish or perhaps both; while in some parts of the south-east, tribal identities may weigh more heavily than ethnic ones (Kirisci and Winrow 1997: 23–27).

Democratic politics and broadened opportunities for education and migration to the more developed western parts of the country have opened the way to upward social mobility for a large number of Kurds. Many have reached the highest echelons of the social hierarchy, on condition of avoiding open expression of their Kurdish identity. It can be argued that the Kurds are fairly represented in the political, administrative, judicial, business, culture and media elites of Turkey. From the early 1980s on, however, it has become increasingly clear that a growing number of Turkish citizens of Kurdish origin seek the right to express their cultural identity freely.

The history of Kurdish nationalism is nearly as old as Turkish nationalism. The nature of the Kurdish uprisings of the 1920s and 30s was mixed, however. Their underlying motives were as much religious as ethnic, opposing both forced assimilation for Kurds and contemporary reforms aimed at relegating Islam to the private sphere. Restrictions on the expression of Kurdish identity were somewhat relaxed after the introduction of multi-party politics and the victory of Democratic Party (DP) in the elections of 1950, in which the DP used its patronage to enlist the support of Kurdish traditional elites (Poulton 1997: 209).

The adoption of the Constitution of 1961 in the aftermath of the 1960 military coup led to a considerable liberalization of Turkish politics. Socialist parties were allowed to operate with relative freedom, and the predominantly-Marxist Turkish Workers' Party (TIP) was founded in 1962. The party embraced the Kurdish cause and welcomed Kurdish intellectuals into its ranks. The idea that all the ills of Turkey including the denial of Kurdish identity would be solved by the establishment of a socialist regime prevailed among both the Turkish and the Kurdish left throughout the 1960s and 70s. The TIP was banned, however, by the Constitutional Court following the military intervention of 1971, on the grounds that it had supported separatism by openly recognizing the existence of Kurds as a group in Turkey.

The military regime established in 1980, moreover, clamped down harshly on manifestations of Kurdish identity. The Constitution of 1982, and laws adopted in accordance with it under the military regime, banned publication, broadcasting and instruction in the Kurdish language. The laws on associations and political parties outlawed organizations claiming 'the existence of minorities based on differences of race, religion, sect, culture or language within the nation of the Turkish Republic or [aiming] to create minorities by promoting and disseminating languages and cultures other than the Turkish language and culture'. A law strictly implemented since 1949 stipulated that 'village names . . . that are not Turkish shall be changed as soon as possible'. Another law adopted in 1977 required that names given to children should conform with 'national culture'. A law of 1983 criminalized even the private use of the Kurdish language (it was not lifted until 1991). The Anti-Terrorism Law adopted in 1991 stipulated prison sentences of 2–5 years and large fines for any written or spoken propaganda aimed at 'dividing the Turkish state or nation'.

There is no doubt that the harshness of the measures taken by the military regime of 1980–83 to suppress the Marxist left in general, and Kurdish activists in particular, and the excessive restrictions on the expression of Kurdish identity, were among the main causes of the violent outbreak of Kurdish nationalism in the early 1980s. The Kurdistan Workers' Party (PKK) that was to start an armed insurgency against the Turkish state was formed clandestinely in 1978 by a group of Kurdish nationalists led by Abdullah Öcalan, a former Marxist-Leninist. The PKK's original programme was the establishment of an independent Marxist-Leninist Kurdish state that would unite all the Kurds of the region. The organization has, however, changed its ideology and tactics over time in accordance with the requirements of regional conditions. It first abandoned its Marxist-Leninist discourse, switching to the exploitation of Islam, in the late 1980s, before moving on to adopt ethnic nationalism in the 1990s. The separatist aim was abandoned as an avowed goal in 1993, to be replaced by demands for federation or devolution within a fully-democratic Turkish state. After the capture of Öcalan in 1999, the PKK seems to have limited its demands to reforms which would recognize the linguistic and cultural rights of Kurds within the borders of a democratic republic.

The PKK's armed uprising was launched in 1984. Although it undoubtedly relied on the support of at least part of Turkey's frustrated Kurds, it would not have been able to step up its insurgency without the covert support of Syria and Iran, or of hostile governments like those in Greece and Armenia. In addition, the possibility of using the predominantly-Kurdish north of Iraq as a base for its operations against Turkey, in the aftermath of the Western-led invasion of Iraq in 1991, was a contributing factor to the PKK's success in spreading the violence to the Kurdish regions of Turkey. The financial and political support of Kurdish communities and sympathizers in Western Europe, particularly in Germany, has also been an important resource. The German authorities' attitude to the PKK was ambiguous throughout the 1990s. While banning the PKK on German territory in 1993, they turned a blind eye to pro-PKK organizations as long as they did not provoke violence (Kramer 2000: 239).

The State and the Kurds

In February 1999, the Syrian regime's decision, under threat of Turkish military force, to abandon its policy of supporting the PKK led to the seizure of the party's leader, Öcalan. During his subsequent trial in Turkey, Öcalan apologized for the past violence and offered to serve the Turkish state. He was nevertheless convicted and sentenced to death in June 1999 (a sentence commuted to life imprisonment after the abolition of the death penalty in Turkey in August 2002). After his conviction, Öcalan called for a cessation of hostilities and the withdrawal of PKK fighters from Turkish territory by 1 September 1999. The PKK announced in February 2000 a formal end to its war against the Turkish government, and declared that it would henceforth adopt 'democratic political struggle'. These events brought to an end a conflict which had cost the lives of about 30,000 Turkish citizens, most of them Kurds. During the 15 years of hostilities, over 3500 villages and hamlets had been forcibly evacuated in the south-east of Turkey, displacing nearly 3 million people. According to official statements the Turkish government had spent about $100bn in fighting the PKK-led insurgency.

The official stance adopted by the Turkish authorities during these years was that they were dealing with the 'security problem' of a terrorist campaign supported by foreign powers, aimed at destabilizing and dismembering Turkey, and as such a problem requiring a primarily military solution. As regards the unrest in the predominantly Kurdish south-east, this has been depicted as arising out of socio-economic backwardness. Several investment packages have been assigned to the region to alleviate its widespread poverty and unemployment. It remains, however, the least- developed part of the country.

Throughout the 1990s various political leaders made attempts to address Kurdish demands and reach a broader political solution (Poulton 1997: 213–17). The military, which has played a decisive role in the shaping and implementation of Kurdish policy, resisted such initiatives. Yet there have been signs in recent years that 'the military itself may recognize the need for some kind of broader political solution than the civilian leadership has been able to formulate'; the problem for the military, 'as the most Kemalist of Turkish institutions, lies in the recognition of a Kurdish reality that violates the very essence of their "Kemalist ideology"' (Barkey and Fuller 1998: 142).

The public debate on the Kurdish problem has contributed over time to an increased readiness in Turkish society to accept the ethnic (and religious) heterogeneity of the country, to such an extent that any statement short of advocating separatism and violence has become acceptable. Legal pro-Kurdish parties in existence since the early 1990s (despite a restrictive legal framework for ethnically-based political organizations, and continuous harassment by the authorities) have greatly contributed to that debate. The first legal pro-Kurdish party was founded when 7 Kurdish MPs elected for the centre-left Democratic Populist Party (SHP) were expelled for attending a Kurdish conference in Paris. They reacted by forming the People's Labor Party (HEP) in June 1990. The HEP was, however, banned in July 1993 by the Constitutional Court for allegedly functioning 'against the indivisible integrity of the state and of the nation'. HEP was consecutively replaced by OZDEP (1992–93), DEP (1993–94), and HADEP (1994–2003). Following the banning of DEP, 13 former DEP parliamentarians were sentenced to 15 years' imprisonment. They are still in prison. Another pro-Kurdish party, DKP (Democratic Mass Party), founded in 1998 by a former minister, Serafettin Elci, was also banned by the Constitutional Court, though it has clearly distanced itself from separatism in general and the PKK in particular.

HADEP raised its share of the national vote to 4.8%, and succeeded in winning most of the important mayoral posts of the south-east region, including the regional centre of Diyarbakir, in the elections of 1999. It managed to become the longest-surviving pro-Kurdish party, but was also banned for separatism by the Constitutional Court in March 2003. Its replacement, DEHAP, in the national elections of November 2002 increased the pro-Kurdish vote to 6.2%—which, however, still fell below the 10% threshold for party representation in parliament. DEHAP, which is facing proceedings with a view to its closure, may face the same fate as the previous pro-Kurdish parties.

As Nicole Watts puts it:

> A complex and subtle struggle is occurring within the Turkish political establishment over how to treat Kurdish identity politics. While some state actors continue to promote and enforce policies crafted around the belief that ethnic heterogeneity threatens the unity, if not the existence, of the republic, others have moved to incorporate an openly multi-ethnic discourse into the framework of mainstream politics under the rubric that suppressing alternative voices would weaken Turkish democracy and fuel separatism (Watts 1999: 632).

TIME FOR REFORM

A debate on democratic reform in Turkey started soon after the end of military rule in the early 1980s, and intensified in the 1990s. That debate has greatly contributed to the understanding that in the globalizing and democratizing contemporary world, modernity no longer means uniformity but recognition of pluralism, not only in the political and economic but also in the cultural sphere. In the light of that continuing debate on democratic reform, it seems possible to put forward some arguments for the kind of reforms which are likely to gain the approval and consent of the great majority of Turkey's population.

There is no doubt that official secularist policies are flawed in many respects, and are indeed 'in need of secularization' (Özdalga 1997: 21). This would mean the state being truly divorced from religion, an end to promotion of the officially-sanctioned Sunni-Hanafi doctrine over others, and full respect for the religious freedom of all citizens irrespective of faith. It can be said that Kemalist secularism has caught the Turkish state in a dilemma: official promotion of Sunni-Hanafi Islam has greatly contributed to the growth of forces pushing for a greater public role for Islam, while the state authorities have struggled to suppress those forces by introducing prohibitions on the expression of Muslim identity. If that dilemma is to be resolved, the *Diyanet* needs to be taken out of the state apparatus, as advocated even by Deniz Baykal, the current leader of the CHP, the party which introduced *laiklik* in the 1920s (*Radikal* 27 August 2001). The assignment of an independent, autonomous status to the *Diyanet* seems more feasible than its abolition (which part of the Alevi community has called for), since the institution has evolved into a sort of a 'state church' with a vast organization and following.

The current Law on Political Parties (Article 89) states that 'political parties shall not pursue any goal contrary to the provisions of Article 136 of the Constitution which stipulates the status of [the *Diyanet*] as an entity within the general administration'. The Constitutional Court has, however, rejected a request by the Chief Prosecutor to ban the Democratic Peace Movement Party for making propaganda in favor of the abolition of the *Diyanet*, in direct violation of this law. The Court decision can be interpreted as an indication of the public's readiness for a review of the status of the *Diyanet*, which began to be hotly debated during the latter half of the 1990s.

'Secularization of secularism' in Turkey also requires that the ban on religious brotherhoods, the *tarikat*, in force since 1925, be lifted. This is necessary if people of various beliefs are to be allowed to practice their religion freely. It would also make it possible to effectively monitor the compatibility of the activities of the *tarikat* with human rights. There is, at the same time, evidence that some of the brotherhoods and communities are involved in efforts aimed at a reinterpretation of the teachings of Islam so as to bring them in line with the requirements of modern life, including respect for individual freedom and choice, human rights, and pluralism (Atacan 1992, Demirci 1996, Yavuz 1999a, 1999b, 2003, Özdalga 2000). This makes it all the more necessary that they be allowed to operate freely and openly, if Turkey is to develop further as a predominantly-Muslim country with a liberal-democratic regime.

The responsibility for religious education, schools for the training of religious personnel (prayer leaders and preachers) and Qur'an courses may be left to an autonomous *Diyanet* and other religious groups as well as institutions of civil society. Religious teaching in public schools should no longer be compulsory, and either removed altogether or replaced with courses aimed at the teaching of religion in general. It was recently reported in the press that the Ministry of Education is preparing to restructure religious courses in public schools to involve the teaching of religion in general, and not specifically of officially-sanctioned Sunni-Hanafi Islam (*Hurriyet* 11 July 2004).

Such measures may be expected to go a long way towards meeting the demands of both the Sunni majority and the Alevi minority. Aside from a restricted group that is asking for representation in the *Diyanet* and public funding for cultural activities, the vast majority of Alevis in Turkey seem to demand nothing more than the full recognition of Alevi cultural identity, full religious freedom, and an end to state support and sponsorship for Sunni-Hanafi Islam.

Restriction of the headscarf ban to public employees and to students of primary and secondary state schools seems necessary, not only out of respect for basic individual democratic rights, but also to avoid an increasingly divisive, provocative and destabilizing controversy. In a secular state it is reasonable to demand that persons in public service abide by a certain dress code. A headscarf ban for public employees can thus be defended on grounds of secularism. On the other hand, a ban which applies even to university students and members of parliament clearly violates their basic rights as individual citizens, is an open case of discrimination against women, and denies education to those among them who choose to wear headscarves for religious (or any other) reasons. In her analysis of the headscarf controversy in Turkey, Arat concludes:

> There is heterogeneity, rather than homogeneity, regarding the meaning and significance of headscarves. The ban assumes that there is one headscarf and that its meaning is clear. In this context of heterogeneity and flux, where even many who would like to see Islamic law implemented have internalized secular concepts of equality and liberalism, the ban itself can be a threat to the foundations of liberal democracy (Arat 2001: 45).

EVOLVING A LIBERAL, CIVIC NATIONALISM

There are Kurdish nationalists in Turkey whose aims range from Kurdish independence (and a pan-Kurdish state) to the establishment of a Turkish-Kurdish federation within the borders of Turkey. These goals are not, however, embraced by the vast majority of Kurds in Turkey, who have lived together and intermingled with Turks for centuries as people sharing the same religious beliefs. At the height of the PKK insurgency in the late 1990s only 13% of Kurds favored secession from Turkey (Kirisci and Winrow 1997: 197). If, indeed, the 15–year armed insurgency failed to trigger a Turkish-Kurdish civil war, with the conflict largely limited to clashes between Turkish security forces and PKK militants in the mountains of the south-east, then this is because the great majority of Turkey's Kurds approved of neither the PKK's goals nor its methods. There is, nevertheless, no doubt that the great majority of Kurds demand the recognition of their ethnic identity, and the freedom to use their mother tongue and enjoy their culture—as stressed by two of the most comprehensive studies of the Kurdish problem in Turkey (Kirisci and Winrow 1997: 209–15, Barkey and Fuller 1998: 221–23). The scale of support for pro-Kurdish parties, especially in the south-east, provides the most convincing evidence for this view. Failure to address these demands may lead to a loss of legitimacy for the Turkish state among a growing number of Turkey's Kurds, and perhaps to yet another armed revolt.

The Kurdish problem is very much part of the general problem of further democratization of the Turkish regime. Its resolution requires, first and foremost, a civic conception of nationalism in Turkey, or a definition of Turkishness as citizenship of Turkey irrespective of ethnic or religious origin, and the lifting of all prohibitions on the expression by Turkish citizens of their religious and/or ethnic sub-identities.

In the case of the Kurds, this would mean allowing the use of the Kurdish language on radio and television, and in educational institutions (which has in principle been allowed in the print media since the mid-1990s). It would also mean recognition of Kurds' right to give Kurdish names to their children and to use Kurdish place-names in their regions, the creation of university institutions for the study of the Kurdish language, and the clearing-away of all obstacles to the further development of the existing Kurdish cultural associations.

The lifting of all legal and extra-legal restrictions preventing pro-Kurdish parties from organizing and working freely is also necessary, as long as these parties do not advocate violence to achieve their aims. The lowering of the threshold for parties to be represented in parliament from 10 to 5%, and the lifting of the ban on election alliances between parties, would greatly enhance the democratic representation of the pro-Kurdish parties which receive the majority of

Kurdish support in the south-east. One must also recognize that the Turkish state is over-centralized, with Ankara being the locus of all administrative decisions. The south-east, together with all other major regions of the country, should be allowed a greater say in its local affairs in the context of a general and gradual process of devolution which would contribute not only to broadened democratic participation, but also to enhanced administrative efficiency.

The Debate Over Group and Individual Rights in Turkey

The reforms suggested above simply require the recognition of the basic individual rights of Turkish citizens. Group or minority rights—in terms of Will Kymlicka's 'self-government' or 'special representation' rights (Kymlicka 1995: 6–9)—may be regarded as largely irrelevant in the Turkish context since both Kurds and Alevis view themselves not as minorities, but as constituent parts or even founding elements of Turkish society (Barkey and Fuller 1998: 202). Representatives of both Kurds and Alevis have reacted strongly to the recent European Commission report which referred to these groups as minorities. The demand by the Cem Vakfi, a largely upper-class foundation, for the reshaping of the *Diyanet* to include Alevi representatives seems to be the only case so far of a demand for 'special representation rights' raised by minority groups in Turkey. The majority of the Alevi community, however, seems to be content with the lifting of restrictions on expression of their identity and religious freedoms.

Administrative reform, and some degree of devolution of the centre's powers to local government, is indeed desired by society at large, and has been on the agenda of the public debate at least since the 1990s. The demand for the formation of a Turkish-Kurdish federation raised by some Kurdish groups, on the other hand, is likely to create insurmountable difficulties, for the following reasons. Turks and Kurds have mingled for centuries in such a way that it is not easy to determine who is a Kurd in Turkey. An estimated half of all Kurds reside in the western, predominantly Turkish parts of the country. Although part of the population of Kurdish origin indeed recognizes itself as a separate ethnic group, another has been entirely assimilated into Turkish society (especially in the west), while still another considerably large part regards itself as both Kurdish and Turkish (Kirisci and Winrow 1997: 24). Even those who recognize themselves as a separate ethnic group do not consider themselves as a minority, as already pointed out above. In this context, Barkey and Fuller observe:

> The federal solution gives rise to as many problems as it pretends to resolve. What regions would be considered Kurdish—merely those with a Kurdish

> majority? What would be the cultural rights and minority protection granted to Turks in the Kurdish regions of the country, and what would corresponding Kurdish cultural rights be in the Turkish regions? . . . What are the implications of such an arrangement for those Kurds who have settled in such places as Istanbul and Izmir? It might further aggravate inter-communal tensions or create ones where none existed before (Barkey and Fuller 1998: 203).

Demands for what Kymlicka calls 'polyethnic rights', basically, state funding for cultural activities, have in fact been raised by some groups within both the Kurdish and Alevi communities. The broadly-shared demand of the Kurdish community in Turkey, however, remains the lifting of prohibitions on the expression of Kurdish identity. An announcement entitled 'What do the Kurds want in Turkey?' placed in the *International Herald Tribune* and *Le Monde* newspapers on 9 December 2004, signed by prominent Kurds representing the entire political spectrum of pro-Kurdish parties and groups in Turkey, stated the basic demands of Turkey's Kurds as follows: 'A new and democratic constitution, recognizing the existence of the Kurdish people, and guaranteeing it the right to a public school system and media in its own language, and the right to form its own organizations, institutions and parties with the aim of contributing to the free expression of its culture and its political aspirations'. It seems reasonable to argue that legal recognition and full implementation of basic individual citizenship rights is likely to go a long way towards satisfying the demands of an overwhelming proportion of Turkey's minority peoples, and meeting the minimum requirements of a liberal-democratic regime.

THE EU PERSPECTIVE: A CATALYST FOR CHANGE

Turkey was declared a candidate for EU membership at the Helsinki European Council of December 1999. The goal of EU membership received strong support in Turkish society. Opinion surveys indicate that not less than two-thirds of the electorate covering all segments of society favor EU membership. The bulk of the political establishment, in fact, perceives this as the crowning measure of the Westernizing and Europeanizing mission launched by Mustafa Kemal Atatürk early in the 1920s. It is, moreover, increasingly sending signals of its awareness that today, modernity no longer means uniformity but recognition of diversity and pluralism. The post-Islamist AKP which came to power in the elections of 2002 has energetically led the pro-EU reforms, backed by its main rival, the CHP. All major political parties and movements, including the pro-Islamic and pro-Kurdish ones, have given their support to the reform process.

The Accession Partnership for Turkey document approved by the European Council in 2000 stipulated, among other things, that Turkey in the short term should 'strengthen legal and constitutional guarantees for the right to freedom of expression, association and assembly . . . remove any legal provisions forbidding the use by Turkish citizens of their mother tongue in TV-radio broadcasting . . . develop a comprehensive approach to reduce regional disparities, and in particular [. . .] improve the situation in the Southeast, with a view to enhancing economic, social and cultural opportunities for all citizens'.

The Council document also required the Turkish authorities in the mid-term to 'guarantee full enjoyment by all individuals without any discrimination and irrespective of their language, race, colour, sex, political opinion, philosophical belief or religion of all human rights and fundamental freedoms . . . Further develop conditions for the enjoyment of freedom of thought, conscience and religion . . . Review the Constitution and other relevant legislation with a view to guaranteeing rights and freedoms of all Turkish citizens as set forth in the European Convention for the Protection of Human Rights . . . [and] ensure cultural diversity and guarantee cultural rights for all citizens irrespective of their origin. Any legal provisions preventing the enjoyment of these rights should be abolished, including in the field of education' (EU Council Decision No. 2001/ 235/EC).

In March 2001 the Turkish parliament adopted a National Programme for accession to the EU. It initiated a comprehensive revision of the constitution and laws with a view to fulfilling the so-called Copenhagen Political Criteria. Constitutional and legislative reforms adopted by parliament since October 2001, and particularly after the 2002 elections, have led to a substantial broadening of democratic rights and freedoms in Turkey. Some of these reforms are related to official identity policies, especially with regard to the treatment of the Kurdish minority. The provisions of the Penal Code and Anti-Terror Law have been amended to lift restrictions on non-violent expressions of opinion, leading both to acquittals and to the release of prisoners sentenced for making separatist propaganda. In an effort to foster social peace in the south-east, the parliament passed a law that provided for a partial amnesty and reduction in prison sentences for persons involved in the activities of the outlawed PKK.

Constitutional amendments have removed the restrictions on the use of Kurdish and other minority languages in public and private radio and television broadcasting. Regulations, however, permit only broadcasting by national television and radio channels, for 4 hours a week on the radio and 2 hours a week on television. The law on teaching of foreign languages has been amended to allow for private courses in Kurdish (though regulations stipulate that private Kurdish courses can only be taken by high-school graduates with their parents' written approval). The civil registry law has been amended to permit parents to give their children Kurdish names. The Kurdish minority in the south-east is likely also to benefit from the draft law on public administration expected to be adopted in 2005 which will introduce a significant degree of decentralization in public administration (Aydin and Keyman 2004: 27–39).

There is no doubt that the prospect of EU membership has provided a major incentive for the reform of Turkey's semi-liberal democracy and at least partial resolution of what I have called the crisis in Turkey's identity politics. Reforms adopted to fulfill the conditions of EU membership constitute significant steps towards the enjoyment of linguistic and cultural rights by Turkish citizens irrespective of their ethnic origin. There are still important shortcomings in respect of minority and cultural rights and the protection of minorities, as discussed extensively in the European Commission's 2004 report on Turkey's progress towards accession. This report to the European Council and Parliament nevertheless concluded that 'in view of the overall progress of reforms, and provided that Turkey brings into force the outstanding legislation . . . the Commission considers that Turkey sufficiently fulfils the political criteria and recommends that accession negotiations be opened' (*Report of the European Commission on Turkey*, 6 October 2004).

The European Council decided on 17 December 2004 to open accession negotiations with Turkey on 3 October 2005. Even though the negotiations are expected to last at least 10 years, the accession process remains on track. It may be argued that even if Turkish efforts to achieve EU membership fail in the end, the pro-EU reforms in the country are irreversible, and Turkish governments are likely in future to continue on the path of recognition of citizens' fundamental rights and freedoms irrespective of their ethnic and religious origin.

REFERENCES

Alpay, S. (2000). ' "After Öcalan", private view '. *Quarterly International Review of the Turkish Industrialists' and Businessmen's Association* 8.

Andrews, P. A. (1989). *Ethnic Groups in the Republic of Turkey*. Wiesbaden: Ludwig Reichert Verlag, trans. M. Küpüsoglu (1992). *Türkiye'de Etnik Gruplar*. Istanbul: ANT Yayinlari.

Arat, Y. (2001). 'Group-differentiated rights and the liberal-democratic state: rethinking the headscarf controversy in Turkey'. *New Perspectives on Turkey* 25.

Atacan, F. (1990). *Sosyal Degisme ve Tarikat: Cerrahiler.* Istanbul: Hil Yayinlari.

Aydin, S. and E. F. Keyman (2004). 'European integration and the transformation of

Turkish democracy'. *EU-Turkey Working Papers* 2. Brussels: Centre for European Policy Studies.
Barkey, H. J. and G. E. Fuller (1998). *Turkey's Kurdish Question*. New York/Oxford: Rowman & Littlefield.
Bilici, F. (1998). 'The function of Alevi-Bektashi theology in modern Turkey' in Olsson, Özdalga and Raudvere eds.
Bulac, A. (1998). 'The Medina Document' in Kurzman ed.
—— (1999). 'Siyasi Islam bitti!'. *Aktuel* 407.
Camuroglu, R. (1998). 'Alevi revivalism in Turkey' in Olsson, Özdalga and Raudvere eds.
Carkoglu, A. and B. Toprak (2000). *Türkiye'de Din, Toplum ve Siyaset*. Istanbul: Türkiye Ekonomik ve Sosyal Etüdler Vakfi (TESEV) Yayinlari.
Copeaux, E. (1998). *Tarih Tezi'nden Türk: Islam Sentezi'ne*. Istanbul: Tarih Vakfi Yurt Yayinlari.
Davison, A. (1998). *Secularism and Revivalism in Turkey*. New Haven/London: Yale University Press.
Demirci, E. Y. (1996). *Modernization, Religion and Politics in Turkey: The Case of the Iskenderpasa Community*. Unpublished Ph.D. thesis, Manchester University Department of Sociology.
Göle, N. (1997). 'Secularism and Islamism in Turkey: the making of elites and counter-elites'. *Middle East Journal* 51, no. 1.
Kirisci, K. (2000). 'Disaggregating Turkish citizenship and immigration practices'. *Middle Eastern Studies* 36, no. 3.
—— and G. M. Winrow (1997). *The Kurdish Question and Turkey: An Example of a Trans-State Ethnic Conflict*. London: Frank Cass.
Kramer, H. (2000). *A Changing Turkey: The Challenge to Europe and The United States*. Washington, D.C.: Brookings Institution Press.
Kurzman, C. ed. (1998). *Liberal Islam: A Sourcebook*. New York/Oxford: Oxford University Press.
Kymlicka, W. (1995). *Multicultural Citizenship*. Oxford: Oxford University Press.
Mango, A. (1999). 'Ataturk and the Kurds'. *Middle Eastern Studies* 35, no. 4 (October).
Olsson, T., E. Özdalga and C. Raudvere eds. (1998). *Alevi Identity*. Istanbul: Swedish Research Institute.
Önis, Z. (1997). 'The political economy of Islamic resurgence in Turkey: the rise of the Welfare Party in perspective'. *Third World Quarterly* 18.
Özdalga, E. (1997). 'A secularism in need of secularization'. *TASG News* 45.
—— (1998). *The Veiling Issue, Official Secularism and Popular Islam in Modern Turkey*. Richmond: Curzon Press.
—— (2000). 'Worldly asceticism in Islamic casting: Fethullah Gülen's inspired piety and activism'. *Critique* 17.
—— ed. (1999). *Nakshibandis in Western and Central Asia*. Istanbul: Swedish Research Institute.
Poulton, H. (1997). *Turkish Nationalism and the Turkish Republic: Top Hat, Grey Wolf and Crescent*. New York: New York University Press.

Shankland, D. (1999). *Islam and Society in Turkey*. Huntingdon: Eothen Press.
Tarhanli, I. B. (1993). *Müslüman Toplum, 'Laik' Devlet: Türkiye'de Diyanet Isleri Baskanligi*. Istanbul: AFA Yayinlari.
Watts, N. (1999). 'Allies and enemies: pro-Kurdish parties in Turkish politics, 1990–94'. *International Journal of Middle East Studies* 31.
Yavuz, H. (1997). 'Political Islam and the Welfare (Refah) Party in Turkey'. *Comparative Politics*.
—— (1999a). 'The matrix of modern Turkish Islamic movements: the Nakshibandi Sufi order' in Özdalga ed.
—— (1999b). 'Towards an Islamic liberalism? the Nurcu movement and Fethullah Gülen'. *Middle East Journal* 53, No. 4.
——(2003). *Islamic Political Identity in Turkey*. Oxford University Press.
Zürcher, E. J. (2001). 'Ottoman sources of Kemalist thought' at www.let.leidenuniv.nl/tcimo/tulp/Research/MUNCHEN2.htm
—— (2004). *Turkey: A Modern History*. 3rd ed. London: I. B. Tauris.

Chapter Six

Kabyles in History and the Crisis of Contemporary Algeria

Inga Brandell

Every year on 20 August an important commemoration occurs in Algeria at a place called the Soummam Valley. It was here, in 1956, that the small guerrilla group which was fighting French colonialism, the *Front de Libération Nationale* (FLN), gathered for its first congress. A political programme was adopted then which came to stand for the Algerian people's expression of their will to achieve independence and build democracy. This document, the so-called Soummam platform, clearly stated that the political struggle should take precedence over the military one, and the political leadership over the military. After independence, the 'Soummam platform' was subsequently invoked by the opposition to the ruling party in government (which was, by then, the FLN itself). Hence the increasing importance of the Soummam commemoration: it represents the political legitimacy given by this founding moment of the independence struggle, even after that goal has been achieved. Yet in August 2001, for the first time, the commemoration was cancelled.

The Soummam valley is situated in the mountains of Kabylia, an area ideally suited to the secret meeting of the FLN cadres. This was the first part of the country to enter into armed struggle for independence, several years before the official beginning of the uprising on 1 November 1954. Though close to the capital, Algiers, Kabylia was very difficult terrain for the French army to control, being protected by its high mountains and steep-sided valleys. In the summer of 2001, however, the region was in turmoil and roles were reversed. Instead of trying, like the French, to enter the region and control it, the Algerian army and police were putting up roadblocks to prevent Kabyles from leaving their region and travelling down to the capital to demonstrate. In Kabylia itself, hundreds of thousands of people were in the streets, expressing their defiance against their own government. For a time, rumours flew that President Abdelaziz Bouteflika would come in person to enter into a dialogue with local residents; but in the event he did not appear. Nor did the official delegation from Algiers dare to come up to the valley for the traditional commemoration. In a sense, Kabylia at that moment was once again liberated from the authorities in Algiers and the Kabyles themselves were in control of their land. Another deeply symbolic event in Kabyle and perhaps Algerian history had occurred.

The aim of this chapter is to reflect on civil and political rights in Algeria from the perspective of the conflict which has arisen between the Kabyle population and the Algerian state or, more exactly, the current regime. It is a paradox of contemporary Algeria that a claim for group rights is the closest one can come to expanding the freedom and integrity of individuals. Other chapters in this book discuss the issue of 'differentiated citizenship', but this will not be touched on directly here. The superficial reason is that it has not been raised in the Algerian context. More important, what the Kabyle ideological discourse expresses is the claim for simultaneous recognition of linguistic and cultural pluralism in Algeria and of fundamental, equal individual rights for all Algerians. The very idea of differentiated citizenship is unthinkable in the Algerian—and so far the Kabyle—contexts.

Kabylia and the Kabyles, their customs, religion and social structures, and the impact on them of migration and modernity, have been studied for the last hundred years; the Berber peoples in general, of whom they are part, form the object of an even older literature. Ibn Khaldun, the 14th-century Arab scholar best known for the *Muqaddima*, the introduction to his world history, also wrote a history of the Arabs and several volumes on the Berbers, including the Kabyles. Important recent debates have taken place about the Berbers' patterns of social organization and culture and their impact on North African society as a whole: suffice here to mention the Kabyle studies of Pierre Bourdieu (1972), or Ernest Gellner's research on Moroccan Berbers (1969), leading to his general and much-debated theory of the segmentation of North African society. Others have developed these debates—Hugh Roberts in particular criticizing over-extrapolation from special cases to the entire society, and reflecting on the specific impact of political tradition in Algerian history (Roberts 2002, 2003). Here I want to focus on state- and nation-formation, territory and citizenship, and within that framework the question of rights.

After independence, French research refrained from delving into the Kabyle question. Bourdieu, in writing his essays published in 1972, used material gathered from his stay in Algeria more than a decade earlier, before and just after the country's independence in 1962. In Algeria itself ethnography, the discipline covering most academic analysis of Berber and Kabyle society, was suppressed in the early 1970s owing to its allegedly-'colonial' underpinnings and applications. Instead, most research on Kabylia was later undertaken either by North African researchers working in France, or by American and British scholars—among whom Roberts is a pioneer. The aim of this chapter is not to add to the empirical evidence presented by him and others, but to discuss the preconditions, and the general impact on Algerian society and politics, of the social movements within one particular population group. Many important aspects, like the relationship between social movements in Kabylia and Kabyle emigrés in France, have been treated thoroughly by others (Silverstein 2003); these will be part of the picture but not discussed for their own sake. A general narrative of events will however emerge.

My main argument concerns, as mentioned above, the relation between the claim for group rights for the Kabyles and the expansion of respect for individual rights in Algeria as a whole. Two propositions need to be spelled out at the outset. The first is that Islam as a cultural mindset and political framework has a consistent history of integrating various ethnic and religious groups. Of course, there has also been political conflict and division within the lands of Islam, but even this has in its way been part of the strong movement for integration, for the competing positions have had to be formulated in Islamic terms and as an Islamic project. Secession, therefore, is in principle unthinkable, although temporary withdrawal is an option, as will be touched upon below.

This history of integration has not gone untouched by the Westphalian model of state-formation, which was introduced to the whole Islamic world with the end of the Ottoman Empire. But the Islamic and Westphalian models (the latter in its later form of national integration) have tended actually to reinforce each other in contexts where Islam is dominant. This is the case both for states, which have benefited from a double legitimacy for their unifying claims, and for social groups who in other settings might have striven for secession. In this context, one might mention the case of the Kurds, one of the groups presenting, since the fall of the Ottoman Empire, a national project without obtaining a state. Here we have confirmation that even in modern times a Muslim-dominated state is relatively immune to radical secessionism. When one compares the policies of the various Kurdish movements in their respective national settings, it is clear that secular Kemalist Turkey has been more radically challenged, over the years, than its overtly-Muslim neighbors, Syria, Iraq and Iran. The case of the Western Sahara points in a different direction. Here, in spite of the Moroccan monarchy's references to the traditional religious bonds between the king and the inhabitants of formerly Spanish-colonial Western Sahara, a movement refusing Moroccan annexation and seeking independence has proved strong and resilient. But even so, the overall pattern of resistance to secession is detectable: witness some defections among the Western Sahara rebel leaders and the cautious stand taken in neighboring countries. A further aspect of the rejection of secessionism is that, in this region, the individual is not the main agent in politics. On the contrary, modern politics has been collective from the beginning, be the collective 'Muslim' or 'Arab' (Brandell and Rabo 2003).

If this first proposition about Islamic and, later, Arab politics might seem familiar to those who have an interest in the region, my second proposition is connected to newer research. It draws on recent collective work on borders and boundaries in the Middle East, of which one conclusion is that faced with the enforcement of state borders, individuals and groups develop different and sometimes contradictory practices and visions (Brandell 2005). But it also links up with more complex reappraisals of the whole Algerian case, which differentiate between the country's social movements (Colonna 1996), or between several traditions of political rule (Roberts 2002); or which approach the intricacies of Algerian politics by deconstructing crucial events and the actors involved, as in Omar Carlier's interesting study of the Berberist crisis of 1949 (Carlier 1986). In this chapter the focus, as in Carlier's study, is on the issue of territoriality and connected forms of social and political organization. I will argue that Kabylia as a place, its topography and the distribution of its population, has generated a local solidarity and ways of thinking which underpin social movements in the region rather differently from the rest of the country.

THE CONTEXT OF THE ALGERIAN CRISIS

The conflict between Kabylia and the central government in Algiers has to be situated within the deep political, economic and ultimately moral crisis which has racked Algeria since the early 1990s. The Algerian struggle for independence was rightfully presented, internally and externally, as a great and difficult achievement. Historically, one should recall, the territory had been administratively integrated into metropolitan France as three *départements*, that is, not even considered a country on its own. About a tenth of the population were European settlers. In 1954, when small groups started what was to become the war of independence, few would have thought that within eight years Algeria would be an independent country, or that close on a million Europeans would leave in 1962. The turmoil which followed, and persisted for the first few years after independence, was compensated for by brave and radical social innovation and plans for socialist self-management in agriculture and industry. This period, which ended with the coup d'état of 1965 instigated by Minister of Defence Houari Boumedienne, was followed by a series of nationalizations and ambitious development plans. The people's basic needs were taken into account, and Algerians were mobilized for the sake of industrial development, agrarian reform and (with the help of foreign teachers from France and the Arab world) educational expansion. Internationally, Algerian politicians and diplomats played important roles within OPEC, the Non-Aligned Movement and the UN. Algerians, whatever they thought about the detail of their government's policies, its suppression of dissent, or its socialist stance, were generally proud of its achievements in domestic and international politics.

This national consensus weakened under President Chadli Benjedid, who took over on the death of Boumedienne in 1978, but was still sustained by past achievements. It was still present after the youth revolt of 1988, which was rapidly followed by a referendum on a new constitution including a bill of rights, and the reintroduction of multipartism. Algeria was seen as having anticipated a movement for democracy that took off in the following years in Eastern Europe and Africa, and as having set an example for the Arab world and the Maghreb. But this national pride suffered a heavy blow following the coup d'état of January 1992, when parliamentary elections were interrupted before the second round to prevent an Islamist party from winning, and a state of emergency was declared. Violence escalated. With thousands of Islamists imprisoned in desert camps, armed groups attacked first the police and the military, then civilians. Politicians became particular targets, followed, without distinction, by foreigners who lived or worked in Algeria, and Algerian artists and intellectuals. Pro-government militias were created in response to the spreading violence. In the years 1996–98 huge massacres of country people took place. Everyone had to take a stand, whether they placed the blame entirely on the Islamists or on the '*pouvoir*' (by which Algerians meant the official and unofficial decision-makers, but mainly the military leaders). All sense of a common understanding of the country, its inhabitants and its aims was lost. Algeria became, in Roberts' words, 'a broken polity' (Roberts 2002).

The explanation sometimes heard for the catastrophe, especially among young Kabyles in Europe, was that Algeria's implosion was altogether 'the fault of the Arabs'. This interpretation made it possible for them to reread history in a way which placed them as individuals outside the ongoing trauma, while at the same time giving them access to the Algerian nation's heroic struggles against invaders—including Arab ones—and its final fight for independence from France. It gives a measure of the depth of the crisis that some felt the need to bring up and question what had happened more than a millennium ago; for the Muslim conquest and ensuing slow Arabization of most of the Berber population in North Africa dates back to the late 7th century AD.

Berbers and Kabyles

In the early colonial period, during the second half of the 19th century, Kabylia and more generally the Berber populations in Algeria were the object of French colonial interest, both among scientists and policy-makers and later among the public at home (Ageron 1976). This early French interest was evoked later, when Kabyle affairs came to the fore. During the 1930s, the whole Arab world was concerned by French Berber policy. At that time, when the entire Maghreb was under French rule, the Sultan of Morocco was induced by the colonial authorities to sign a decree giving official status to courts ruling according to local pre-Islamic Berber law. Thus, parts of the population were excluded, for the first time for centuries, from the jurisdiction of Islamic law—which, paradoxically enough, in the case of Algeria, had been codified by French jurists. A strong reaction ensued in the Arab and Muslim world, which is considered to have led to the unification and strengthening of burgeoning national movements there, and in particular the the rejection of any colonial manipulation of Berber-Arab divisions (Brandell 1994). The nationalism was Muslim, thus transcending other possible cleavages. In that context, the French colonial involvement in Kabylia was thrown into the political debate. In French public opinion there was a strong conviction that the Berber population of North Africa was closer to Europeans; indeed, that it was descended from Romans or Phoenicians, and/or former Christians, and hence more receptive to the French *mission civilisatrice*. Without doubt there were more Christian converts in Kabylia than elsewhere, but equally, large parts of the region were totally untouched by missionaries and other 'civilisers', or by the French military and civil administrators of the time (Lacoste-Dujardin 1997).

The next time the Kabyle question was politicized was at an early stage of the movement for Algerian independence, in the second part of 1940s. The 'Berberist crisis', described by some as a struggle for democracy and by others as Berber secessionism, ended with the defeat of the 'Berbero-materialists', or in the other version the 'democrats'. In the 'anti-Berberist' version, which became the official Algerian account, Kabyles were splitting the anti-colonial movement by not accepting the necessary unity of the political leadership. This left the impression of them as a potential threat to national unity. In fact, as shown by Carlier and Ouerdane, in their detailed studies of all available sources, the crisis had many dimensions. These ranged from differing approaches to strategy in the mobilization against the French, to the role of leadership—in particular the charismatic leadership of Messali Hadj—and the organizational structure of the nascent independence movement. There was also a latent conflict over the definition of the Algerian nation, in which the pan-Arab and Islamic definition won out. The 'Berber question' then disappeared from the agenda for several decades and the difficult task of defining the Algerian nation was avoided and postponed (Carlier 1986; Ouerdane 1987).

The Kabyle upheaval that led to the cancellation of the Soummam commemoration in August 2001 is often traced back to earlier events. But in general terms the populations of Kabylia, together with Kabyle emigrés in Europe, have since the war of independence been part of a common Algerian political life, the same conflict-lines seeming to go through them as through the rest of the population. It has also been well documented that people of Kabyle background are to be found at every level of decision-making in all spheres of the Algerian society (Quandt 1973, ICG 2003). On the other hand, in the Maghreb as a whole, at least since the 1970s, observers have pointed to a potential 'Berber question', centring on the use of another language than Arabic in the Maghreb.

The Kabyles, it must be stressed, are just one of the groups in which the Berber language is spoken. Most of the inhabitants of North Africa, with the exception of Egypt, could probably be considered of Berber origin. People who speak only *Tamazight*, in one of its varieties, or who are bilingual with Arabic (or sometimes with French), can be found from the oasis of Siwa in Egypt's western desert to the Atlantic coast. In Algeria convention distinguishes four groups. First, the Tuareg nomads of the Sahara. Second, the Chaoui of the Aurès mountains in the north-east of the country. Third, the Kabyles, who have their origins in the mountains behind the Mediterranean coast to the east of Algiers. Fourth, the inhabitants of the M'zab region in the south-west, concentrated in desert oasis cities. This last group, often called Mozabites from the name of the region, adhere to the Kharijite Ibadite tradition, sometimes characterized as the Protestantism of Islam, with an egalitarian and puritanical approach to their faith. After having lost their state in northern Algeria at the end of the 10th century, these Ibadite Berbers withdrew to a place where they could establish their own social and religious order, without fear of attack or domination. Mozabite society therefore differs in important respects from the other three groups of Berbers, who like all other Algerians adhere to the Sunni Malikite religious law school.

Figures for Berber speakers, or for that matter those who consider themselves as Berbers, are very imprecise, varying between 10 and 25% of the population. The latter figure would give more than 8 million people for Algeria. This is perhaps an exaggeration, but with the desert Mozabites and Tuaregs amounting together to no more than a few hundred thousand, the Berbers originally from the mountains of the north must be held to constitute a substantial part of the Algerian population. Of the two northern groups the Kabyles clearly dominate in numbers.

'BERBER SPRING' 1980: 'BLACK SPRING' 2001

In the spring of 1980 Algeria was in transition. Two years earlier, President Boumedienne, the country's leader since the coup d'état of 1965, had died. The new president, Chadli Benjedid, despite having come like his predecessor from the top ranks of the military, was beginning to sketch out a different course. The second oil-price crisis, linked to the Iranian revolution of 1979, had brought in substantial revenues for the state-owned oil industry in Algeria. Some of this foreign currency was used to import consumer goods—a step inconceivable in earlier times but necessary now, given the needs of a growing middle class. Algerian state socialism was seeming to lose its grip, and plans were afoot to give some nationalized agricultural land back to smallholders, owing to a rampant crisis in agricultural production and a rapid increase in the national population. Yet 'Chadli' was widely perceived to be lacking in the former president's leadership qualities.

Against this background, at the new university of Tizi-Ouzou, the principal town in Kabylia, Mouloud Mammeri, a famous Kabyle author and intellectual, was to lecture on his recent translation and publication of ancient Kabyle poetry. Late in the day, however, the authorities intervened to cancel the lecture, ordering the police to stop his car and bring him to the governor of the region to be notified of the cancellation (Chaker 1982). The decision was met with student protests, which in turn resulted in repression, imprisonments and counter-demonstrations. This period of high political mobilization, later named 'le printemps berbère' (Berber Spring), was the starting point for several Kabyle or Berber associations and initiatives. It also gave birth to the first human rights group in Algeria, a Committee against Repression at the universities of Tizi-Ouzou and Algiers.

The Committee against Repression was followed in 1986 by the foundation of the Algerian League for Human Rights, an organization rapidly suppressed by the government. A mass trial against its founders and militants took place the same year in Algiers, under the official accusation of 'threatening the authority of the State with a view to overthrowing the regime' and setting up an illegal association (Collectif contre la Répression 1989). This led to adverse international publicity and protests, and a new government-sponsored organization with the same name was created shortly afterwards. The movement of the 'Berber Spring' and its human-rights militants were also instrumental in founding the *Mouvement Culturel Berbère* and much later a political party, the *Rassemblement pour la Culture et la Démocratie*. However, barely a year after these events, political life in the country was dominated by the surprise of the first big Islamist demonstrations. During the later 1980s, other student movements erupted in different regions without any specific cultural or linguistic reasons or demands (Colonna 1996, Brandell 1998), and Kabyle issues remained solely of Kabyle concern.

This was still the case in the 1990s, although a school and university strike in Kabylia lasted for the whole year of 1994–95. The strike was a protest against the enforcement of the law on Arabization of the education system and civil service, which still used French. The Arabization project had begun in the late 1960s but proved difficult and still contained many exceptions. Now, new instructions to rapidly enforce the law were perhaps meant to weaken public sympathy for the Islamist opposition, by taking over the Islamists' agenda. The political situation, however, was so volatile, and the unrest in the country so great, that the protest in Kabylia against enforced Arabization and for the recognition of *Tamazight* as a national language remained a cause with largely local resonance. This was also the case when Matoub Lounès, a very famous singer and radical defender of Berber language and culture, was murdered in 1998. The reaction in Kabylia, and also elsewhere, was immediate and strong. Yet Lounès had been abducted, only to be released, on an earlier occasion, supposedly by Islamists. Outside Kabylia the murder was viewed as another in the series of murders of singers, actors, theatre directors and intellectuals committed by religious extremists with a puritan agenda, and with no specific links to any Kabyle question.

Then in April 2001, a young Kabyle, Massinissah Guermah, died in custody after having been taken to gendarmerie headquarters in a small Kabyle town. His given name, Massinissa, came from a Berber king who bravely fought the Romans two thousand years ago. It was decreed in the 1970s that only Arabic first names could be given, but Massinissa was born after these years of intense policy-making in the field of Arabization. In any case, he was called Momo by his family and friends—as good a sign as any of the seriousness which they attached to a glorious Berber past. Youth in Kabylia live, as elsewhere, in a global MTV-world with not much space for Massinissas.

The gendarmerie, in whose local office Momo received bullet wounds that caused his death two days later, is a paramilitary police force directly under the Ministry of Interior, on the French model. When informed, the Minister of Interior declared that Massinissa's death had been an accident, and that the young man was a criminal (adding nine years to his age to make him 26 instead of 17). The population of the small town, however, knew that Massinissa had been a good and ambitious high-school student. The rage which had already brought them out into the streets grew out of control after the Minister's statement. The building housing the gendarmes' offices and living quarters was besieged, and unrest spread throughout the region, leading to demonstrations and the shooting by gendarmes of several other young people. This is why the spring of 2001 became popularly known as the Black Spring. The protest movement continued uninterrupted until the local elections of autumn 2002. On one occasion in Algiers, and several times in Kabylia, demonstrations numbering up to a million people took place. Eventually a definitive ban on demonstrations was introduced in the capital and enforced by troops.

Three themes dominated the demonstrators' demands. First there were general demands for freedom and democracy and the removal of those in power, who were said to 'despise and kill young people'; second, an insistence that the Berber language become a national language and that Berber culture be 'recognized'; third, a specific demand for the withdrawal of the gendarmerie from Kabylia and its replacement by ordinary municipal police. Great gains were won as a result of these demonstrations. In the autumn of 2001 President Bouteflika announced a revision of the constitution, and in April 2002 the Algerian Parliament confirmed the constitutional change, making *Tamazight* a 'national' language—though not 'official' (a status reserved for Arabic). The gendarmerie was not withdrawn, but individual members who were proven to have a record of violence or extortion against the Kabyle population were transferred or prosecuted. Normal police stations were opened, thus preparing the way for the withdrawal of the gendarmerie. Policy measures in other fields such as the introduction of the teaching of *Tamazight* in schools in the Berber-speaking regions, already decided on after the school strike of 1995, were expanded, as was teaching of *Tamazight* language and literature at university level.

But the question of the responsibility for all the deaths and injuries remained. President Bouteflika nominated an independent commission, led by a well-known judge of Kabyle origin, Issad Mohand. This body was first met with suspicion and calls for a boycott, but gained greatly in legitimacy through its first report, which laid a heavy burden of blame on the gendarmerie for the riots (and totally rejected the President's explanation of a foreign conspiracy to destabilize the country).

Since these events, however, the situation in Kabylia has become less clear. In May 2002 there was a very efficient boycott in Kabylia of the parliamentary elections, with a less than unified boycott of the local elections the following October, and finally in the presidential elections of May 2004 a very low Kabyle participation (17%). This time, however, the media reported on people being hindered from voting and the widespread looting of election offices. Reports have come out of dissent and conflict within different parts of the movement and of fatigue among the population in general. In February 2004 the leadership of the movement was invited to Algiers for a 'dialogue'. On that occasion the delegates presented a programme of 11 points, the so-called El Kseur platform, initially decided upon in June 2001. An agreement was now struck with the government on some of the points, regarding the withdrawal of the gendarmerie and their replacement by other police forces, and compensation for the families of the youngsters who had been killed. But when the government agreed to take into account only a part of the demands contained in the document, the dialogue was interrupted. In particular the government had proposed that the demand to turn *Tamazight* into an official language, on an equal footing with Arabic, be put to a referendum. This was vehemently rejected by the representatives of the Kabyle movement, who claimed that there could not be a vote on a language!

There can be no doubt that the Kabyle crisis is far from solved, or that the existing organizational structure of the Kabyle movement is making it difficult for it to play a part in the political process and avoid total fragmentation. I shall return to this last point.

WHAT IS THE CONFLICT ABOUT?

There are two main interpretations of the Kabyle movement that followed on the Black Spring. The first stresses the long-standing increase in political self-awareness among Berbers in general and Kabyles in particular, beginning with a cultural movement among small groups in the 1970s. In this perspective, the refusal of successive Algerian governments after independence to take account of the Kabyles' distinctive language and culture, the ensuing build-up of frustration, and the conscious work of Berberist groups, are the explanatory factors for a movement which will continue until its demands have been met. Here the Berbers are seen, together with the Kurds, as the last big population in the Mediterranean and Middle Eastern region to see its legitimate claims for nationhood denied. The other interpretation stresses social and political frustrations among Kabyle youth in particular and similar cases elsewhere in the country. Demonstrations against police forces or local authorities, and riots resulting in attacks on state property, are cited as signs of a general dissatisfaction, and of equally-general hopes, throughout Algeria, with events in Kabylia merely being larger and longer-lasting. The key question, then, is: do the phenomena in question represent a Kabyle Berber movement striving for group/ethnic rights, or an Algerian social movement striving for collective social and perhaps also individual rights?

The answer is certainly both. In favor of the first—stressing the distinctively-Berber aspect of the question—one could mention the particular context of the Arabization policy and the presence of the gendarmerie. Jane Goodman asked young Kabyles about how school had 'Arabized' them. They told her the same story as has been heard from so many other minority-language speakers in the world: prohibition of the use of the mother tongue, even in the school yard (Goodman 2004). That children with Arabic as their first language could come under similar pressures (since the classical Arabic taught at school and spoken Algerian Arabic differ substantially) is not something which matters to Kabyle children. To this should be added the recurrent campaigns by the authorities to enforce Arabization—an approach which may have been seen as an attack not only on the Kabyles' mother-tongue but also on the second language of many of them, namely French. As regards the gendarmerie, this force was deployed in Kabylia especially after the events of 1980. Its members are nationally-appointed and tend to come from non-Kabyle areas. They live in isolation from the local population and do not speak *Tamazight*; they behave notoriously as if in conquered territory. During the first two months of unrest in Kabylia they were responsible for the deaths of about 40 young people.

It is sometimes further stressed that Kabylia as a region has a very different political, particularly electoral, record compared to the rest of Algeria. Kabyles boycotted massively the presidential election of 1999 (only 10% voted as compared to 74% in the rest of the country) and, although a little higher, their participation in a referendum on 'civil concord' in 1998 was still very low. This negative record does not necessarily express a sense of distance from the political life of the country, based on a feeling of not belonging; it may equally reflect the much higher level of politicization in Kabyle areas. The leaders of the two political parties with strong followings there were both candidates for the presidency, but together with all the other candidates they eventually withdrew and called for a boycott, because on the eve of the elections they considered that these would not be free and fair. As shown by the figures, the call for boycott was heard in Kabylia, but hardly at all in the rest of the country.

If electoral boycotts represent a high degree of responsiveness to the actions of the political parties, this can also be advanced as a sign of Kabyle specificity, i.e. the consistent presence and impact of two dominating political parties. Particularly so since the two parties, the *Front des Forces Socialistes*, led by Hocine Aït Ahmed, and the *Rassemblement pour la Culture et la Démocratie*, are essentially Kabyle organizations.

WHY ARE GROUP RIGHTS INSTRUMENTAL TO INDIVIDUAL RIGHTS?

Arguments in favor of the second interpretation have to put the Kabyle demands into the Algerian context. As mentioned above, in the early 1980s repression following the events in Tizi-Ouzou and the Berber Spring helped to lay the foundations of the first independent human-rights organization in Algeria.

In 2001 the movement began as a protest against a violation of the basic human right to life, when Momo Guermah was killed. Later the demand for the withdrawal of the gendarmerie from the whole of Kabylia became the central claim on the authorities in Algiers. The fact that this was eventually granted, at least partly, as in the spring of 2002, implies a certain regional autonomy for Kabylia that has not been acknowledged elsewhere in Algeria (ISG 2003). It also implies an acknowledgment of rights—at least to life, and to be left alone—for everyone in Kabylia, Berber or otherwise.

Meanwhile, establishing routine respect for individual rights remains very difficult in the kind of political situation that has prevailed in Algeria (Brandell 1997). Witness in recent years the many obstacles placed in the way of solving the cases of disappearance in custody during the violent times since 1992. The association of family members of the 'disappeared' were depicted as the families of terrorists, which was tantamount to being called terrorists themselves. It was claimed that the disappearances meant individuals had joined terrorist groups, for example, or that deaths in custody resulted from legitimate treatment of terrorists by the police. When statements of this kind were made by organizations claiming to represent the families of people murdered by terrorists, the families and lawyers of those who had 'disappeared' in police or military custody could hardly continue their campaign for clarification. Such widespread fear prevailed anyway, with more than 100,000 dying in the ten years of intense violence, that the disappearance of up to 7000 persons could easily be downplayed, with the authorities delaying their answers to enquiries or not replying at all.

In Algeria, individual *political* rights were severely limited when multiparty elections disappeared after independence. When multiparty elections were reintroduced in 1989 it took only two years before their importance was reduced by the prohibition of the major political opposition, the Islamist FIS, and by the return to power of forces outside the elected bodies. As regards *civil* individual rights, the respect for these has certainly not been enhanced by colonialism first, followed by a war of independence, state socialism and finally civil war. More profoundly, in a society which is not individualistic by culture or tradition; where such rights as have been won have been depicted as the achievement of the Algerian people as a whole (national self-determination), or by the workers and peasants among them (social and economic rights); and where individual political rights have been very briefly enjoyed, it can be argued that claims for group rights tend to carry with them claims for individual rights, both civil and political.

Some, of course, would argue that individual rights in general depend on the construction of a particular social group in opposition to others—whether the group is defined in national, ethnic or gender terms—and that this has always been the case. If this is so, then the Algerian national struggle for independence, and now the Kabyle confrontation of the Algerian state, have helped to advance the cause of individual rights, through the assertion of the rights of these groups.

MODELS OF INTEGRATION AND THE KABYLE UPHEAVAL

It took several decades after Algeria's independence before outside obervers realized the Islamic undertones of the Algerian war of independence. In fact, for the great majority of those who fought and for those who supported them, the justification of the effort to pursue this long and vicious war came from their definition of the French as Christians. (The use of the word *rumi*—Roman—for both French and Christians seems to indicate even more deeply-rooted assumptions, from a time before the existence of Islam and Christianity. In fact, the Roman invasion of North Africa took place well before its partial Christianization). The political leadership of the FLN, and the section of international public opinion which encouraged it, might well have seen the cause as a war for national liberation with no place for religious concerns. Yet Islam constituted the framework within which all people *de facto* could gather. This was also the case in Kabylia, the vanguard of the struggle and a physical stronghold during the war. On the other hand, many Kabyles had, not least through emigration to France, contacts with secular movements, especially socialists and communists. The Berberist crisis of the late 1940s is often described as a result of this exposure to secular values, which made democracy within the national movement an aim.

When, in 1963, the *Front des Forces Socialistes* was founded by Hocine Aït Ahmed, in opposition to the Ben Bella government in Algiers, the official reason was the absence of radical socialist plans for independent Algeria such as had been endorsed during the war. There was no mention, for example, of the question of language and culture. At the same time, the new party's impact, through the mobilization of its members to open a guerrilla front in Kabylia, owed much, paradoxically, not only to Aït Ahmed's position as one of the founders of the National Liberation Front but also to his role as the head of a great religious family, entrusted with the heritage of its ancestors.

Kabylia has, as mentioned above, been described as an electoral exception in Algeria, with two parties totally dominating—the FFS, which was able to emerge from clandestinity in 1989, and the newer *Rassemblement pour la Culture et la Démocratie*. Yet this did not prevent the Islamist party, the FIS (in French, *Front Islamique du Salut*), from winning some victories in the region. The FIS was indeed the only party, together with the two just mentioned, to publish electoral material in *Tamazight* and choose candidates of Kabyle origin. Accordingly, the message was received that these men were Muslims and therefore to be trusted when opposing the government in Algiers, which was accused of being out of touch with the people and responsible for all the country's social and economic problems.

Islam as a near-natural framework for all social life and the basis of belonging underwent more intense exposure to foreign ideas and ways, among Kabyles, than among other Algerians. Kabyles were the first to be recruited to the army and to work in French industry during the First World War, and during the colonial period they constituted the bulk of Algerian immigrants in France. One aspect of the crisis of the 1940s was differing ways of thinking between emigrants and the independence movement in Algeria. Yet Kabyle emigrants in general would almost certainly have signed up to the famous statement of the great reformist leader Ben Badis: 'Islam is my religion, Arabic my language and Algeria my country'—and until recently, perhaps, had no reservations about the middle part concerning language. Even today, most of those Algerians who in their daily life sometimes speak a variety of Berber would consider Arabic to be 'their language' for national and political reasons (Algeria being their country and part of the 'Arab nation') and for religious reasons (Arabic being the language of the Qur'an).

Thus Kabyles have felt able to participate, without any crisis of identity, in the Islamist party and later the armed Islamist groups (active until very recently in the Jijel region). While several Islamist guerrilla groups existed in Kabylia in the 1990s, the largest consisted of former military men and was active in the region of Lakhdaria. There have, however, been limits to their influence, in part because of the domination of the two Kabyle parties. FFS is much stronger than the RCD, which formed part of the government from 1999 until summer 2001, when it withdrew on grounds of the political repression in Kabylia. The Kabyles had accordingly at their disposal one government party supporting the policy of 'rooting out terrorism', and one opposition party very active in iniatives involving the banned Islamist party, as shown by the meetings at San Egidio in Rome in 1995 which brought together all opposition factions and proclaimed a common resolution to confront the government with an alternative. But in addition, limits to the Islamist influence were imposed by the particular geographical, demographic and socio-political conditions of Kabylia.

Territory and a Socio-Political Movement

The mountains of Kabylia are close to the capital, Algiers, to the fertile plains of the Mitidja and the Mediterranean Sea. Even more than other mountainous areas around this sea, the region is densely-populated: lively confrontations and many invasions over the centuries have pushed the population up from the plains into the safety of the mountains.

As a result Kabylia cannot feed its inhabitants. The extraordinary reporting from Kabylia by Albert Camus in 1939, which contributed to the authorities' closure of his newspaper, gives a concrete insight into the social and economic conditions of that time, including conditions of food shortage extending to outright starvation (Camus 1978 [1939]: 278–336). The harsh living conditions provide one explanation of why Kabyles have been at the forefront of emigration not only to France, but also to the towns and cities of Algeria. More Kabyles are today living in Algiers than in the capital of their own region, Tizi-Ouzou. Nonetheless, the short distance to the national capital, and the fact that emigration to France until the 1970s often was not definitive (rotating within families), has enabled most emigrants to keep close ties to their mountains and their people.

In historical times topography alone meant that no domination could be imposed from the outside. The political organization of villages and small towns was one of primitive republicanism, with decision-making in the hands of the general assembly of male inhabitants, where elders had most influence. The relations between these villages and small cities, often quite conflictual, were kept at a tolerable level by the mediation of *m'rabet* families, descendants of holy men. Visits to the tombs of these venerated forebears gave an opportunity for gatherings and negotiations outside the villages of parties in conflict. By the same token, when a foreign invader pushed into the mountains unity was rapidly created among all those more or less autonomous villages. Groups of villages were also permanently allied within an *arch,* a Kabyle concept sometimes translated by 'tribe', referring to the idea of a common ancestry.

On top of this traditional republicanism, which was either tolerated or enforced under French colonial rule, the whole system of state institutions was added after independence. At the municipal level these were sometimes close in form to the older organizations. In any case, when crisis came, first through the armed confrontations, then the upheaval of the spring of 2001, it was possible to put the old concepts back into use. The Kabyle movement was organized through village committees and coordination between them. The political parties, the FFS and the RCD, faced with what they considered political rivalry, initially claimed that some of the committees had been established by pro-regime elements to weaken them. Whether or not this was the case, the local logic was without doubt crucial.

Today's Kabyle youth refer ironically to the old concepts of *arch* and *arouch*. Those structures have, however, proved a strong instrument of organization, co-ordination and decision-making, and also, not least, of restraint on a movement which in the Algerian setting could easily move towards civil war, with or without provocation from outside the Kabyle movement itself. In a subtle analysis, coinciding with the concern to understand the Kabyle upheaval in its Algerian context, Mohamed Brahim Salhi (2002) seems to conclude that the movement was using the old concepts and modes of decision-making, but acting in a totally modern way (painting graffiti, for example, or organizing demonstrations). Salhi also points to the limitations of the 'traditional' model in explaining Kabyle politics, and discusses more broadly the changes introduced by the economic crisis, which has forced people back to the village and 'retraditionalized' part, but only part, of their lives. As regards the whole movement of committees and coordinations, he stresses the tension within it between the individualistic and democratic values needed to bring forth a modern citizenry, and the consensus model of decision-making, which tends to refuse entry to, and sometimes even proscribe, those within the movement who express divergent views. The organizational and decision-making aspects of the movement, drawing on tradition, may create cohesion and efficiency, but are problematic from the point of view of democratic debate in Kabylia and in Algeria as a whole. Finally, the refusal of party politics puts the movement in an awkward and difficult position of *face-à-face* with the regime, hindering the mediations, negotiations and compromises which are also part of building democracy.

CONCLUSION AND EPILOGUE

What has happened in Kabylia is undoubtedly of great importance for the future of Algeria. While continuing to defend the autonomy of the territory and its inhabitants, the ongoing movement has imposed limitations on the central authorities that may foreshadow a wider movement for individual rights in the country as a whole. The issue of group rights—in this context the *Tamazight* language and the teaching of it—opens a space for the recognition of pluralism which has been almost completely proscribed in Algerian politics since independence. At the same time, the specific blend of a tradition of republicanism in the assembly-led villages, together with contemporary links to a huge polyglot emigration, creates very special conditions for social and political movements. These conditions do not exist elsewhere in Algeria, either in general or among other Berber groups.

The Kabyle movement has not, in the end, developed into separatism, but has presented itself instead as a common project for the whole of Algeria. This should be understood against the background of the national and Muslim integration of the Algerian people through colonialism, and the mobilization for independence and for development after independence. It is also to be understood as a result of the high level of local autonomy within the movement. These advances can, however, easily be undermined if the central authorities, faced with difficulty in pursuing any domestic policy in a situation of revival of terrorist violence, were to opt for exacerbating latent conflicts between regions and local groups. Or, for that matter, if internal power struggles in Algiers were to spill over onto and exploit the Kabyle terrain, as some claimed was the case in 2001 when the gendarmerie responded so disproportionately to local demonstrations in Kabylia.

A two-day general strike in February 2003 united the whole country, however, as did in early 2005 protests against a major government-decreed increase in energy prices. It also seems that the groups pursuing clarification of cases of disappeared persons have had some success of late and are being met with more understanding among the rest of Algerian society. An official report, moreover, on the cases of disappearances is due for early 2005. This is expected to bring more solid information into the public domain and, for the first time, acknowledgment of the armed forces' responsibility for crimes against Algerian citizens. If this means that respect for the individual right to life and dignity is slowly getting recognition in Algeria, then this is certainly a consequence of the collective fight for group rights in Kabylia.

In mid-January 2005 a new dialogue was opened at the invitation of the government led by Ahmed Ouhayia. Representatives of the co-ordinated Kabyle village committees met the Prime Minister and his staff. Surprisingly, within a short time an agreement was struck to set up a common committee in order to implement *all* the demands of the El Kseur platform, including the total withdrawal of the gendarmerie, an economic programme for Kabylia, and an end to arbitrary and authoritarian rule. This would entail the return of all the security forces and civil service to the control of the elected bodies, meaning, in effect, the installation of a working democracy and the rule of law in Algeria. Critics within and without the Kabyle movement point, in response, to the upcoming referendum on a general amnesty which President Bouteflika has prepared, and explain away the government's co-operative mood as an attempt to disarm its opponents at this delicate time. They have also stressed that the government is hardly constitutionally qualified to put into reality all the different demands of the El Kseur document.

This is certainly true. It remains, however, the case that a certain recognition of cultural pluralism, and the first steps towards respect for the individual, have taken place in Algeria as a consequence of the Kabyles' demands and actions in favor of group rights. Moreover, the official government agenda now displays a document emanating from this very movement, containing both harsh criticism of the Algerian civil and military executive and the basic principles for a more democratic future for the country. Time alone will tell whether young Kabyles will be able to look on themselves in future times as the spearhead of democratic Algeria.

REFERENCES

Ageron, Ch.-R. (1976). 'Du mythe kabyle aux politiques berbères'. *Le Mal de Voir*, Cahiers Jussieu/2. Paris: Université de Paris-VII.

Bourdieu, P. (1972). *Esquisse d'une Théorie de la Pratique, précédée de Trois Etudes d'Ethnologie Kabyle.* Geneva: Librairie Droz.

Brandell, I. (1994). 'Islam och politik bland Maghrebs berber' in Svanberg and Westerlund eds.

—— (1997). 'North Africa: from social to political citizenship?' in Linjakumpu and Virtanen eds.

—— (1998). *Algeriet: demokratins och islamismens tid.* Stockholm: Tranan.

—— and A. Rabo (2003). 'Arab nations and nationalism: dangers and virtues of transgressing disciplines'. *Orientalia Suecana* LI-LII (2002–2003). Uppsala: Uppsala University Department of Asian and African Languages.

Camus, A. (1978 [1939]). 'Misère de la Kabylie'. *Cahiers Albert Camus 3*, Fragments d'un Combat, 1938–1940 Alger Républicain, Le Soir Républicain.* Edition établie, présentée et annotée par Jacqeline Lévy-Valensi et André Abbou. Paris: Gallimard.

Carlier, O. (1986). 'La production sociale de l'image de soi: note sur la "crise berberiste" de 1949'. *Annuaire de l'Afrique du Nord 1984.* Paris: Editions du CNRS.

Chaker, R. (1982). 'Journal des événements de Kabylie (mars-mai 1980)'. *Les Temps Modernes* 39, no. 432–33 (July-August).

Chaker, S. (1987). 'L'affirmation identitaire berbère à partir de 1900: constantes et mutations (Kabylie)'. *Berbères, Une Identité en Construction*, *Revue de l'Occident Musulman et de la Méditerranée* 44.

Chaulet, C. (2002). 'Le "local", l'origine et le terme'. *Insaniyat: Revue Algérienne d'Anthropologie et de Sciences Sociales* VI, no. 16.

Collectif Contre la Répression en Algérie (1989). 'Au Nom du Peuple, Vous êtes accusés d'atteinte à l'autorité de l'Etat. Qu'avez-vous à dire?' Paris: Imedyazen.

Colonna, F. (1996). 'Sur le passage de l'émeute à l'attentat collectif (1978–1996)'. *Monde Arabe, Maghreb-Machrek*, no. 154 (October-December).

Gellner, E. (1969). *Saints of the Atlas.* Chicago: Weidenfeld & Nicolson.

—— and C. Micaud eds. (1973). *Arabs and Berbers: From Tribe to Nation in North Africa.* London: Duckworth.

Goodman, J. (2004). 'Reinterpreting the Berber Spring: from rite of reversal to site of convergence'. *Journal of North African Studies* 9, no. 3 (autumn).

International Crisis Group (2003). *Algeria: Unrest and Impasse in Kabylia.* ICG Middle East/North Africa Report no.15 (10 June).

Lacoste-Dujardin, C. (1997). *Opération Oiseau Bleu: Des Kabyles, des Ethnologues et la Guerre d'Algérie*. Paris: Editions la Découverte.

Linjakumpu, A. and K. Virtanen eds. (1997). *Under the Olive Tree: Reconsidering Mediterranean Politics and Culture.* Tampere: University of Tampere.

Quandt, W. (1973). 'The Berbers in Algerian political elites' in Gellner and Micaud eds.

Ouerdane, A. (1987). 'Un conflit à plusieurs faces: la "crise berbériste" de 1949'. *Berbères, Une Identité en Construction*, *Revue de l'Occident Musulman et de la Méditerranée* 44.

Roberts, H. (1980). 'Towards an understanding of the Kabyle question in contemporary Algeria'. *The Maghreb Review* 5, nos. 5–6 (September-December).

—— (1982). 'The unforeseen development of the Kabyle question in contemporary Algeria'. *Government and Opposition* 17, no. 3.

—— (1983). 'The economics of Berberism: the material basis of the Kabyle question in contemporary Algeria'. *Government and Opposition* 18, no. 2.

—— (2002a). 'La Kabylie à la lumière tremblotante du savoir maraboutique' (review of Kamel Chaouchoua: *L'Islam Kabyle: Religion, Etat et Société en Algérie*, Paris: Maisonneuve et Larose). *Insaniyat: Revue Algérienne d'Anthropologie et de Sciences Sociales* VI, no. 16.

—— (2002b). *Embattled Algeria 1988–2002: Studies in a Broken Polity*. London: Verso.

—— (2003). 'De la segmentarité à l'opacité: à propos de Gellner et Bourdieu et des approches théoriques quant à l'analyse du champ politique algérien'. *Insaniyat: Revue Algérienne d'Anthropologie et de Sciences Sociale* VII, nos. 19–20.

Salhi, M. B. (2002). 'Local en contestation, citoyenneté en construction: le cas de la Kabylie'. *Insaniyat: Revue Algérienne d'Anthropologie et de Sciences Sociales* VI, no. 16.

Silverstein, P. A. (2003). 'Martyrs and patriots: ethnic, national and transnational dimensions of Kabyle politics'. *Journal of North African Studies* 8, no. 1.

Svanberg, I. and D. Westerlund (1994). *Majoritetens islam.* Stockholm: Arena.

Chapter Seven

Democracy, Religion and Minority Rights in Nigeria

Jibrin Ibrahim

The development of democratic culture is dependent on the existence of a modern state that can protect the rights of its citizens and extract duties from them. Modern democratic states are characterized by equity, the rule of law and a search for legitimacy. The latter is dependent on the state's capacity to provide necessary public goods and, more important, neutral arbitration that guarantees the security of all sections of society. When the state is generally perceived as serving the particular interests of one group, this legitimacy begins to erode, along with its authority. As state capacity declines, fear of 'the other' increases, and citizens resort to other forms of solidarity—religious, ethnic and regional—in search of security. Religious insecurity is particularly insidious because it touches on people's fears not just in their present lives but also for the hereafter. Some provisions of the 1999 Nigerian Constitution, and statutory provisions subsequently enacted in some Nigerian states, have given rise to serious insecurity. Before addressing these issues, however, it will be useful to examine the dynamics of religious movements in contemporary Africa.

RELIGION AS THE ARENA FOR CIVIL-SOCIETY STRUGGLES

The dynamics of religious movements in contemporary Africa are very complex. They cannot be reduced to a simple 'revivalist tendency' or mechanical response to political and economic crisis. What is known is that there has been a multiplication of religious movements in the continent and an intensification in their fervor. The prevailing context is not only one of serious economic and social crisis; it also includes the collapse of ideological frameworks that previously provided meaning and helped to guide social development. How does religion fit into the attempt by ordinary people and political entrepreneurs to produce alternative autonomous spheres of meaning and action? How can we understand the relationship between growing and wide-ranging struggles for democratization and the multiplication of religious movements and the intensification of their activities? We need also to consider the threat which fundamentalist religious movements pose to democracy and human rights.

The religious sphere in contemporary Africa is open to a wide range of actors and a broad spectrum of social projects. It produces intensive social dynamics in which people's attachments shift continuously, but usually from established traditional religious organizations towards new and more populist sects. Contemporary social movements are the products of more open-ended processes of socialization which are replacing traditional structures rooted in the family, school, church and workplace (Magala 1992: 180). New elements such as the mass media and computer technologies are taking centre stage. The significant characteristic which they share is that they challenge the hitherto-pervasive system of control by states and transnational corporations.

Civil Society

If we accept that civil society is an alternative social sphere relatively autonomous from the state and the family, then most of civil society in Africa is located within the religious sphere. According to Shils, the idea of civil society has three main components:

> The first is a part of society comprising a complex of autonomous institutions—economic, religious, intellectual and political—distinguishable from the family, the clan, the locality and the State. The second is a part of society possessing a particular complex of relationships between itself and the State and a distinctive set of institutions which safeguard the separation of State and civil society and maintain effective ties between them. The third is a widespread pattern of refined civil manners (1991: 4).

The third aspect, in my view, has been insufficiently emphasized in the current literature. For civil society to exist, the conduct of members of society towards each other must be characterized by civility. Polished and refined manners are expressions of respect for other members of society. This is also a precondition for democratic practice, as citizenship cannot be effective if the rights and dignity of the person are not respected. Part of the African tragedy is that refined civil manners, an essential characteristic of most traditional societies, have been eroded by state terrorism, war, poverty and the parochial politics of authoritarian leaders. But many active religious movements have an even worse record of inculcating intolerance, contempt and exclusion and, indeed, incitement to annihilate the other.

A further important attribute of civil society is that it is necessarily pluralist. The world of African religious movements is the highest expression of difference and plurality in civil society. The three broad categories of Islam, Christianity and traditional religions encompass a plethora of different belief-systems and socio-economic practices, all competing for followers and by the same token maintaining a certain autonomy from the state and other institutions that seek control over society.

Globalization and The Rise of Fundamentalism

We are living in a world in which urbanization is growing very rapidly. Cities everywhere resist all attempts to limit them. African cities have chiefly grown through an increase in shanty towns, which are a focal point for the aggravation of poverty. The major characteristic of the urban crisis in contemporary Africa is the precariousness of life. Daily subsistence-needs such as food, housing, healthcare and education are lacking for a large proportion of the population. There is serious pressure on livelihoods, both formal and informal. More and more people are being pushed into the informal sector. The breakdown of the social fabric and family bonds is producing a lumpen culture, characterized by delinquency, violence and prostitution, that only religion seems to have an effective cure for.

The conditions created by urbanization and social transformation have created ideal conditions for the proliferation of informal as well as formal religious activities. Sufi orders in West Africa, for example, provide many survival functions—shelter, medical support and economic networks—that neither the family nor the state can secure in these times of crisis (Kane 1997: 48). Religious actors are also social agents who provide some meaning for those living in the new and difficult conditions in the squatter towns. New forms of bonding and differentiation have to be created; new social networks are needed to provide comfort and emergency relief to those in distress; new lucrative spheres for accumulation, both legal and criminal, are being created—and for all of these and more, the religious sphere provides the most effective framework. It also offers salvation for the African soul, arguably the most vital of needs in the post-modern age. Fundamentalist movements typically cater for anxiety created by such conditions.

Globalization refers to the universalization of certain practices, identities and structures and more significantly, the current global restructuring of modern capitalist relations (Aina 1996:8). Central to these phenomena is the emergence—and contestation—of a new world order in which inequities in the distribution of power and resources are growing wider. Rudolph reminds us that

> religious communities are among the oldest of the transnationals: Sufi orders, Catholic missionaries and Buddhist monks carried word and praxis across vast spaces before these places became nation-states or even states . . . In today's post-modern era, religious communities have become vigorous creators of an emergent transnational civil society (1997: 1).

Consequently religion has not faded away with modernity or the triumph of science and rationalism. On the contrary, it has expanded, fuelled largely by global secular processes such as urbanization, migration, transnational capital transfers and the mass media. Religion today is a product of modernity as well as a response to it.

That said, the major forces of propulsion in contemporary Nigeria are internal rather than external. Foreign religious organizations and money were influential in the 1970s, especially American Pentecostalism and Wahhabism from Saudi Arabia. They still retain contacts in Nigeria but have a very marginal impact today. Indeed, Nigeria is now a major exporter of religious fundamentalism to the rest of Africa, Europe and even the United States, where the power of Nigerian Pentecostal churches is growing. The church, for example, with the largest congregation in Europe today, Kingsway Ministries in London, is run by a Nigerian. The Redeem Christian Church of God from Nigeria runs regular tele-evangelist broadcasts in the United States. Similarly Islamic fundamentalism rooted now in Nigeria exercises influence in the neighbouring countries.

The Democratic Paradox of Religion

Now, religious movements are veritable arenas for expressing democratic demands in contemporary Africa. Because of the informal character of the religious sphere, entry into it is easy. Actors use the space and voice created by religious movements to make political demands, contest secular and religious authorities and mobilize the population for political and social action. The paradox, however, is that actors have a limited voice within the religious movements themselves. The system of authority within these movements is based on divine ordination and total obedience to the persons with constituted spiritual control. Dissent can only be exercised when members exercise their right to exit the space. A contradiction therefore seems to be developing between a democratising external environment and an increasingly-authoritarian internal religious environment for members. This process is heightened by growing tension between rising religiosity in society and demands for greater secularism. The central problem that emerges is the place of religious minorities in areas of the country where religion and law have been integrated in ways which do not fully respect these minorities' rights. One clear example is that of the Christian minorities in Muslim-dominated areas of Nigeria, whose freedoms are being particularly threatened by the adoption of *sharia* penal laws in some states of the federation.

Another example is the excessively authoritarian culture of fundamentalist religious movements. One of the most common phrases used by Pentecostal leaders in Nigeria has been popularized by Ruth Marshall: 'God', as she puts it, 'is not a democrat' (Marshall 1992). She argues, with justification, that the form of authority exercised in Pentecostal organisations is personal and charismatic. Those who establish a fellowship or exercise leadership do so on the basis of claims to having seen visions or dreams, or having somehow received a message directly from God. The routine governance of Pentecostal organisations is transmitted on the basis of such claims. For example, when Bishop Idahosa of the Church of God Mission died a few years ago, the leadership of the organisation was passed on to his wife. The succession was effected by a simple declaration, by an American friend of the Church, that he had seen a vision in which God had said Idahosa's wife should take over the mantle of leadership. Similarly, in the Family Worship Centre in Abuja leadership was passed from Mr to Mrs Omaku in 2003 following the death of the founder-general and overseer of the church.

In Pentecostal organizations there are no elections, and even consultations are very limited, because direct messages from God transcend earthly questions of democratic governance. Often the only option for dissent is that of exit, which those wanting to exercise their own charismatic power are obliged to take. Thus, although the points of entry into the religious arena are open, the internal political culture of most of the organisations there is anti-democratic. Similarly, although the Islamic revival and fundamentalism permeates society through informal as well as formal means it undeniably fosters an undemocratic mindset. The antinomies between religion and democracy in Nigeria have been futher widened by the growing profile of *sharia* in politics and public law.

THE *SHARIA* QUESTION IN NIGERIAN POLITICS

Since 1978, the question of the *sharia*, or Islamic religious law, has become a major bone of contention in Nigerian politics. During the 1978 Constituent Assembly, the most contentious debates were aroused by this issue. Specifically, Christian and Muslim members differed over a proposal for the establishment of a *sharia* Court of Appeal. Many Christians saw the suggestion as the first step towards the establishment of an Islamic state in the country, while Muslims argued that it would be a logical extension of the lower *sharia* courts which Muslims had been demanding for a long time. In the compromise that emerged, the *sharia* Court of Appeal was indeed established, but its appellate jurisdiction was limited to civil law. The situation at that time seems to have been that Christians accepted the federalization of the *sharia* juridical structure, while Muslims accepted its restricted application to civil matters.

The *sharia* question, however, developed into a major political confrontation in October 1999 when Governor Yerima of Zamfara state inaugurated the adoption of the *sharia* legal system, to take effect from 27 January 2000. The Zamfara Law extended the application of *sharia* from personal law to criminal law. Following this example, similar laws were adopted in eleven other Muslim-dominated states in the north of Nigeria. The attempt by the Kaduna State House of Assembly to pass a *sharia* bill led to a series of demonstrations, first by Muslim supporters and then by Christian opponents. The demonstration on 21 February 2000 led to a major conflict, resulting in massive killings of people on both sides, the destruction of religious buildings, arson and the destruction of property. People were said to have organized the killing of their neighbors simply because they belonged to a different religious order. This event led to a major demographic restructuring of the town, with people congregating in areas where their religious faith had a majority of inhabitants.

The Kaduna conflict demonstrated the fundamental problem posed by the adoption of the *sharia* legal system. It created acute insecurity among Christian minority groups in the affected states, who feared that the new legal regime would affect them adversely, despite claims to the contrary by Muslim supporters. Indeed, many voices on both sides called for the partition of Nigeria rather than the adoption, or abandonment, of the *sharia* legal system. The Kaduna mayhem led to retaliatory killings and burning of mosques in Aba and Owerri, in which Igbo youths targeted northerners, whom they accused of killing their kith and kin. As the conflict was assuming state-threatening dimensions, a meeting of the National Council of State was called to seek a solution to the problem. (The Council is composed of the Head of State, former Heads of State and state governors.) At the end of the meeting on 29 February, it was announced that the *sharia* laws being enacted would be suspended and there would be a return to the *status quo ante*—the Penal Code.

However, two members of the Council and former Heads of State, Shehu Shagari and Mohammadu Buhari, denied that such a decision had been taken and contended that Muslims were not ready to compromise on the *sharia*.

Tensions mounted once again and riots were reported in Sokoto and Borno States. Non-Muslims started fleeing the Muslim-dominated parts of the north. Finally, at the beginning of April, northern governors met and agreed to set up a joint Muslim-Christian Committee to align the *sharia* with the penal code and counter the threats to northern and national unity posed by the issue. Their communiqué, read by Governor Bafarawa of Sokoto state, announced: 'We have resolved to uphold the whole North as one indivisible geographical entity within the Federation of Nigeria'. Yet shortly after this announcement, a thief, Buba Bello Jengede, had his right hand amputated on the orders of a *sharia* court judge in Zamfara state—for stealing a cow. Other cases were soon to follow. The most spectacular were those of two women, Safiya Husaini and Amina Lawal, who were sentenced to death by stoning for alleged adultery, as described below.

In some sense, the *sharia* debate has always been about the nature of the Nigerian state as a whole, because Muslim activists have consistently campaigned for the extension of *sharia* law to the domain of criminal law. As pointed out by Ben Nwabueze, professor of constitutional law and a member of the 1978–79 Constituent Assembly:

> In civil law, the state, through its judicial arm, the courts, merely interposes its machinery as an impartial disinterested arbiter between parties in a dispute; it lacks the power to initiate the process of adjudication, and must wait until it is moved by one of the disputants. So the enforcement through the courts of the civil aspects of *sharia* does not involve the support, promotion or sponsorship by the state of the Moslem religion in preference to other religions. In criminal law, however, the position is entirely different. The state invokes its coercive power to arrest and detain an alleged offender, to initiate a criminal charge against him in court, and to see to the effective prosecution of the charge. Thus, as complainant, initiator of the criminal process and prosecutor, the state is an interested party. Accordingly, the enforcement by the state of the *sharia* criminal law under the Qur'an involves the use of its machinery to aid, support and sponsor the Islamic religion in preference to other religions (*Post Express* 13 April 2001).

The application of *sharia* criminal law has had a significant impact on the rights of women, who have been subjected to standards significantly different from those applied to men.

Women's Rights Under *Sharia* Penal Law

There has been much debate regarding the most effective campaign strategy on *sharia*-related human-rights issues in Nigeria. Some activists have argued for a generalized national and international campaign on the basis of international human-rights standards (Mahdi 2004: 173). Others have argued for a culturally sensitive campaign using progressive Muslim advocates and jurists relying on Islamic jurisprudence and the demonstrated difference between Islamic law and Muslim laws (Ibrahim 2004). To illustrate this latter argument, though the same Islamic sources were used in all twelve states in northern Nigeria where the *sharia* penal code was adopted, the codes themselves have significant differences in terms of procedure, the definition of offenses and the composition of courts as one moves from state to state. This reality led to human-rights organisations in Nigeria adopting a strategy of choosing the most favourable texts and sources when they rose to the defence of the two women sentenced to death for adultery (*zina*). I shall briefly present these two cases as they show that the category of minority can also be applied in a gendered context, because the two women clearly had fewer rights than the men who had been jointly accused with them.

Safiya Husaini Tungar Tudu

Safiya Husaini was born between 35–38 years ago. A divorcee and mother of four children, she lived in the rural and largely illiterate society of Tungar Tudu village in Gwadabawa, a local government area of Sokoto state. Her saga began on 23 December 2000, when an informant reported her to the police authority in Gwadabawa. The informant alleged that a 35-year-old divorced woman had been pregnant for eight months outside wedlock. He also denounced one Yakubu Abubakar, a 53–year-old married man in the same village, as responsible for the pregnancy. The informant was a close relation of Safiya who apparently felt an obligation to report her in conformity with the *sharia* penal code that had recently been introduced in the state.

Both Safiya and Yakubu were summoned to court to defend themselves against the allegation of *zina*. By the time of her appearance, Safiya had already given birth to a seven-month-old bouncing baby girl. She had no possible defence, according to the judge, who ruled, under the Maliki school of Islamic jurisprudence routinely applied in northern Nigeria, that the manifestation of pregnancy in a divorced woman was sufficient proof of guilt of adultery. Safiya's co-accused, Yakubu, on the other hand, denied even knowing her, let alone having had sexual relations with her; and he swore an oath to this effect.

On 9 October 2001, Safiya Husaini was sentenced to death by stoning for adultery by a *sharia* upper court in Gwadabawa, while Yakubu Abubakar was acquitted and discharged 'for lack of evidence', as there were no witnesses to invalidate his avowal of innocence. (The evidence required to convict a man, under *sharia* law, is that of four respected witnesses who observe actual penetration during love-making, an almost impossible requirement, while the evidence required to convict a woman is pregnancy).

Immediately after Safiya Husaini's conviction, there erupted national and international condemnation from governmental and non-governmental organizations, owing to the blatantly biased nature of the judgement in her case. The federal government, through its Minister of Justice and Attorney General, Chief Bola Age, warned the Sokoto state government that it would not allow the punishment to be carried out. Also, with the help of Baobab for Women's Human Rights, a vibrant NGO, Safiya appealed against her conviction. Her lawyer, barrister Abdulkadir Ibrahim, applied for a stay of execution pending the determination of the appeal. The case was heard in November at the Sokoto state *sharia* court of appeal.

The case of Safiya Husaini also raised concerns among learned Islamic scholars and legal professionals who felt due process had not been followed even within the context of Islamic law (Ismail 2004). When the case went to appeal, Safiya was freed on technical grounds, namely that the offense of which she had been convicted had been committed before the enactment of the *sharia* penal code in Sokoto state. The appeal court therefore did not address the substantive issues.

Amina Lawal Kurami

On 20 March 2002 the *sharia* court in Bakori sentenced Amina Lawal of Kurami village (Katsina state) to death. The First Information Report reads that 'a charge of adultery was brought against Amina Lawal and Yahaya Muhammed by one Cpl Idris Adamu on behalf of the Katsina State Commissioner of Police' (Yawuri 2004: 185). The accused persons were arrested on suspicion of having committed adultery in the course of their one-year courtship, which resulted in the birth out of wedlock of a baby girl, contrary to the Islamic law of Katsina state.

The case had been brought before the court on 15 January 2002. Initially, Amina admitted that she had committed adultery with Yahaya, which resulted in the birth of the baby. But Yahaya denied the accusation, while admitting that he had been courting Amina with a view to marriage. He argued that there were no witnesses to prove that he had had sexual intercourse with Amina. He was asked to swear to an oath on the Qur'an that he was not guilty, which he did. The court accepted his oath and he was discharged.

On 30 January the court re-assembled for continuation of the case with Cpl Idris on the stand. He presented the 25-day-old baby, Wasila, as evidence, which the court admitted as proof of Amina's adulterous relationship. On 20 February, the court sat to pass judgement. The sole judge sitting throughout the proceedings, Alhaji Nasir Bello Dayi, found Amina guilty of adultery based on: 1) her confession of *zina* (adultery), 2) the evidence of the baby presented by the prosecution, and 3) the charge against her, quoting verse 32 of the Qur'an ('And come not near unto adultery. Lo! It is an abomination and an evil way' (Yawuri 2004:186).

The judge sentenced Amina to death by stoning, based on the punishment prescribed in *Al-Risala*: 'Whoever, being of in full possession of his/her faculties, commits the offence of *zina* should be stoned until he/she dies'.

The Women's Rights Advancement and Protection Alternative (WRAPA), a local NGO, took on a lawyer, M. A. Yawuri, to defend Amina. A strategy group composed of interested parties, including human-rights organizations, lawyers and the National Human Rights Commission, was established to work on the case. The lawyers filed a notice of appeal to the Upper Sharia Court in Funtua, Katsina state, on the grounds that the Sharia Court in Bakori had erred, when it convicted the accused and sentenced her to death, by not clearly defining the offence or explaining it to her; and indeed that the court had found the appellant guilty even before she had been convicted and sentenced. The judgement, therefore, was null and void in that under Islamic law, neither the police nor any other person had the authority either to investigate or to prosecute a Muslim for the offence of adultery. Further, the judgement was given in error because pregnancy does not serve as conclusive proof of adultery.

The Funtua appeal court judges, however, knocked down all 11 grounds of appeal. They thereby upheld the decision of the lower court and sentenced Amina to death by stoning, ruling that the sentence would take effect after she had finished weaning her child. A notice of appeal was then filed at the Court of Appeal in Katsina state to challenge the judgement. The strategy team, drawn from women's rights NGOs, Islamic researchers and scholars, and Senior Advocates of Nigeria (SAN), developed a comprehensive strategy to ensure victory at the next level of appeal. The final outcome of the case in the Katsina state Court of Appeal, on 25 September 2003, was that Amina Lawal's appeal was upheld. The decision of the lower court was set aside and the death sentence quashed. The Katsina appeal court judges made clear their view that the lower court had not observed the principles of *sharia* law, thereby denying Amina a fair trial. The defence team had been able to use the significant corpus of arguments available within Islamic law to make a convincing case and save the life of the accused, acquitting her of a criminal offence and establishing an important legal precedent (Mahdi 2003).

The significant lesson of these two cases is that group rights should be applicable not just to minority or other religious groups but also to groups within a dominant religion—in this case, women within Islamic societies. The cases also highlight the problem of legal asymmetry in the application of criminal law. For the same act, a Muslim woman is routinely sentenced to a slow and painful death, while a Muslim man is routinely acquitted because the evidence required to convict him is almost impossible to obtain.

Federalism and the 1999 Constitution: Contested Terrain

The debate over the *sharia* has posed in clear terms the contest over the definition of Nigeria's political community. Section 10 of the 1979 and 1999 Constitutions has a very short prohibition section, which states: 'The Government of the Federation or of a state shall not adopt any religion as a State Religion'. Christians have argued that this provision means that the country is secular—a position rejected by Muslim activists. In my view the Section 10 formulation was deliberately made ambiguous by the Obasanjo Administration in 1979. The major problem with it is that it appears to allow for preferential treatment to be accorded to particular religions without formally adopting any given one as a state religion.

The 1989 Constituent Assembly tried to clarify the situation, formulating a less ambiguous provision: 'No Government shall overtly or covertly give preferential treatment to any particular religion'. This formulation, however, was rejected by President Babangida's Armed Forces Ruling Council which decided to retain the 1979 formulation, as also happened with the 1995 and 1999 Constitutions. The implication of this retention is a deliberate political choice in favor of ambiguity, allowing more room for public policy choices on the ground. But this ambiguity underlies the current political crisis over the introduction of *sharia* criminal law in some states of the Federation, for each side has interpreted it in a manner that supports particular conceptions of Nigeria's political order.

Ben Nwabueze reads Section 10 of the Constitution as a consecration of the multi-faith nature of Nigerian society. He has argued as follows:

> We must be honest with ourselves and accept the plain truth that state enforcement of *sharia*, in all the plenitude of its injunctions, cannot in the multi-religious society of Nigeria co-exist with a truly federal form of political association. If, therefore, any of the federating units now feel that they can no longer abide by the condition of our association as enshrined in section 10, then all the constituent units should come together and renegotiate another form for our continued association, whatever that other form might be . . . If the states in the North are bent on adopting *Sharia* criminal law, and refuse to be persuaded to drop the idea, they must be taken to have to have opted for a confederal arrangement or a complete break-up of the association. It is better to pull apart and break up in peace than fight over the issue (*Guardian* 3 July 2000).

Muhammeed Tabi'u contests this interpretation:

> Neither Section 10 nor any part of the constitution uses the word secular or secularism. The onus therefore of proving the assertion that that prohibition of state religion means secularism and that it further translates into prohibition of *Sharia* courts and the sourcing of laws from Islam rests on those who make the assertion. If we examine Section 10 in the context of the whole constitution we are forced to conclude that it is impossible to sustain that assertion. A Constitution that itself sets up *Sharia* Courts of Appeal to enforce *Sharia* laws cannot logically be assumed to make the application of *Sharia* its violation (Tabi'u 2001: 4–5).

Ali Mazrui seems to steer a course between these two positions. Pointing out that Nigeria is a former British colony, he argues that Britain leads the world in legal asymmetry:

> The United Kingdom virtually invented asymmetry as a constitutional order. Scotland has its own law, its own currency, and more recently, its own regional assembly . . . On the other hand, Northern Ireland has had a separate regional assembly long before either Wales and Scotland. As for England, it has no separate regional assembly distinct from the national parliament of the whole country. In short, the United Kingdom has never tried to have symmetrical constitutional arrangements for its main constituent regions . . . What all this means is that federalism is able to accommodate a lack of constitutional symmetry even when the areas of disagreement are about matters of life and death. The *hudud* [Qur'an-prescribed set of punishments] in Nigeria and Sudan includes matters of life and death. So does the debate about capital punishment in the United States (*Weekly Trust* 11 May 2001).

If, therefore, he continues, such divergent constitutional paths can co-exist in the United Kingdom (which is not even a federal country), then they should be able to do so in Nigeria.

The *Sharia,* Rights and the Nigerian Constitution

Section 38 of Chapter 4 of the Constitution, dealing with fundamental human rights, has clear provisions on religious rights:

1. Every person shall be entitled to freedom of thought, conscience and religion, including freedom to change his religion or belief and freedom (either alone or in community with others, and in public or in private), to manifest and propagate his religion or belief in worship, teaching, practice and observance.

2. No person attending any place of education shall be required to receive religious instruction or to take part in or attend any religious ceremony or observance if such instruction, ceremony or observance relates to a religion other than his own, or a religion not approved by his parent or guardian.
3. No religious community or denomination shall be prevented from providing religious instruction to pupils of that community or denomination in any place of education maintained wholly by that community or denomination.

Early in the debate on the *sharia* and rights, however, the then Minister of Justice, Mr Kanu Agabi, declared that the Federal Government had no constitutional powers to take to court the states that had established the *sharia* legal code. It was incumbent on those who felt that their rights had been violated to seek redress:

> If *Sharia* violates the fundamental rights of an individual, it is the duty of that individual to sue for the enforcement of his or her rights. The right to dignity and life are fundamental rights vested in the individual, but not the state or the federation. So when people are calling on my office to seek for a declaration on the *Sharia* in a court, I could not oblige because the court has no jurisdiction to entertain such a case. I have to comply with the Constitution (*New Nigerian* 1 June 2000).

While this position might make sense to some lawyers, it seems to allow the state to abdicate its responsibility to protect the rights of its citizens. Following this refusal of the Federal Government to challenge *sharia* in court, the Christian Association of Nigeria took the matter to court on behalf of Christians who felt their rights had been violated by the introduction of the new legal regime. However, the suit was soon withdrawn. The CAN Vice-President, Archbishop John Onaiyekan, explained the decision as follows:

> The northern state governors hiding under the canopy of religion to introduce laws that negate the security of the country and threaten the corporate existence of Nigeria as a united country should hold themselves responsible for the consequences of their unfortunate action which could lead to the disintegration of the country. To hide under religion and introduce unconstitutional laws that limit respect for the fundamental rights of citizens is an insult to God (*Guardian* 10 July 2000).

Throughout history, religious laws have provided rules, regulations, moral precepts and standards of the highest nature to keep humankind along the narrow and difficult path of devotion to God, moral probity and selflessness.

As Chindo Kani writes:

> *Sharia* is not just about amputation. It is a divine welfare programme. It is for peace, social security, good healthcare, responsible parentage and dignified childhood. It is all about transparent honesty, sincerity in high and low places, responsible leadership, probity and accountability. Above all, *Sharia* enshrines equity, justice, fair play, goodwill and equity before the law (*Post Express* 13 July 2001).

The extension of *sharia* into the criminal domain, however, poses a number of questions relating to human rights. Can non-Muslims feel safe in an environment in which the prevailing criminal law is directly based on Islamic religious texts? Can minorities fully practice their religious rights in a society in which one particular religious order has been elevated to a privileged legal status?

The problem with religion-based laws is that they have almost always been applied by human beings whose spiritual and moral standards have been far below the requirements of what was necessary to faithfully and truthfully implement the divine imperative that was originally ordained. Much of the concern over the extension of *sharia* to criminal law, therefore, is about the possibilities for abuse of the system. One of its effects in northern Nigeria has been an assault on culture. Blanket bans have been imposed not merely on alcohol and prostitution, but also on cinemas, video production, drumming, singing and dancing. In Katsina State a number of clashes occurred between Muslim musicians and Yan Hizba, a group of vigilante enforcers of *sharia* law. While the musicians argued that the *sharia* code did not ban drumming and singing, the enforcers took the view that all traditional music, singing and dancing in Muslim Hausaland must cease immediately (*Trust* 6 June 2001). The state authorities finally pronounced that the *sharia* code permitted drumming and singing on specific occasions such as marriages and naming ceremonies. The vigilantes, however, refused to accept this and have continued to attack Muslim performers and deny the Hausa Muslim community access to their culture. A related development is the attack on 'Soyaya' writing (and video-production), a vigorous form of romantic literature which emerged in the early 1990s in central Hausaland, especially the Kano area.

In a further instance, Sheikh Kabo of the Kano Council of Ulama issued an ultimatum to all foreign NGOs in Kano to leave town within 24 hours or face the wrath of Muslims. His threat followed the attempt by the Johns Hopkins University Centre for Communications Program to organize a workshop on early pregnancy and HIV/AIDS, which the cleric took to be a promotion of sexual liberty and contraception. Kabo called for 'war against NGOs who teach and propagate anti-*sharia* doctrine'. The Programme Officer of the organization, however, Hadiza Babayaro, pointed out that the rights of Muslims would be violated if the Sheikh's instructions were carried out. Consultations, she said, had been held even with the chairman of the Ulama. Moreover, 'there was no basis for the Ulama to attack the programme of the NGO because the organizers were also Muslims who would not do anything to harm the provisions of the *Sharia* legal code' (*Comet* 9 January 2001).

Meanwhile, Christians in the *sharia* states have been complaining that their rights are constantly violated by the legal regime, especially the right to Christian worship and proselytizing in the Muslim Emirates. It is not a new problem. At colonization, Lord Lugard, the Governor of the colony, signed a pact with the Emirates promising that Christian proselytizing would not be allowed among Muslims within the Emirates, and permission to build churches would not be given in the 'Muslim/traditional' parts of the colony. While a Reverend Miller was allowed to establish a church in Zaria city in 1906, this was an exception because on that occasion, the Emir of Zaria had given express permission for the church to be established in spite of the standing order. The church was, moreover, moved out of the city to Wusasa village in the 1930s.

Following the modern introduction of *sharia* in Kano (2000) and the destruction of seventeen churches in the Bompai area of the town, the Christian Association of Nigeria petitioned for justice. Over the previous two decades, the Kano state government had taken a number of measures limiting the right of Christians to operate in the state. According to CAN Kano, the following churches had been demolished: Baptist Church, Mujik village; Assemblies of God Church, Bada village; and four ECWA Churches in Rogo, Yar Tofa, Tudun Wada and Jarkaya (*Vanguard* 23 June 2001). These churches belonged to Maguzawa Christians—indigenous inhabitants of the region who were being discriminated against not because they were outsiders, but because they had converted from their traditional African religion to Christianity.

Since the early 1980s, the Kano State Government has refused to allocate plots for the building of churches in the state. Christians have therefore been obliged to buy empty plots or residential houses for new or converted buildings. Since they have no authorization to build these churches, the buildings are continuously under threat. In 1999, a year before the introduction of the *sharia*, the Kano State Environmental Protection Agency issued letters to fifty-four churches in the state threatening to demolish them for non-possession of building permits. The concern among the Christian community is that even before the re-introduction of the *sharia*, there had been a long tradition of the violation of the constitutional rights of Christians in the region to freedom of worship; the re-introduction of the *sharia*, they felt, would give legal teeth to these violations. It was reported, for example, that five churches were destroyed in Dutse, Jigawa state, following an accusation on the state-owned radio station that some local Christians had launched a book on Christianity. 'Jigawa', the radio said, 'is a *sharia* state (where) Christian teachings should not be tolerated' (*Post Express* 12 July 2001).

MULTI-FAITH SOCIETY, GLOBALIZATION AND GROUP RIGHTS

One motive behind the adoption of *sharia* in the north of Nigeria could be a fear of the forces of westernization and globalization, on the one hand, and the fear of a decisive power-shift to the south of the country on the other. In early 2002 an advertisement from the Supreme Council for *sharia* in Nigeria argued that the forces of globalization were organizing under the United Nations a covert campaign against Islam, ostensibly through international human-rights conventions, which were held to be in contradiction with Islamic norms. Singled out for condemnation on this occasion were UN agreements to outlaw torture, discrimination against women and child-abuse (*Weekly Trust* 22–28 February 2002) .

Shortly afterwards, in an article in the same publication entitled 'Shariacracy and Globalization', Ali Mazrui commented:

> The *Sharia* under this paradigm becomes a form of Northern resistance—not to Southern Nigeria, but to the forces of globalization and to their westernizing consequences. Even the policy of the privatization of public enterprises is probably an aspect of the new globalizing ideology. Privatization in Nigeria may either lead to new transnational corporations establishing their roots or to private southern entrepreneurs outsmarting Northerners and deepening the economic divide between the North and the South (*Weekly Trust* 18 May 2001).

The so-called 'power-shift' that occurred in 1999 in Nigeria has remained a sore point among the northern Muslim political establishment. This refers to the calls from southern Nigerians that the occupant of Aso Rock (the name for the Presidential Palace) should move from the north to the south. According to Charles Ibiang, out of the twelve Heads of State Nigeria has had, only four have been from southern Nigeria (*Thisday* 11 February 1999). The four southern Heads of State have ruled for only six of the thirty-eight years that the country has been independent. As Alex Ekwueme, Vice-President during the Second Republic, has argued, the phrase 'power-shift' was invented as an alternative to the concepts of zoning and rotation, which dominated the National Constitutional Conference of 1994–95 (*Guardian* 26 January 1999). Section 229 of the 1995 Draft Constitution had stipulated that the Presidency should be rotated between the north and the south, gubernatorial power between the three senatorial districts in each state and the chairmanship of local governments between three zones to be created in each of them. These constitutional proposals were seriously weakened when it became clear that General Abacha had no intention of vacating power, but planned to continue as 'elected President'. Since Abacha was from the Muslim north, the implication was that the zoning was going to start from the north, the region that had already monopolized power for a long time.

The swearing-in of President Obasanjo in May 1999 nevertheless marked the implementation of a power-shift from north to south. A political pact had been worked out by the political class in which northern politicians, whose constituencies were a numerical majority in the country, agreed not to run for the Presidency so that a Southerner would emerge as President, thus calming political tensions. The pact 'allocated' the presidency to the Yoruba of the south-west, and the two candidates who competed for the Presidency were Falae and Obasanjo, with Obasanjo winning. Thereafter, however, the problems began. The hardcore Yoruba political elite felt that Obasanjo, although Yoruba, was a northern candidate who might be subservient to the northern political machine. They had therefore voted in bulk for the unsuccessful Yoruba candidate, and Obasanjo won the election in spite of, rather than because of, the Yoruba vote. Although Yoruba candidates had been struggling to win this exalted post for forty years, Obasanjo's victory created anger rather than joy in Yorubaland. Ethnic mobilization and chauvinism intensified and the Yoruba militia, organized in the Odua People's Congress, increased its attacks on Nigerians from other ethnic groups living in Yorubaland, especially Hausa Muslim settlers.

As a result of these events, the northern Nigerian political establishment felt that it was not deriving dividends from its decision to loosen voluntarily its traditional hold on central power. Appointments in the military, the police, the civil service and government boards and parastatals brought in many of the hitherto-marginalized groups, especially the Yoruba and people from the petroleum-producing delta in the south and the Middle Belt. This meant that many Muslim northerners were being displaced from positions of influence. The policy, for example, of retiring all military officers who had previously held political positions removed a significant part of the northern Muslim officer corps, a body which had long marched down the corridors of power. What President Obasanjo presented as modernization, therefore, was read by many as a political purge. *Sharia* in this context can be understood as symbolizing a wished-for return, for northerners, to an ideological framework which they felt they could control.

The President of the Supreme Council for Sharia in Nigeria, Dr Datti Ahmed, has insisted that aside from the interventions of the Zamfara and Niger state governors, *sharia* was introduced in all the other states in accordance with the will of the people, and called on Muslims to vote out leaders who had reservations about its full implementation. This would include President Obasanjo and most of the governors of states in which the *sharia* has been adopted (*Vanguard* 11 August 2001). This activity of elite manipulation and competition remains an important aspect of the *sharia* problem.

Another aspect is its continued capacity to evoke strong emotions nationwide, as in the conflicting passions generated by the attempt to hold the Miss World Competition in Nigeria at the end of 2002. This event was planned as an opportunity to show off the more positive aspects of the country. In November 2002, however, an article appeared by a young female reporter, Isioma Daniel, publicizing the coming show and promising its success, in the face of fears expressed within Nigeria and without. Ms Daniel was apparently unaware of complaints by several Muslim organizations about the timing of the event—during the holy Ramadan month of fasting—and its content—showing scantily-dressed women on prime-time television. Matters were made worse when she went on to remark, in the face of the incipient furore, that even the Prophet Mohammed would have chosen a wife from among the bevy of beauties who would visit Nigeria for the Miss World Competition. Many Muslims immediately expressed their anger at what they considered a highly-sacrilegious remark. There were calls for an economic boycott of Ms Daniel's newspaper and for the Government to cancel the event. In Kaduna, groups of Muslim youths began rioting. Hundreds of innocent lives were lost and quantities of property were destroyed. Within a few days, the riot reached the capital, Abuja, causing a national crisis. This was followed by a *fatwa* from the Zamfara state judicial authorities to the effect that Ms Daniel should be executed. She was forced to flee the country, and before long the organizers of the event resigned themselves to cancelling it and transferring it to London.

CONCLUSION

Throughout history, it is women who have suffered the worst from strictures in the name of religion. When one examines the introduction and extension of *sharia* in the north of Nigeria, one cannot avoid the conclusion that the over-riding aim has been to restrict and punish the behaviour of women. The imposition of dress codes, the chasing of female prostitutes out of the states, restrictions on freedom of movement, and cruel and unnatural punishments for adultery are among the measures directed at women. Moreover, the legal process has been laid wide open to abuse. There is also the problem of law enforcement. The police in particular have seized on the re-introduction of the *sharia* as an opportunity to practice extortion, particularly in respect of women.

Is Nigeria destined to live with *sharia*? On the one hand, it is difficult to escape the conclusion that religious laws are culture-bound and resistant to change—inimical, in fact, to modern multicultural society. On the other, the very dynamics of such societies as they develop can give rise to genuine demands for such laws, perhaps as a sincerely-felt desire to slow and monitor change, rather than resist it outright. In such cases, religious laws such as the *sharia* should be seen as provisional systems awaiting redefinition of the source of their validity. Following the violence that accompanied the attempt by the Kaduna State government to introduce integral *sharia* law in the country, the state government opted for an expressly-multicultural approach based on a tripartite legal system, involving the simultaneous application of *sharia*, customary and common law in that state. This action points the way to a possible model for the future.

REFERENCES

Aina, T. A. (1996). *Globalization and Social Policy: Issues and Research Directions*. Dakar: Council for the Development of the Social Sciences in Africa.

Alkali, N. *et al.* eds. (1993). *Islam in Africa*. Ibadan: Spectrum.

Enwerem, I. (1995). *A Dangerous Awakening: The Politicization of Religion in Nigeria*. Ibadan: French Institute for Africa.

Ibrahim, J. (1989). 'Politics and religion in Nigeria: the parameters of the 1987 crisis in Kaduna State'. *Review of African Political Economy* 45/46.

—— (1991). 'Religion and political turbulence in Nigeria'. *Journal of Modern African Studies* 29, no. 1.

—— ed. (2004). *Penal and Family Laws in Nigeria and in the Muslim World: A Rights-Based Approach*. Zaria: Ahmadu Bello University Press.

Ismail, M. (2004). 'Sharia sources and the defence of women's rights' in Ibrahim ed.

Ilesanmi, S. O. (1992). 'Religious pluralism, identity and political legitimacy in Nigeria'. London: School for African and Oriental Studies unpublished seminar paper.

Juergensmeyer, M. (1993). *The New Cold War? Religious Nationalism Confronts the Secular State*. Berkeley, CA: University of California Press.

Kane, O. (1994). 'Izala: the rise of Muslim reformism in northern Nigeria' in Marty and Appleby eds.

—— (1997). 'Muslim missionaries and African states' in Piscatori and Rudolph eds.

Kukah, M. H. (1993). *Religion, Politics and Power in Northern Nigeria*. Ibadan: Spectrum Books.

Ludwar-Ene G. ed. (1991). *New Religious Movements and Society in Nigeria.* Bayreuth African Studies Series 7.

Magala, S. J. (1992). 'Movementization of social change' in Mizstal and Shupe eds.

Mahdi, S. (2003). Text of press conference on the successful outcome of the appeal of Amina Lawal. Abuja, 30 September.

—— (2004). 'Women's rights and access to justice' in Ibrahim ed.

Marshall, R. (1992). ' "Power in the Name of Jesus": social transformation and Pentecostalism in Western Nigeria'. Unpublished paper, St. Peter's College, Oxford.

Marty, M. E. and R. S. Appleby eds. (1993). *Fundamentalisms and the State: Remaking Polities, Economies, and Militance*. Chicago: University of Chicago Press.

—— eds. (1994). *Accounting for Fundamentalisms: The Dynamic Character of Movements*. Chicago: University of Chicago Press.

Misztal, B. and A. Shupe eds. (1992). *Religion and Politics in Comparative Perspective.* Westport, Conn.: Praeger.

Muazzam, I. and J. Ibrahim (1997). 'Religious identity under Structural Adjustment Programme in Nigeria'. Paper for Centre for Research and Documentation and Nordic Africa Institute National Seminar on 'The Transformation of Popular Identities Under SAP'. Kano, February.

Piscatori, J. and S. H. Rudolph eds. (1997). *Transnational Religion and Fading States.* Boulder, Colo: Westview Press.

Ranger, T. O. (1980). 'Religious movements and politics in sub-Saharan Africa'. *African Studies Review* 29, no. 2.

Robbins, T. (1988). 'Cults, converts and charisma: the sociology of new religious movements'. *Current Sociology* 36, no. 1.

Rudolph, S. H. (1997). 'Religion, states and transnational civil society' in Piscatori and Rudolph eds.

Shils, E. (1991). 'The virtue of civil society'. *Government and Opposition* 26, no. 1.

Shupe, A. and J. Hadden (1989). 'Is there such a thing as global fundamentalism?' in Shupe and Hadden eds.

—— eds. (1989). *Secularization and Fundamentalism Reconsidered.* New York: Paragon.

Tabi'u, M. (2001). 'Religious laws and the 1999 constitution'. Paper for Centre for Research and Documentation Workshop on 'Religious Pluralism in Nigeria'. Kano.

Yawuri, A. (2004). 'Issues in defending Safiyyatu Husaini and Amina Lawal' in Ibrahim ed.

Yusuf, B. (1993). '*Da'wa* and contemporary challenges facing Muslim women in secular states: a Nigerian case study' in Alkali *et al.* eds.

Chapter Eight

Hindu Nationalism and The Quest for a Uniform Civil Code

Henrik Berglund

Ever since independence, the Indian state has wrestled with the political implications of group identity. Though founded on the liberal principle of equal individual rights, the country is so large and culturally-diverse that a discussion of group rights has naturally opened up. Moreover, the use of group identity for political purposes has led to demands for special rights and benefits for religious and ethnic groups, so defined.

In the case of religion, the late 1980s saw a reorientation of national politics, in which political parties increasingly drew on religion as a constituent of identity. While large segments of the political establishment contributed to this development, the Hindu nationalist movement, spearheaded by the *Rashtriya Swayamsevak Sangh* (RSS) and its political wing, the Bharatiya Janata Party (BJP), has been the most open critic of the historically-dominant form of Indian secularism. Advocating a Hindu state, the party has challenged the established notions of Indian democracy, and for the last decades actively propounded its position on national integration and the role of the minorities of India. This chapter is an attempt to analyze the implications of Hindu nationalist ideology, with special reference to minority rights.

The division of British India in 1947 was largely the result of a massive politicization of religion, and the tragedy of Partition still casts its shadow over regional relations in South Asia. Despite this, the multicultural Indian state did not collapse. In the decades following independence, the issue of rights for religious minorities was debated, as were the sensitive questions of reserved employment for lower castes and protection for regional languages. While sometimes violent, these conflicts were solved or at least postponed. Instead, the real challenge to the Indian state came in the 1980s, when demands for increased political influence were voiced by a number of groups.

Based on different identities, they all reflected a change in the political climate which allowed increased ethnic and religious mobilization. The explanation for this development, according to most political analysts, is to be found in a change of strategy in the Congress Party, led by Indira Gandhi, in the early 1980s. Challenged by various ethnic and regional forces, Mrs Gandhi progressively abandoned the traditional secularism of Indian politics in her attempt to gain Hindu votes in Punjab and in Jammu and Kashmir. These tactics largely backfired, provoking strong opposition in the form of armed insurgencies in Kashmir, Punjab and Assam. The number of ethnic, religious and caste-based political movements swelled. Within a few years, the general change in the political climate helped bring Hindu nationalist parties to the fore, notably the Bharatiya Janata Party and Shiv Sena.

The BJP is part of a broader Hindu nationalist movement which for nearly a century has been promoting the idea of Hindu supremacy (Jaffrelot 1996, Hansen 1999, Bhatt 2001). The core of the movement is a mass-based cultural organization, the *Rashtriya Swayamsevak Sangh* (RSS). The RSS is, according to its leaders, non-political, but it usually supports the political wing of the movement, now embodied in the BJP. In addition, it incorporates a number of organizations, such as the *Vishwa Hindu Parishad* (World Hindu Council) and its youth wing, the *Bajrang Dal*; the Hindu nationalist trade union (*Bharat Mazdoor Sangh*); and the student organization, *Akhil Bharatiya Vidyarthi Parishad*.

The BJP itself draws on an ideological tradition dating back to the early 20th century, when the first Hindu nationalist texts were published, putting forward an alternative form of Indian nationalism and rejecting the liberal-socialist ideas of the Indian National Congress. The BJP's overall goal has been to found an Indian state based on Hindu values and traditions. The Party is very critical of the current Indian state, which it regards as being anti-Hindu and pro-minority, especially insofar as the Muslim minority is given preferential treatment over the Hindu majority. One such example is special family laws. The issue has been debated for decades, but came to a head in 1985 in the Shah Bano case.

In this chapter I shall focus on the BJP stand on minority rights, with special reference to separate family laws and the Shah Bano case.

ALTERNATIVE DEFINITIONS OF SECULARISM AND NATION

The stand of the BJP in the Shah Bano case is one example of how the party has been trying to increase its influence by redefining key concepts such as secularism, the nation, and democracy. Forming a coherent pattern, these redefinitions may be interpreted also as a challenge to the established form of Indian democracy—defined theoretically by full civil and political rights as well as free and fair elections. Full rights would also include the right to religious freedom and to protection from discrimination on the basis of religion, culture and ethnicity—enshrined, in the Indian case, as fundamental rights in the constitution.

Given the form of the modern state, religious faith may seem difficult to combine with democracy, since a choice between secular or divine law must be made on both the national and individual levels. The solution to this has generally been some kind of secularism, in which the state either is essentially *non*-religious or is uncommitted to any particular faith. In India there has been long-standing and broad-based support for the latter approach (Bhargava 1998, Ganguly 2003). This consensus has now been challenged by the BJP in its proposals for a Hindu state.

The relation between nationalism and democracy in general has been a topic for debate for more than a century. Most observers regard the Western form of nationalism, with territorially-defined membership, as more easily combined with democracy. Cultural nationalism, developed mainly in central and eastern Europe, is seen as more problematic owing to its emphasis on language, ethnicity or culture as the defining features of nationality and citizenship. This may come to clash with respect for individual political rights, as well as with the established practice within democracies to leave it to citizens to form their own cultural, religious or ethnic identities. Not surprisingly, therefore, in many multicultural states the issue of minority rights has been a serious source of political problems, and India is a case in point.

While the cultural-nationalist ideal is a state whose borders are congruent with those of 'cultural nations', most states in practice include a number of minorities within their borders. The solution to this problem largely determines the relationship between a cultural-nationalist ideology and democracy. In order to qualify as a democracy, a state is expected to guarantee the political, cultural and religious rights of all groups, while often coming under pressure from the dominant community not to extend these rights too far. In the Indian case this relates to discussions concerning special rights for both castes and religious communities.

THE HISTORICAL BACKGROUND TO THE SHAH BANO CASE

The legal controversy which arose in the Shah Bano case touched on an important and sensitive issue in Indian society: the question of a common civil code. In pre-independence India, a multitude of social and legal practices concerning family relations co-existed. The British authorities introduced no uniform legislation in the subcontinent, so that the law varied from place to place depending on the faith of the Empire's subject. After independence, the question arose of whether a uniform civil code should be introduced, or whether family law should remain within the religious sphere, with different legislation for each community. The first Constitution of independent India, in its 44th article, stated: 'The State shall endeavor to secure for the citizens a uniform civil code throughout the territory of India.' Despite this, legal practice ever since has been to operate separate civil codes for each community, largely owing to the resistance among Muslims to the introduction of a uniform civil code (Sangari 1995, Rajan 2000).

Article 44 was placed in the fourth part of the Constitution, under the heading 'Directive Principles of State Policy'—i.e. guidance for public policies, both legislative and administrative, but not enforceable by the courts. This solution was criticized at the time from both ends of the spectrum of opinion, by those in favor of establishing a uniform civil code and by those rejecting it even as a Directive Principle. In the Constituent Assembly debate of 23 November 1948, for example, some Muslim members opposed the idea of uniformity spilling over into the civil sphere, while others defined it as a necessity both for national integration and for respect for individual rights, especially those of women (*Manthan* July 1986).

The same section of the Constitution prescribes a number of other general goals for a future Indian welfare state, such as the right to work, protection of the environment and the promotion of international peace and security. These too are principles which the government has a duty to follow, but they do not carry the same status as the fundamental rights in Part Three of the Constitution. Moreover, though the original ambition was to include more rights than fundamental political and civil ones, the enforcement of more general goals has been held up by economic and political constraints.

In the case of a uniform civil code, the political constraints have been severe. The Hindu code was reformed after independence, but with great difficulty. The work begun in the last years of British rule was continued by the Nehru government. A comprehensive revision was undertaken in 1941, and what began as the Hindu Code Bill was later divided into four separate bills. Resistance came from conservative Hindus, reinforced by the fact, as noted above, that different laws and customs prevailed in the various regions of India. The bills were finally passed in 1955 and 1956, with substantial changes in Hindu family law, notably the rights to divorce and adoption.

The next step would have been reform of family law concerning non-Hindus, but apart from reforms concerning the Parsee community in 1988 no further changes have been introduced. The introduction of the Hindu Code

Bill signified an intention from the Congress leadership to reform other civil codes, but it was also known that there would be widespread resistance. The idea of a common civil code had not been seriously discussed in the freedom movement. On the contrary, because of the animosity between Hindus and Muslims, which threatened the effectiveness and legitimacy of the whole movement, the possibility of separate personal laws came to be seen as a guarantee that the rights of minorities would be respected in a future independent India.

For the Hindu nationalist movement, by contrast, the demand for a universal civil code has been on the agenda for decades. The movement has argued that no community should have any privileges or separate laws. The issue has been used, in fact, to agitate against 'anti-national elements', usually Muslims or politicians in general who have supported the institution of separate family laws. This agitation increased in the mid-1980s, when the BJP used the change in the political climate to reactivate the issue of a universal civil code. It was helped greatly by the debate on the ongoing Shah Bano case (Engineer 1987, Hasan 1989, Berglund 2004).

The case originated in a petition filed by a Muslim lady, Begum [Mrs] Shah Bano, in 1978. This lady had been divorced by her husband after 43 years of marriage, in which she had borne him five children. In her petition, Begum Shah Bano claimed her right to maintenance under section 125 of the Indian Criminal Procedure Code. This section covers the right to maintenance of wives, children and parents, and establishes that any man with sufficient means is obliged to provide financial support to his divorced wife, unless she has remarried. The Judicial Magistrates' Court of Indore, ruling in favor of Begum Shah Bano, set her maintenance at 25 rupees per month. The High Court of Madhya Pradesh subsequently upheld the lower court's decision and raised the level of maintenance to 179.20rs per month. Against this decision the former husband appealed, and the case came before the Supreme Court, attracting widespread public attention, in April 1985.

The Supreme Court Verdict

The claim of the appellant before the Supreme Court was that he had fulfilled his duties toward his former wife, because he had acted according to Muslim personal law; and since the legal practice in India was to respect religious faith and customs, secular law would not be applicable. The Supreme Court rejected these arguments and ruled in favor of Begum Shah Bano. The ruling was widely regarded as an attempt to strengthen secular law by giving preference to the secular Criminal Code over religious family laws, thus implicitly supporting the idea of a uniform civil code. The Supreme Court judges did not, however, address directly the issue of whether secular or religious law should prevail when the two clashed, but argued instead that the problem did not arise in this particular case. The appellant had argued that Indian Muslim law clearly stated that alimony was to be given during one *iddat* (a period covering three menstrual cycles or three months). The Court found support for this in various sources (Mulla's *Mahomedan Law*, Tyabji's *Muslim Law*, and Dr. Paras Niwan's *Muslim Law in Modern India*), but argued that Muslim law was not applicable in this particular case: as this was an instance of a divorced woman being rendered unable to support herself, the Criminal Code was applicable. The works of Muslim jurisprudence called in aid by the appellant were 'inadequate to establish the proposition that the Muslim husband is not under an obligation to provide for maintenance of his divorced wife, who is unable to maintain herself.'

While avoiding addressing the principle of whether secular law should prevail over religious, the Supreme Court took the controversial stand that Muslim law on family matters was not all-encompassing, since it did not explicitly deal with the issue of divorced women facing destitution. To strengthen its argument, the Court referred to the Qur'an, whose guidelines were found to be of too general a character. In verses 240–242, for instance, pious Muslims are urged to provide maintenance to their divorced wives 'on a reasonable scale'. Nowhere, however, is there any mention of a recommended sum or of a period appropriate for the maintenance. The conclusion drawn by the Court was that the current laws and traditions amongst Indian Muslims did not address the issue at stake in the Shah Bano case (where the wife had actually been rendered destitute by the divorce), hence there could be no clash between religious and secular law. The court therefore rejected the plea of the appellant, ordering him to pay the costs of the appeal. It also declared that it would consider an application from Begum Shah Bano for an increase in the allowance decided earlier by the Madhya Pradesh High Court.The court concluded the verdict by expressing its dislike of the fact that a uniform civil code had not been introduced in the country:

> It is also a matter of regret that Article 44 of our Constitution has remained a dead letter . . . It is the State which is charged with the duty of securing a uniform civil code for the citizens of the country and, unquestionably, has the legislative competence to do so. As a counsel in the case whispered, somewhat audibly, that legislative competence is one thing, the political courage to use that competence is quite another. We understand the difficulties involved in bringing persons of different faiths and persuasions on a common platform. But a beginning has to be made if the Constitution is to have any meaning.

The religious leadership of the Indian Muslim community expressed strong displeasure at the ruling of the Supreme Court in the Shah Bano case. The issue of a common civil code was now on the public agenda again, and this seemed likely to lead to a general debate on the special rights of minorities. Communal tensions had been on the increase in the 1980s, and even those Muslims with little interest in the case feared both the loss of their rights as a minority and a new wave of riots, with violence directed against them. Some groups within the Muslim community, mainly academics and intellectuals, supported a change in the law, but the majority of the Muslim voices heard, both in the streets and in the media, were very negative towards the Supreme Court ruling (Ahmed 1996: 110–112). These feelings were further strengthened by the fact that the court had made use of the Qur'an to develop its arguments, an intervention which some Muslims regarded as blasphemous.

Sections of the Muslim leadership had previously sensed the danger of the criminal code taking precedence over religious family laws. Resistance to the abolition of these laws was primarily organized under the All-India Muslim Personal Law Board (AIMPLB), which included two of the most important Muslim national organizations, the Muslim League and the *Jamaat-e-Islami*. Large rallies were held against the Supreme Court verdict in the autumn of 1985, but equally important was the political pressure applied by the AIMPLB on the Congress (I) government. The prime targets were Prime Minister Rajiv Gandhi and the Interior Minister Arif Mohammed Khan. It was of course impossible for the government to change the Supreme Court ruling, but it was possible to nullify its effects by the introduction of a new law, exempting Muslims from Section 125. Although himself a Muslim, Arif Khan rejected all such moves, as did initially the Prime Minister. Eventually, however, Rajiv Gandhi gave in to the pressure, deciding in December 1985 to amend section 125 in accordance with the AIMPLB's wishes. The result was the Muslim Women (Protection of Rights on Divorce) Bill in February 1986, which recognized the practice of maintenance only for the duration of the *iddat*, and thus made the law against forced destitution inapplicable to divorced Muslim women.

The short-term consequence of Rajiv Gandhi's decision was to tie the Muslim leadership closer to the Congress (I), through which he expected to retain the majority of Muslim votes in the forthcoming election. The move was occasioned by the challenge posed by the secular opposition, mainly the Janata Dal, which was making inroads amongst traditional Congress (I) supporters such as Muslims and low-castes. The cost for Gandhi, however, was that he alienated both the liberal and the radical elements within the Muslim community, among them Arif Mohammed Khan, who resigned after the decision to introduce the bill. Rajiv Gandhi also continued along the road paved by his mother in the early 1980s, towards the increased exploitation of religion for political gain (Noorani 1990).

HINDU NATIONALIST IDEOLOGY AND MINORITY RIGHTS

The BJP reacted strongly to the introduction of the Muslim Women Bill, interpreting it as the acceptance of a legal practice extending special rights to Muslims. Hindu nationalists rejected these alleged special rights, which would come into conflict with their concept of a unified nation based on Hindu culture. The idea of national unity is evident in the Hindu nationalist critique of the caste system (which is seen as an obstacle to the unification of all Hindus against common enemies), but even more so when defining the status of minorities in a future Hindu state. Much of the minority-rights vs. national-unity debate has revolved around the position of Indian Muslims, the largest religious minority in the country who have, in addition, played a historically prominent role since the Moghul conquests.

Hindu nationalism, from its beginnings in the late 19th century, was inspired by reform movements like the *Arya Samaj*, which emphasized the need for a reformed Hinduism while at the same time strengthening the communal identity of its members. The first coherent presentation of Hindu nationalism is found in the writings of Veer Savarkar, who in 1923 published the treatise *Hindutva* stressing the importance of Hindu unity and resistance against foreign influences. Savarkar defines *Hindutva* as a form of 'Hinduness' in which loyalty to the nation is placed above everything else. His writings, however, contain strong anti-liberal features which firmly establish Hindu nationalism as the archetype of cultural nationalism.

In Savarkar's vision, the citizen of the Hindu state is recognized as an individual, but his or her duty is primarily to strengthen the community: he/she lives for the community but also through it. With this strong emphasis on culture, rites and religion, there is very little room for the self to develop outside the parameters decided by the community. The liberal and atomistic individual is impossible. According to Savarkar, all human beings need to respond to the cultural context in which they exist, and any deviation from the values of the community will lead to the demise of both the individual and the community. In *Hindutva* this is seen as the natural order: every human being tends to conform to his or her primordial identity. Savarkar advocates a mono-communitarian solution to the problem of competing majority and minority interests. He is in fact reluctant even to recognize the possible rights of minorities, as against the supremacy of Hindu culture. The language used in his discussion of multiculturalism, as well as the historical examples chosen, indicates that the relation between Hindu nationalist ideology and democracy is strained, especially when analyzed from the perspective of minority rights.

Savarkar's ideas were developed by M. S. Golwalkar, leader of the Hindu nationalist cultural organization RSS. In his *Bunch of Thoughts*, first published in 1966, Golwalkar is very clear in his rejection of what he calls 'Western thinking', on the grounds that it includes too much individualism and competition. Instead, he wants a value-based society built around Hindu culture. The respect for the individual he sees as second to that of the community, and he is highly distrustful of the idea of a social contract amongst equal individuals. This distrust is also obvious in his rejection of territorial nationalism. Golwalkar uses the terms 'territorial' and 'cultural' when discussing nationalism, firmly advocating an Indian nationalism based on Hindu culture. The most aggressive statements against Indian Muslims are found in his *We, or, Our Nationhood Defined*, where he asserts that they cannot expect fair treatment unless they adapt to mainstream Indian culture, which in practice means Hindu culture:

> [T]he non-Hindu peoples in Hindusthan must either adopt the Hindu culture and language, must learn to respect and hold in reverence Hindu religion, must entertain no ideas but those of glorification of the Hindu race and culture i.e. they must not only give up their attitude of intolerance and ungratefulness towards this land and its age-long traditions but must also cultivate the positive attitude of love and devotion instead—in one word, they must cease to be foreigners, or may stay in the country, wholly subordinated to the Hindu nation, claiming nothing, deserving no privileges, far less any preferential treatment—not even citizen's rights. There is, at least should be, no other course for them to adopt. (Golwalkar 1945: 52–53.)

It is interesting to note that this book is no longer reprinted by the RSS or the BJP, nor is it generally referred to by members of these organizations. The quotation is from the third edition of 1945, where the text has been slightly altered compared to the first edition. Other remarks by Golwalkar, containing positive references to Nazism, have been used to found a critique of Hindu nationalism as a non-democratic ideology (Jaffrelot 1996: 55).

Though the mainstream of Hindu nationalist writing is less extreme, the attitude towards the Muslim minority is generally hostile. The general attitude of the BJP and other members of the Hindu nationalist movement has been to reject special treatment of minorities in favor of a uniform civil code, which, they claim, would promote a common Indian identity: with no community receiving preferential treatment or feeling discriminated against, the argument goes, the underpinnings of ethnic politics would be removed. That the party sees Muslim separatism as a real threat to national unity—or at least promotes the idea of such a threat—is evident from many remarks by national leaders. Sikander Bakht, Member of the Rajya Sabha (Upper House of Parliament), describes Indian Muslims as living in a 'psychosis' which has to be lifted before any real national integration is possible, while both Arun Jaitley, Party Spokesperson, BJP, and Jay Dubashi, Member of the National Executive of the BJP, have asserted that the Muslim community still today harbors both separatist and fundamentalist ideals (interviews with the author in Delhi, November 1994).

This view was not, however, actively promoted in the decades after independence. Instead, religious issues like the demand for a ban on cow-slaughter, and general nationalistic issues like a strong military defence, dominated the BJP's predecessor, the Jana Sangh, and the BJP's own early years. When the Shah Bano case reached the Supreme Court and the debate caught on, the reaction from the Hindu nationalist movement was almost uniformly positive towards a change in legal practice. The issue dealt with the very core of Hindu nationalist ideology: the unity of the nation. Special treatment of any part of the population, whether from the majority or the minority community, was seen as negative for national integration. One interesting exception to this trend was Golwalkar himself, who in a surprisingly conciliatory interview in 1972 rejected the idea of a uniform civil code as necessary for national integration (*Manthan* July 1986: 6–8).

THE UNIFORM CIVIL CODE AND NATIONAL INTEGRATION

In the views generally expressed by Hindu nationalists, the integration of the Indian people will suffer if one community is favored over another. In this lies the assumption that the Muslim community is actually benefiting from having its old family laws preserved. Since these laws are regarded by many, inside and outside India, as discriminatory towards women, one must strongly question the Hindu nationalist view. It implies that the rights of men are to be considered more important than the rights of women. Moreover, since Muslim family laws give (Muslim) men the possibility of acting unilaterally towards women, making it easier to divorce them and limiting their maintenance after divorce, they provide them with a latitude not afforded to Hindu men. The tendency among Hindus is to resent these privileges as representing a special right for Muslim men, rather than as an injustice against Muslim women. Many BJP members and sympathizers do claim that the concern for Muslim women is the main reason for demanding a uniform civil code. This argument is present in most of the articles written by Hindu nationalists, either explicitly or implicitly (*Manthan* April and July 1986, Shourie 1993, Malkani 1989). It also came up during my interviews with party officials in Delhi, and was especially emphasized by Sushma Swaraj, Party Spokesperson (interview, November 1994). Gender issues are not, however, generally promoted by the party, and the claim that it cares especially for Muslim women fits awkwardly with its general attitude towards Muslims.

My interviews with party members in Varanasi suggest that the debate on separate civil codes is connected, in fact, to their own images both of gender relations and of Hindu-Muslim relations. All of those interviewed were men, most of them Hindus. All the Hindus felt that it was important for family laws to be made uniform. Many mentioned the Muslim's right to have more than one wife as an example of undue privilege. Their statements evince very little concern for Muslim women, but rather the feeling of an affront to Hindu masculinity. Muslims are often caricatured by Hindu nationalists as aggressive, but also sexually potent. These prejudices are usually spread in order to show Muslims as barbaric, and often use examples from Muslim invasions and present-day riots. However, they also carry with them the image of Muslim strength, and therefore corresponding Hindu weakness. The claim that Muslims have a much higher birth rate, and will form the majority in the country, is widespread, and although it is false, surprisingly-large segments of the Hindu community tend to believe it, or at least continue to spread corresponding rumours.

The BJP presented the manoeuvring of the Rajiv Gandhi government over Muslim family law as an example of how minorities were pampered by the Congress (I) and left-wing parties. The introduction of a uniform civil code was included in the constitution, it said, and now it was time to honour this commitment (interview with Sushma Swaraj, Delhi, November 1994). According to Party Spokesperson Arun Jaitley, the verdict from the Supreme Court was welcomed by the party, and seen as a test of the secularism of the Indian state (interview in Delhi, November 1994). Yet in the light of its poor showing in the 1984 Lok Sabha (Lower House) elections, the party could at that time expect to wield very little influence if the matter reached parliament.

Some Hindu-nationalist reactions to this debate could be found in the RSS mouthpiece *Organiser*, which soon after the Supreme Court verdict in the Shah Bano case began reporting on how Muslim organizations were pressing the Rajiv Gandhi government to legislate to reverse the effects of the ruling. In the summer of 1985 came an interview with Begum Shah Bano herself, in which she claimed to have been pressured by Muslim leaders to change her stand. Later, the magazine published articles highly critical of the decision to introduce the Muslim Women Bill, claiming that even a majority of the Congress (I) MPs regarded it as a surrender to Muslim separatism, and that the Bill was fundamentalist and a threat to the unity and integration of the nation (*Organiser* 11 May 1986: 1). According to the same article, a majority of the Muslim community was also against the Bill. Although dissatisfied with the turn of events, the BJP was still not ready to put its full weight behind a campaign for a uniform civil code. Party President L. K. Advani remarked in April 1986:

> [W]e have not demanded that there should be a uniform civil code here and now. All that we have said is that the commitment to the uniform civil code is a part of our commitment to the Constitution. Nothing should be done that weakens this commitment. And I regard an attempt to undo the Shah Bano judgment as such an attempt. (*Organiser* 13 April 1986).

This captures the essence of the Hindu nationalist stand on the issue: no overt agitation, but support in principle for a uniform civil code. Note also the reference that Advani makes to the constitution.

The BJP has at various points in its history been accused of extremism and engaging in political violence. It is evidently because of this that the party's spokespersons have found it necessary to stress their loyalty to the political institutions of the country, in this case the constitution. Such a stance gives the BJP an air of respectability, and of a party which is able to lift itself above the turmoil of daily politics. In the interview Advani also explained the party's policy for the implementation of a uniform civil code. He denied the accusations that the party would recommend a code which would in practice be a Hindu code. Instead, he said, a commission should examine all personal laws and come up with a proposal for a common code acceptable to all communities. This position was held also by leading BJP members Sushma Swaraj and Arun Jaitley: the future universal code is to some extent open to negotiation. One example concerns marriages between cousins, which are alien to a majority of citizens, but not unusual within the Muslim community or amongst some Hindus. Statements by BJP vice-president K. R. Malkani on this matter show no significant differences compared to the stand taken by Advani. He makes clear that the issue of a uniform civil code is non-negotiable in principle, but that the party is willing to wait if the Muslim community is not ready for a major reform of its family laws. These laws should, however, be reformed to the extent of banning such practices as instant divorce and polygamy (Malkani 1989: 21).

Despite the willingness to wait for reform initiatives from the Muslim community, the BJP and its allies continue to spread material which is hostile to current Muslim legal practices, as well as to Muslims in general. One of the most important websites of the Hindu nationalist movement published in 1997 a text by Balraj Madhok, categorically denying minorities any special rights, in which he simply told Muslims they had had their chance in 1947: if they chose to stay in India they must accept that India was a Hindu nation (*Global Hindu Electronic Network*: 1997). This is a common assertion from the BJP and its allied organizations. Some are more moderate, while others display open hatred for Muslims, but we can conclude that the principle of a uniform civil code has been important as propaganda for the BJP.

During the period after independence, the BJP and its predecessor Jana Sangh had promoted its Hindu-nationalist solution to the Hindu-Muslim conflict, initially with limited electoral success. In the early 1980s, however, the political climate changed, largely as a consequence of the increased exploitation of ethnic and religious identity in party politics. A number of issues relating to the conflict between majority and minority rights were taken up in the political debate, and due to the changes in the political climate, it was now possible more forcefully to mobilize around a Hindu identity.

HINDU NATIONALISM AS A COMMUNITARIAN THEORY

The position of the BJP in the Shah Bano case follows the Hindu nationalists' logic, in the sense that it reflects their generally hostile attitude towards minorities as well as the ideal of a unitary state going back to the heritage of *Hindutva*. Thus, the party has argued that its demands for changes in Islamic family law are not anti-Muslim, but simply part of the search for a modern and civilized state, based on the principle of equal treatment for all. This stand is projected by the party as liberal, but on closer analysis the connection with liberalism appears tenuous.

The demand for a uniform civil code is long-standing, and although it has not been pressed the issue is often commented on by both high officials and the party's rank and file. All my interviewees were very clear on this issue, giving national integration and the suffering of Muslim women as reasons for their position, while male-chauvinist and anti-Muslim sentiments appear more plausible explanations. The BJP's position cannot be seen isolated from a general Hindu nationalist ideology, where the idea of a neutral and liberal state is rejected. When analyzed within the framework of communitarian theory and cultural rights, the position of the BJP in the Shah Bano case is more appropriately defined as *mono*-communitarian.

Within political theory, the issue of cultural and religious rights has been addressed from several different angles, perhaps most notably in the liberal-communitarian debate. Liberal ideas are part of an almost-universally recognized form of democracy, centring on the notion of the autonomous individual, whose rights are seen as best protected by centralized political and civil rights, rather than by the extension of special rights to cultural groups. The contemporary communitarian critique of liberalism was developed partly in response to Rawls' *Theory of Justice*, first published in 1971. Rawls argued that a universal idea of justice could be applied in all democratic societies. He refuted notions of cultural relativism and suggested a procedure from which this universal justice could be derived.

The current communitarian critique should not, however, be seen as a challenge to the whole idea of liberal democracy, but rather as a debate between thinkers who largely accept the framework of liberal democracy yet differ over both its design and its content. Communitarian theory questions the hegemonic position of liberal democracy and what is seen as its over-emphasis on the individual, stressing instead the values and traditions of the community in which individuals exercise their rights. The individual is seen as part of the community—incapable, in fact, of attaining fulfillment outside his or her community-based practices, traditions and values. Within this perspective, every community has the right, perhaps even the duty, to define and protect what it feels to be common values identified through interpretation of its traditions. The most-widely acknowledged proponents of communitarian philosophy are Alasdair MacIntyre, Michael Walzer, Charles Taylor and Michael Sandel, whose ideas on the definition and protection of common values are connected to debates on nationalism, minorities and citizenship (Mulhall and Swift 1996).

In seeking to understand the relation between Hindu nationalism and democracy, we may use the liberal-communitarian debate as a tool to identify the theoretical issues and conflicts that are opened up. For communitarians a neutral state is either an illusion or an abomination, possibly both. Instead, the state should protect the common values derived from what its citizens define as a good way of life (Sandel 1982). In order to ensure both the possibility of fulfillment for individual members, and the long-term survival of the community, any values or lifestyles which are incompatible with the established norm should be discouraged, or at least not encouraged. In practice, these communities are often based on culture, language, ethnicity, or perhaps religion —in short, some primordial factor—and are sometimes congruent with nations. Michael Walzer uses the Greek and German states as examples of political entities which are based on the idea of national sentiment, extending to non-residents the moral right to seek assistance from them in times of need, as long as they are of Greek or German nationality (Walzer 1983). These states are making use of a communitarian definition of the nation: that is, as an entity obliged to protect not only its citizens but also the culture of the nation and its members living outside the political borders of the state.

The debate between liberals and communitarians is not referred to by the Hindu nationalists, and it is basically a North American debate with little input from the sub-continent. It is of course known to Indian academics with an interest in political theory, but is generally not applied when discussing Hindu nationalism. One exception is Thomas Blom Hansen, who in his study of

Hindu nationalism uses the term 'communitarian nationalism' when defining the nationalism of the Hindu *Mahasabha* and the Muslim League (Hansen 1999: 45–46). The term 'communitarian' is not explicitly defined in his study, nor is the concept of 'communitarian nationalism' further applied there. The purpose of analyzing the BJP with reference to the liberal-communitarian debate is to analyze its ideology and practice within this framework, in order to understand what issues at the level of political theory are activated by Hindu nationalist claims and how these claims relate to the question of minority rights and democracy.

CONCLUSION

The impact of cultural nationalism is evident in the development of Hindu nationalism both historically and at present, and the concept is used by the party itself as a definition of its ideology. Within cultural nationalism, the nation is ideally seen as congruent with the nation-state, which is regarded as the protector and bearer of the national culture. How this relates to democracy depends on the scope and nature of the rights extended by the state. If far-reaching political, social or economic rights are extended to one community and denied to others, we have a case of discrimination. Usually the groups discriminated against are minorities, defined as being non-members of the national cultural community. This is of course a violation of their democratic rights, which marks out this version of cultural nationalism as anti-democratic.

Equally problematic is a case of the constitution and laws of the state being built solely on the values and traditions of the dominant community. Although cultural nationalism in its most extreme form would seem to favor such solutions, or even favor ethnic cleansing to obtain the desired congruence between the 'cultural' and the 'political' nation, there are also democratic alternatives for those with strong cultural nationalist convictions. If they accept existing borders, they have the possibility of building a state based on the culture of communities. The only condition would be that this state showed respect for the culture of *all* communities.

While the ideal state advocated by the BJP is based on a definition of the Hindu nation heavily influenced by cultural nationalism, the relation to communitarian theory is less direct. The communitarian approach in its Western form is largely seen as an integral part of a democratic tradition. Communitarianism may, however, also develop into an undemocratic political theory, depending on how the community and its relation to the state is defined, with Hindu nationalism and the conflict between majority and minority rights being a case in point.

Communitarian solutions to the issue of cultural rights may be divided into two categories: multi-communitarian and mono-communitarian. If one particular community is defined as the bearer of the national culture, and if the state is explicitly established to promote the cultural values and traditions of this community, then the state is mono-communitarian. Every member of the state should theoretically be a member of both the nation and the (dominant) cultural community. The role of the state is then to work for the realization of the common goals of this community and to uphold its values; its role is not simply to be neutral. The equal treatment of all citizens could prevail, but this would then no longer be a liberal state, since it would be based on a specific culture. If an attempt was made, in an existing multicultural society, to establish or even promote such a state of affairs, the potential for friction between the different cultural groups would be obvious. Above all, those outside the (dominant) 'national' community would feel alienated in relation to the culture promoted by the state.

If, on the other hand, it were decided that no cultural group should be defined as the 'national community' or as having a special relation to the state, this solution would recognize every community's right to its own culture, traditions and common values. In this case, the different communities, defined by language, race, religion or ethnicity, could as far as possible be given the right to manage their own affairs; and the state could be replaced in those spheres by the structures and values of the society as a whole. The state would then not be neutral in the liberal sense but rather be based on a principle of equal treatment of all communities: a multi-communitarian solution.

The BJP offers assurances that it recognizes and respects the Muslim faith and that a Hindu state would by no means be a threat to the freedom of religion. However, when the party defines such a state, it is first and foremost a Hindu one: the Muslims may stay in it, but they must adapt to the Hindu way of life. No full adoption of Hindu customs and traditions is requested, but the vast majority of Muslims, it should be obvious, would be alienated by a state set up on these terms.

For the BJP and its supporters, the state cannot be neutral since the whole basis of Hindu nationalism and *Hindutva* is built on a rejection of the principle of separate spheres for politics and religion. In its solution to the conflict between majority and minority rights, therefore, the party has been trying, quite simply, to pressure the Muslims to give up their minority rights; one example of this is the BJP's support for a uniform civil code. At the same time, though party leader L. K. Advani argues that a future common civil code would not be a Hindu code, the strong mono-communitarian tendencies of Hindu nationalism suggest that all legislation within a Hindu state would be decisively influenced by Hindu culture.

India includes a number of distinct communities defined by caste, religion, region and ethnicity. After independence, the established practice of handling the multi-religious character of the country was to respect the right of the various communities to a certain autonomy, although limited to the spheres of religious and cultural matters. Both the Indian National Congress and the left-wing parties have historically supported this solution. Despite the strong liberal tendencies within both these camps, this model can be interpreted as an example of multi-communitarianism, since it recognizes that the needs of the various communities cannot be met in all respects in a unitary state. It simultaneously rejects the idea of a single Indian cultural and religious community.

The problem with this course of events, beginning in colonial times, from a Hindu nationalist point of view is that it has led, or seemed to lead, to the crystallization of a distinct Muslim community, and in the writings of the Hindu nationalists this is seen as a wound in the Hindu body. In their definition of the nation, they reject the idea of having religious minorities within the borders of the state, unless they demonstrate their loyalty to India—to *Hindu* India, that is—by accepting Hindu culture as the basis of national identity. As the conflict between majority and minority rights has been placed on the political agenda, it is clear that the BJP has made it a part of its electoral strategy to side with the Hindu majority in the country and that the party's demand for a Hindu state is based on a mono-communitarian approach to the whole problem of cultural rights.

How strong the Hindu bias would be in a state dominated by Hindu nationalists is difficult to say, but with regard to the situation of the Muslim population, the Babri Masjid-Ramjanmabhoomi controversy may be an indication of how the ideology of the Hindu nationalist forces works in practice. The Ramjanmabhoomi movement was mobilized by Hindu nationalist forces in order to force the Muslim clergy to relinquish ownership of the Babri Masjid, a small mosque allegedly built on top of an ancient Hindu temple in Ayodhya, Uttar Pradesh. Although virtually no archaeological or historical evidence supported their hypothesis, the Hindu nationalists claimed that the prior temple had been constructed on the birthplace of Ram, one of the most important Hindu gods. In the wake of the agitation, communal violence plagued large parts of the country, reaching its peak after the destruction of the Babri Masjid Mosque on 6 December 1992. While the Shah Bano case was an example of how the BJP would make changes to legislation, the Babri Masjid-Ramjanmabhoomi controversy signifies how Hindu nationalists see respect for Hindu culture as the appropriate framework for the implementation of legal and administrative decisions. This may also indicate how a Hindu state would act on issues of minority rights.

According to the BJP, the reason for the tensions between the Muslim and Hindu communities today is not increased propaganda from the Hindu nationalist movement but instead the Muslims' feelings of their own uniqueness and superiority. This separatist mentality was, according to BJP, encouraged both by the British and by some Muslim leaders before Partition. The creation of Pakistan is a central theme in Hindu nationalist agitation, both directly and indirectly. Developments in Pakistan are used as an excuse to argue that India should be proclaimed a Hindu state, which strengthens the image of Hindu nationalism as mono-communitarian. The party supports a vision based on the existence of two hostile communities on the subcontinent: Muslims and Hindus. No room is left for multi-communitarian solutions where minorities of both faiths are equally respected. Indirectly, the party uses Partition to challenge the Muslim minority, claiming that the feelings of separateness are still alive, encouraged by the Muslim leadership and the 'pseudo-secularist parties' for the sake of electoral gain (BJP 1993: 11–12).

The alleged feelings of Muslim separateness are interpreted by the BJP as an aggression against both the Hindu community and the Indian state, while Hindu culture is presented as in essence non-violent. The theme of Hindu non-violence appears in the writings of both Savarkar and Golwalkar, although they both conclude that violent resistance is necessary to protect the Hindu nation. In my interviews the Hindu tradition of non-violence was often contrasted with the alleged aggressiveness of Muslims, both at the level of the relations between Hindus and Muslims in India, and in relation to Pakistan (interviews with Sikander Bakht, BJP, Delhi, November 1994, and Om Prakash Singh, BJP, Member of Uttar Pradesh Legislative Assembly, Varanasi, 7 December 1996). It is also notable that many BJP officials see separatism as representative of Indian Muslims in general. Qualifications are sometimes made, but most of my interviewees preferred to see the Muslim minority in India as a uniform mass. Likewise, the party shows a distinct refusal to draw a line between what has happened in the past and what is relevant for a solution to Hindu-Muslim problems today, but it also disregards the complexity of the Indian Muslim identity today. Within the Muslim community there is a wide range of opinions on how to relate both to the Indian state and to the majority community, but few Indian Muslims support the separatist ideas claimed by the BJP to be typical of them. Yet the BJP continues to promote stereotypical images, which in turn form the basis of its own constructions of Hindu and Muslim identities.

Within Hindu nationalism, Hindu values and traditions are important, but they are overshadowed by the strong influences of cultural nationalism. The fascination for the idea of the nation-state, and the acceptance of it as a necessary prerequisite for the successful development of independence, democracy and prosperity, produced the Hindu nationalist ideal of a largely unitary state. While recognizing the importance of a cultural and religious identity for all individuals, the main Hindu nationalist party today denies minorities the right to express their collective identity at a political level. Instead, it argues for a mono-communitarian state in which Hindu values, symbols and traditions would form the core and would command the respect of all citizens.

Inspired by the cultural nationalism of *Hindutva*, the party construes the Indian political scene according to the premise that the individual is subordinated to his or her religious community. This perspective is in itself not a problem for Hindu-Muslim relations, as a multi-communitarian solution could be designed where the interests of the various communities were guaranteed, possibly by allowing each community to deal with its own cultural and religious affairs. Yet as soon as the BJP brings in the quest for a nation-state, its political theory runs the risk of clashing with minority rights. In the present political setting, this risk has been turned into a violent conflict in which the BJP-proposed solution to the issue of majority and minority rights must be seen as a serious threat both to the rights of the Muslim minority in India and to the established practice of Indian secular democracy.

REFERENCES

Ahmed, I. (1996). *State, Nation and Ethnicity in Contemporary South Asia*. London: Pinter.

Berglund, H. (2004). *Hindu Nationalism and Democracy*. Delhi: Shipra Publications.

Bhargava, R. ed. (1998). *Secularism and Its Critics*. Delhi: Oxford University Press.

Bhatt, C. (2001). *Hindu Nationalism: Origins, Ideologies and Modern Myths*. Oxford and New York: Berg.

BJP (1993). *White Paper on Ayodhya and the Rama Temple Movement.*

Engineer, A. A. ed. (1987). *The Shah Bano Controversy*. Bombay: Orient Longman.

Ganguly, S. (2003). 'The crisis of Indian secularism'. *Journal of Democracy* 14, no. 4.

Global Hindu Electronic Network (1997).http://rbhatnagar.ececs.uc.edu:8080/~archives/hvk/books/whr/ch4.htm downloaded 10 December.

Golwalkar, M. S. (1945). *We, or Our Nationhood Defined.* 3rd ed. Nagpur: M. N. Khale.

—— (1980). *Bunch of Thoughts.* 2nd ed. Bangalore: Jagarana Prakashana.

Hansen, T. B. (1999). *The Saffron Wave: Democracy and Hindu Nationalism in Modern India*. Delhi: Oxford University Press.

Hasan, Z. (1989). 'Minority identity: Muslim women bill campaign and the political process'. *Economic and Political Weekly* 7 January.

Jaffrelot, C. (1996). *The Hindu Nationalist Movement and Indian Politics, 1925 to the 1990s*. London: Hurst.

MacIntyre, A. (1985). *After Virtue: A Study in Moral Theory*. London: Duckworth.
Malkani, K. R. (1989). 'Justice for all and appeasement of none'. *Manthan* 10, no. 9 (September).
—— (1993). *The Politics of Ayodhya and Hindu-Muslim Relations*. Delhi: Har-Anand.
Mulhall, S. and A. Swift eds. (1996). *Liberals and Communitarians*. 2nd ed. Oxford: Blackwell.
Noorani, A. G. (1990). 'Indira Gandhi and Indian Muslims'. *Economic and Political Weekly* 3 November.
Rajan, R. S. (2000). 'Women between community and state'. *Social Text* 18, no. 4.
Rawls, J. (1971). *A Theory of Justice*. Cambridge, MA: Harvard University Press.
—— (1993). *Political Liberalism*. New York: Columbia University Press.
Sandel, M. (1982). *Liberalism and the Limits of Justice*. Cambridge: Cambridge University Press.
Sangari, K. (1995). 'Politics of diversity: religious communities and multiple patriarchies'. *Economic and Political Weekly* 23 December.
Savarkar, V. D. (1942). *Hindutva*. 2nd ed. Poona: S. R. Date.
Shourie, A. (1993). *A Secular Agenda*. New Delhi: ASA Publications.
Taylor, C. (1989). *Sources of the Self*. Cambridge: Cambridge University Press.
Walzer, M. (1983). *Spheres of Justice*. New York: Basic Books.

Chapter Nine

The Politics of Group Rights in India and Pakistan

Ishtiaq Ahmed

Group rights in India and Pakistan are rooted in religious culture—the two main traditions being Hinduism, which dominates in India, and Islam, which dominates in Pakistan. In the British colonial era, before India split into two countries, these two cultural traditions co-existed uneasily and evolved slowly, affecting the structure of power and law both at a local level and through some key individuals. Colonialism focused minds not only on the national issue of achieving independence, but also on the political issue of national cultural identity after independence. In the event, a unified cultural identity proved impossible to achieve, and the traumatic events of Partition, with widespread population-transfers and loss of life, ensued. Today, communal heterogeneity with full formal political rights has been achieved only in India (the larger part of the original whole), while the problems of co-existence between the various religious and caste groups there are far from being resolved. Meanwhile, in Pakistan, while the threat of a 'problem of minorities' to a national cultural identity has been painfully removed, serious splits have emerged within that identity itself under the pressures of Islamic fundamentalism.

HINDUISM IN PRE-COLONIAL TIMES

The classic Hindu *dharma-karma* theory presents an idea of justice in which right action in one life results in the reward of a higher birth in the next life, and the converse. From the time of the Laws of Manu (ca. 800 BC), therefore, there has in theory been no scope for social mobility, up or down, in one lifetime (*The Laws of Manu* 1971). In reality, mobility was possible, with some groups being able to elevate their standing in the caste order through 'Sanskritization'. This concept implies adherence to Hindu food (and other) codes and thus a slow process of assimilation into Hindu society. Nevertheless, the *dharma-karma* theory created a vast number of low-caste and casteless people based on ethnic and racial criteria.

The Indo-Aryan tribes that poured into the Indian subcontinent between 1500 and 1000 BC defeated the Dravidian and proto-Astraloid aboriginal inhabitants (now known as Adivasis). The Hindu social order that came to constitute the resulting orthodoxy consisted of four *varnas* or status groups. At the apex, the Brahmin priests were held to be of the purest Aryan stock. The warrior and princely caste of Kshatriyas followed them. These castes together constituted the nobility. Below them were the ordinary members of society, called Vaiyshas. These three *varnas* were considered 'clean' and accorded the status of 'twice-born'. Lower still, the Dasas (ostensibly, those of mixed Aryan-Dravidian race) were placed at the bottom of the caste system, and named Sudras. Outside the pale of caste society altogether were the 'untouchables' (the term they prefer for themselves nowadays is Dalit, which means an oppressed person).

Under *dharma-karma* provisions, upper-caste Hindus enjoyed impunity for crimes—up to and including murder—against lower-caste persons and untouchables. Hindu reform movements against Brahminical domination began, however, to spring up in ancient times. Two Kshatriya princes, Siddhartha Gautama and Vardhamana Mahavira, founded Buddhism and Jainism respectively during the 6th century BC. Much later, during the 8th century AD, the Bhakti movement emerged in South India as a popular protest against Brahminism. It gradually spread to the north, with its mainstay from individuals in both upper and lower castes who were dissatisfied with established Hinduism. In time, the Bhaktis opened their movement to Muslims too, and sections of Muslim society were attracted to its fold. Its most famous exponent was Kabir (1440–1518), a low-caste Muslim weaver (Antonova, Bongard-Levin and Kotovsky 1979: 225–27). Later, however, even the Bhakti movement was infiltrated by Brahminic influence and slipped quietly into oblivion.

ISLAM IN PRE-COLONIAL TIMES

The Muslim presence in South Asia dates from 711 AD. For the greater part of the period between the early 13th century AD and the Great Mutiny against British rule in 1857, Muslim dynasties dominated the northern part of the Indian subcontinent. Under Islamic rule, a sharp line was drawn between Muslims and non-Muslims; the latter were referred to as *dhimmi*. Among them, Christians and Jews were recognized as legitimate minorities and accorded communal autonomy and other rights, while political and military power remained in Muslim hands. In return for this 'protection', these minorities were required to pay a special tax (*jizya*).

Some Muslim theologians and jurists in India interpreted Islamic law liberally, classing Hindus as monotheists and thus creating scope for a proto-pluralist society (Naqvi 1995: 46). But there was also movement in the other direction, leading to calls for Muslim strictures against polytheism and idol-worship. The practice of slavery further complicates the picture. Although the institution of slavery was present during Muslim rule it seems to have been rather loosely organized. Generally conversions to Islam won freedom for slaves, and several Muslim dynasties of foreign origin, founded by former slaves, ruled in India.

The leading personages in the Muslim social order were the so-called *ashraf*, while local converts were known as *ajlaf*. The former, tracing their descent to Turkish, Afghan, Persian or Arab ancestors, kept their distance from local converts. According to one (perhaps over-precise) estimate, during the Mughal period (1526–1857), 86% of the imperial services were manned by Muslims, of which 70% were foreign-born (or their descendants) and 16% were drawn from the much larger group of indigenous converts (Talha 2000: 16). Upper-caste Hindus who became Muslims were accorded respectable status and in due course assimilated into the *ashraf*.

Since Islamic theology did not recognize untouchability, the social esteem of local converts to Islam from lower castes and rural-dwelling tribes went up significantly, though the *ashraf* for their part continued to keep their social distance. Thus it was that British colonial officers found upper-class Muslims in the United Provinces to be, in practice, above Islamic law relating to murder, adultery, and evidence-giving (Singha 1998: 42), while the same group was orthodox in observing strict segregation of the sexes.

Meanwhile, sectarian differences between Sunnis and Shi'as were to some extent carried over into Muslim rule in South Asia. The differences date from the time of the death of Muhammad in 632; they concern the right of succession to leadership of the Muslim community and remain unresolved today. Persecution of Shi'as in predominantly Sunni societies was widely practiced for many centuries after the birth of the Prophet. In order to evade persecution Shi'as practiced *taqayya* (or 'pious' dissimulation, whereby they could conceal their true faith and outwardly conform to Sunni beliefs). But the official adoption of Shi'ism under the Iranian state at the beginning of the 16th century led to the ethnic cleansing of Sunnis from that country. In the Indian subcontinent, Sunni-Shi'a differences were certainly the basis of court intrigues and similar divisive practices; at the time of the annual Ashura processions to mark the death of Imam Hussain, Sunni-Shi'a clashes took place among the populace; but otherwise, in the peculiar cultural diversity of India, the two groups lived side-by-side in relative peace.

The pre-colonial political order was constituted by an autocratic ruler, Muslim or Hindu, at the apex of a segmentary power structure. Within this, a descending power hierarchy of lesser princes, chiefs, caste leaders and tribal headmen presided over the mass of peasants, craftsmen, artisans and menials (Ahmed 1987:67–8). On the whole, the popular fiction prevailed that the ruler, Hindu or Muslim, was the guardian of all his subjects and an impartial judge in personal and communal conflicts. Terms like *nyaya* (Sanskrit/Hindi) and *insaaf* (Arabic/Urdu), meaning justice, gained currency and became associated with notions of good government. Moreover, terms such as *adhikara* (Sanskrit/Hindi) and *haqq* (Arabic/Urdu), referring to a right or entitlement, have been part of everyday parlance and legal vocabulary, in association with the idea of 'to each his due', since pre-British times. Yet the concepts underlying *haqq* and *adhikara* were rooted not in a shared sense of common citizenship or of equality, but as a general claim to justice upheld (in theory) in traditional practices, and for that reason should not be confused with the modern concept of 'rights' (Anderson and Guha 1998: 5–6).

As for Muslim theologians, there is little evidence to suggest that in pre-colonial times they seriously questioned the applicability of dogmatic Islamic law as interpreted by the various recognized schools of Islamic jurisprudence. In fact, whenever the state was perceived to have deviated from its Islamic character some form of censure sooner or later ensued from the orthodox establishment.

It should also be stressed that traditional South Asian society comprised various groups formed around religion, caste, ethnic origin, and sect. Individuals were notional members of these entities, and both high culture and local affinities claimed their allegiance. In everyday life, it was the network of immediate family, clan and *biradari*, or putative common lineage based on descent, that provided succour and protection to members. Despite widespread inequality, the various social layers interacted with one another through the division of labor, and lower castes and classes were in principle entitled to some material rewards. In substantive terms, however, the terms *adhikara* and *haqq* seem to have had greater relevance for interaction between social equals, whether Hindu or Muslim, than between social ranks at large.

BRITISH COLONIAL RULE AND THE MODERN CONCEPT OF RIGHTS

The British had since at least 1757 been expanding their hold over several parts of the subcontinent, but it was only after 1857 that India was annexed by the Crown and the London government assumed direct control. Thereafter colonial policy became centralized, being enforced through a bureaucratic system based on elaborate rules and procedures. This had important consequences. Although the British were reluctant to foster active citizenship among the natives, and Indians remained mere colonial subjects of the Crown, reforms fashioned on liberal constitutional theory and English Common Law were introduced. This led inevitably to the emergence, among the natives, of modern educated classes, including a large number of lawyers trained in British schools and universities and developing for themselves a sense of citizenship and rights under the law. Such ideas gained wider currency as education spread and political activity acquired a more popular character.

In the colonial polity, religious law was supplanted with modified versions of Common Law, with the exception of personal matters—a crucial distinction. This meant that Hindus could observe Hindu religious law, as well customary laws, in respect of personal matters. Similarly the Islamic *sharia* code was confined to the private sphere, where it covered personal matters such as worship, marriage and divorce. Deviation was allowed to the extent that, under customary law, Muslim agricultural castes in the Punjab were able to deny a share of parental property to female descendants and dependants (Anderson 1990: 205–24). While the practice of *suttee* (widow-immolation) was outlawed, untouchability was not, and it was left to Christian missionaries and British reformers, especially at local levels, to provide these unfortunates with some relief through conversion. In the political sphere, representative institutions were gradually introduced, though suffrage remained narrow and subject to property and educational qualifications.

Political strategies to keep the various communities apart, as well as the desire to give them some representation, led the British to give official recognition to certain cultural groups. Thus, in 1909, the system of separate electorates was introduced whereby the Muslim community was granted separate representation on municipal and legislative councils. The Indian National Congress objected to this policy, arguing that it gave constitutional sanction to cleavages between Muslims and Hindus. Muslim leaders in general, however, welcomed it out of a fear that in mixed constituencies the Muslim minority would be at a disadvantage. Later, other minorities began to clamour for separate electorates; among them the untouchables and the Sikhs of Punjab were the most prominent. The Sikhs were granted separate electorates in 1921. As regards the untouchables, however, Congress leader M. K. Gandhi began a fast-unto-death protest against the establishment of such a right, which would, he asserted, formalize their exclusion from the Hindu social order. Gandhi succeeding in convincing the untouchables' leader, Dr Ambedkar, that an independent India would ban untouchability and take measures to meet their outstanding grievances. The Poona Pact, as this agreement came to be known, was reached in 1932 (Mallick 1998: 238–40).

Modernization of British ruling practices in the wake of annexation also impelled the perturbed Hindu, Muslim and Sikh leaders to contemplate the question of social reform. Among Hindus, the aggressive campaigns of Christian missionaries in the late 19th century and continuing conversions to Islam led to a number of reformist initiatives. The *Brahmo Samaj* movement in Bengal pressed for greater adaptation to Western rationalism, while its circle of supporters remained upper-caste Hindus. The more populist *Arya Samaj* movement sought to rid Hinduism of idol-worship and caste prejudices through a revised interpretation of scripture, ancient history and folklore. It was successful mainly in removing social taboos among the upper three 'twice-born' castes and in winning back some recent converts to Islam and Christianity (Bhatia 1987: 114–20: Farquhar 1967). In different parts of India, a number of assertive lower-caste movements also emerged, such as the *Staya Shodhak Samaj* movement in Maharashtra, the SNDP in Kerala, and the *Dravida Kazam* and *Ramaswami Naicker* in Tamil Nadu. However, it was Gandhi who from 1915 onwards launched a number of movements to positively change upper-caste Hindu attitudes to untouchability. For example, in place of the deeply-offensive name of *acchout* (untouchable) he introduced the word *harijan* ('Child of God').

The Congress party itself spelt out new ideas of citizenship in 1928 with the publication of the Motilal Nehru Report. This clearly envisaged universal citizenship based on equal civil and political rights, although communal representation was to be retained for special circumstances. In the subsequent years, Motilal Nehru's son Jawaharlal was to add social and economic dimensions to citizenship based on universal criteria. The younger Nehru believed strongly in the state as a medium of progressive, even egalitarian reform and had little sympathy for religiously-charged argumentation in the area of rights-claims. Gandhi, on the other hand, was more in tune with the notion of equal status for all religious communities based on the philosophical notion of *sarva dharma samabhava* (equal respect for all religions). Such a position suggested that the various communities would have substantial internal autonomy and could apply their religious law to their internal affairs. Nehru, Gandhi and the Congress Party solicited the support of nationalist Muslim clerics in this regard, by promising not to interfere with their personal law (Mahajan and Sheth 1999: 3–5).

Among Muslims, the earliest reaction to the British takeover had been one of despair. The old *ashraf* families of northern India, in particular, found themselves losing power and influence. The *Aligarh* movement of Sir Syed Ahmed Khan went on to pioneer a number of reforms in favor of modern education; Sir Syed went so far as to proclaim that Islam was in conformity with science and nature. Yet while such ideas made some impression on modern-educated Muslims, the clerics remained steadfast in their belief that *sharia* was just, rational and divine and therefore there was neither need nor scope for its reform. The famous Deoband seminary (founded in 1867) and similar seats of learning prescribed reforms based on the restoration of the *salaf* model of government associated with the first four successors of the Prophet Muhammad (Faruqi 1980).

On the other hand, the All-India Muslim League, founded in 1906 by upper-class Muslims and professionals, reached a different conclusion, with directly-political implications: it held that the Muslims of India constituted a separate nation by virtue of their distinct Islamic faith and culture. From 1940 onwards the League leaders, basing themselves on the 'Two-Nation' theory, concentrated on stressing the differences between Hindus and Muslims. In the 1945–46 elections a clear mandate was given by Muslim voters in favor of a separate Muslim state. Meanwhile the supreme leader of the League, Mohammed Ali Jinnah, skilfully avoided giving a clear idea of the ideology this independent state would be based on. In some statements and speeches he spoke of a modern democracy based on Islamic values, in others of *sharia* being applied solely to the Muslim community's affairs (Ahmed 2002a). But overall, he successfully argued for separate nationhood on a religious basis and in mid-August 1947 India was partitioned into two separate and independent states, India and Pakistan, amid communal riots that claimed the deaths of 1–2 million people.

INDIA AFTER PARTITION

The failure to keep India united left the Congress ideal of a composite Indian nation in a shambles. When discussion began on the constitution, the notion of a modern individual-rights-oriented civic body was very much in evidence. The Hindu nationalist lobby argued in favor of Hindu cultural hegemony, but was overruled. The trauma of Partition had left everybody in the Congress high command over-sensitive to the question of unity (Chaube 1989: 298–9).

On the whole, therefore, the founders of independent India decided to continue working within the constitutional framework initiated by the British. A secular-democratic state, upholding civic nationalism, universal human rights and the political principle of centralized development, within a federal administrative and power-sharing structure, would characterize the public face of independent India. In formal terms no particular religion or cultural tradition would be given priority. Today, the Indian constitution declares that freedom of speech, expression, assembly, association, occupation, property and religion are to be enjoyed within the requirements of public law. A number of welfare and economic rights are also mentioned but these are, properly speaking, directive principles rather than entitlements open to enforcement through the courts. Article 44 envisages the adoption of a 'uniform civil code throughout the territory of India' at some future date (The Constitution of India 1992).

Such a code implies a comprehensive set of human rights enjoyed by all citizens on a universal basis without regard to caste, creed, colour or sex. The state also encourages inter-caste and inter-religious marriages and the laws of the land recognize their validity. By contrast, Hindu nationalists have in recent decades intensified their pressures for special constitutional privileges for Hindu civilization and culture, which would, they say, reflect India's 'national' identity. Naturally enough, such calls for 'cultural authenticity' have been perceived as a threat by non-Hindu minorities. In addition, ideas of seceding from India have given birth to several separatist movements. It is against this socio-political background that we need to examine the politics of group rights (Ahmed 2002b: 16–18).

Linguistic nationalities

Prior to independence, the Congress Party accepted the idea of a federal structure for India and committed itself to re-organizing the country on the basis of linguistic nationalities. Partition, however, resulted in the break-up along religious lines of British-ruled India. After this, Nehru and his close associates were reluctant to alter existing provincial boundaries, fearing it would lead to a resurgence of divisive competition along ethnic and cultural lines. They were particularly opposed to the creation of states (here, provinces) in newly-independent India in explicit recognition of separate religious identities. Nevertheless, popular pressure throughout the country forced the government to implement the principle of linguistic nationalities, and the process of re-organization began in the mid-1950's. In the case of East Punjab, where Sikhs were in a majority, statehood was reluctantly conceded as late as 1966; it was long held that Punjabi and Hindi were not sufficiently distinct from each other to justify separation on a linguistic basis (Brass 1974: 320).

Separatist movements have in fact always existed in India. In the 1950's the Dravidian movement emerged in the southern part of the sub-continent as a strong force resisting the domination of upper-caste Aryan Hinduism; in the 1970's Sikhs began to agitate for a separate state of Khalistan. The latter movement resulted in a protracted armed confrontation with the central government which claimed at least 60,000 lives, including Prime Minister Indira Gandhi who was assassinated by her own Sikh bodyguards on 31 October

1984. In the predominantly-Muslim Kashmir Valley a separatist movement has been present since at least the late 1980's; this region too has seen the use of violence and terror-tactics by both central government and separatist militants. The number of people killed in this conflict has been estimated at 70–80,000 (Ahmed 1998: 120–36).

Dalits and Adivasis

The Dalits (untouchables) and Adivasis (tribal and indigenous peoples) are described as the 'scheduled castes' and 'scheduled tribes' respectively by the Indian constitution. Article 46 states: 'The State shall promote with special care the educational and economic interests of the weaker sections of people, and, in particular, of the Scheduled Castes and Scheduled Tribes, and shall protect them from social injustice and all forms of exploitation' (The Constitution of India 1992). In 1955 the Union parliament passed the Untouchability (Offences) Act, criminalizing discriminatory practices. Also by act of parliament, quotas were fixed for the scheduled castes and scheduled tribes in government services, central and provincial legislatures and educational institutions. Consequently some 22% of posts have been reserved for them.

Such reservations apply to Hindus, Sikhs, Buddhists and Jains, but not to Muslims and Christians of Dalit and Adivasi origins. This is something of an anomaly. The argument goes that Muslims and Christians of scheduled caste and tribal background belong to religions that do not recognize caste. Yet most of the adherents of these religions are of lower-caste, untouchable or tribal origin. Unsurprisingly, in recent years human-rights activists have demanded that all people of a culturally-underprivileged background should be considered for affirmative action.

Notwithstanding these measures, it has been a slow process of upward mobility for Dalits and Adivasis. Social taboos are still widely prevalent in society and brutal attacks on them by upper-caste Hindus continue in different parts of India. Also, given the narrow scope for admission generally to higher educational institutions and government employment, the reservation system has drawn a great deal of criticism from upper-caste Hindus, not all of whom are materially well-off. Upwardly-mobile Dalits, in consequence, are more frequently attacked than those who remain at the bottom of society (Alavi 1989: 233–34). In recent years a mainly Dalit party, the *Bahujan Samaj* ('Party of the Majority Society'), has made some impact on state and local elections. Along with a category of peasant and artisan castes known as the Other Backward Castes (or OBCs), the Dalit politicians have been striving to achieve greater political influence. Meanwhile, among radical Dalits there are strong reservations about Gandhi's insistence that untouchables be seen as an integral part of Hindu society. Some have suggested that the only way forward is to use democratic power acquired through elections to promote the interests of untouchables and aborigines (Mallick 1998: 233–73). They have also sought international attention. At the World Conference Against Racism, Racial Discrimination, Xenophobia, and Related Intolerance held at Durban, South Africa from 31 August to 7 September 2001, they lobbied against the continuation of casteism in Hindu society.

Women

Under traditional Hindu law the position of women was very weak and vulnerable. Jawaharlal Nehru's reformist government made various changes in the laws governing marriage, divorce and inheritance which brought improvements in women's rights (Smith 1963: 241–3; 277–91). This example demonstrates that although the main ideological thrust of the Indian political system is to confer rights on an individualistic basis, it has been possible to consider ways and means of rectifying historical disadvantages faced by a group of people. In particular, the question of women's representation has been given considerable attention in recent years. In the early 1990's, 33% of seats were reserved for women in village and local councils. A bill reserving 33% of seats in the Union and state legislatures has also been debated keenly in the Union parliament. Apparently a consensus exists in favor of passing the bill into law, but some parties claiming to represent Dalit and Adivasi interests have insisted that reservation should give proportional representation to women of the lower orders. At present the discussion continues in parliament and the latest reports suggest that some parties are insisting that the fixed representation of women should be reduced to 15–20%. Meanwhile, widespread violence against women persists in Indian society. Young women, especially those of Dalit origin, are subjected to harassment, rape and other indignities by people of upper castes. Cases of wife-burning by husbands and in-laws disgruntled with the dowries brought at the time of marriage have figured prominently in the media in recent years.

The Muslim minority

As mentioned above, some Muslim clerics supported the Indian National Congress's idea of a united India and opposed the Muslim League's demand for a separate homeland for Muslims. In return they were given assurances by Congress leaders that the government would not interfere with the internal matters of the Muslim community, while it was hoped that in due course Muslims would voluntarily assimilate into mainstream political life and thus partake in the democratic nation-building project. Consequently, when Nehru initiated a number of reforms to modernize and democratize the Hindu marriage and inheritance laws (reforms which were also applicable to Sikhs, Buddhists and Jains), the Muslim community was exempted. The new changes forbade Hindu men to take more than one wife, child-marriage was prohibited, and regarding inheritance from parental property daughters were given equal shares along with sons. Later, more general changes in family affairs were introduced, in respect of which it was not clear whether only Hindus or all Indian citizens were concerned. Thus for example it was laid down that if a man divorced his wife and she had no source of income to support herself, the divorcing husband was obliged to provide her with means of sustenance in accordance with his income.

Nevertheless, the exemption of the Muslim community from reformed personal laws has been the subject of considerable criticism both from Hindu cultural nationalists and from human-rights groups. The line of criticism of the Hindu nationalists was that such a policy served to strengthen separatist tendencies among Muslims and was therefore inimical to national consolidation. Further, it typically favored men, who could not only take more than one wife but also marry girls classed as minors (since no age limit for marriage existed in Islamic law). To such objections were added sensationalistic claims, to the effect that the Muslim population was increasing at a faster pace because of child and multiple marriages, which in the long run would threaten the 'Hindu identity' of India.

At the same time, many Muslim clerics and conservative leaders remained reluctant to allow the Indian state to legislate on personal matters within their faith-group (Kunda 1989: 203–220), asserting that Muslims need merely be guided by the holy Qur'an, the *Sunna* (the acknowledged acts of the Prophet Muhammad) and *Fiqh* (Islamic jurisprudence). Thus, they insisted, marriage, divorce and inheritance must comply with Islamic injunctions—although ironically, the first of these is only a civil contract in Islam with no sacred status. On the whole, such leaders also advocated adherence to strict rules of segregation between men and women and therefore discouraged modernistic change. The Muslim community of India, moreover, is not only poor but also economically and educationally well behind other religious communities; and their difficulties are compounded by the suspicion of Hindus who feel that their sympathies and loyalties are with Pakistan.

Matters in this area came to a very public head in 1985, when Begum Shah Bano, a middle-aged Muslim woman of Madhya Pradesh, was divorced by her husband, M. A. Khan. On the advice of some well-wishers she filed a petition in the state High Court that as an Indian citizen she was entitled to financial support from her former husband. A detailed account of this *cause célèbre* in Indian legal history is given in Henrik Berglund's chapter in this book. The plight of Begum Shah Bano, rendered destitute by her husband's actions after 43 years of marriage, and his mobilization of the conservative *ulama* (clerics) in his favor, led to conflicting demonstrations all over India. When the Supreme Court eventually ruled conclusively in the wife's favor, Syed Shahabuddin, the President of the influential All-India Muslim *Majlis-e-Mushawarat* (Muslim consultative assembly), and other Muslim leaders vehemently condemned what they saw as intrusions by the Indian state into the internal domain of Muslim communal life.

Many liberal and progressive Muslims, including academics, lawyers, jurists, members of parliament, women activists and political workers came out boldly in favor of the Supreme Court judgment. Both sides of Muslim opinion put arguments forward, but the conservative forces greatly outnumbered the modernists. Unwilling to antagonize the large Muslim vote-bank, Prime Minister Rajiv Gandhi went along with the traditional standpoint and a special law exempting Muslims from such obligations to ex-wives was passed by the Indian parliament (Aggarval 1986). Matters did not end there, for within the Muslim community at large voices had begun to be raised against the application of *sharia* law to marriage and divorce. Moreover, Hindu nationalists' vocal championing of the uniform civil code had made many reformist Muslims apprehensive, while strengthening the resolve of traditional leaders to maintain the structure of *sharia* unchanged.

Shabana Azmi, a leading Indian Muslim film-star, feminist and member of the Upper House of the Indian parliament, has since set out her views on the uniform civil code and the disputes which have arisen in the country around this issue:

> The laws of all religions discriminate against women. The Convention on the Elimination of All Forms of Discrimination Against Women (1979) is the most pertinent framework for developing uniform civil laws on women. In India, the ground will have to be prepared gradually for a proper and substantial application of the Convention. It would be desirable to draw upon all the positive aspects of religious laws, whether Hindu, Muslim, Christian, Sikh and so on, to develop an argument in favor of gender equality. All Indian women should participate in formulating a programme on women's rights which can be given legal effect as part of a uniform civil code in India. In short, I am for gender justice being included in the uniform civil code.
>
> I have never withdrawn my support for the idea of a uniform civil code. What has happened is that the majority [Hindu] community continues to harass, intimidate and attack the minorities. No culprit from the Hindu community has been found guilty and subsequently punished. Consequently the minorities become even more apprehensive and therefore do not participate towards the acceptance of a uniform civil code because they fear that the majority com-

munalists will use it to further weaken minorities. (Author interview August 2001).

Meanwhile, it is interesting to note that growing pressure from different directions has led to a review of the traditional standpoint on marriage and divorce among members of the *Majlis-e-Mushawarat*, and the beginning of a discussion about how to minimize the abuse of traditional Islamic law with regard to Muslim individuals.

Leaving aside the complicated legal aspects of group rights, the Muslim minority has since the beginning of the 1990's been targeted by virulent Hindu nationalists who seek to purge India of Western secular rights and replace them with an 'authentic' indigenous version deriving from Hinduism. Typically, they allege that Nehruvian secularism favors the non-Hindu minorities at the expense of the Hindu majority, pointing out that whereas the Hindu marriage and divorce laws have been modernized in an egalitarian direction, the Muslim minority has been allowed to practice Islamic law, which favors the position of men. Right-wing Hindu movements such as the *Rashtriya Swayamsevak Sangh* and the *Vishwa Hindu Parishad*, in particular, have demanded constitutional privileges for Hinduism, and further, advocated a system in which all Indian citizens would accept Hinduism as their national cultural identity, while non-Hindus could continue, in their private spheres, to practice their beliefs (Ahmed 2002d). Organized communal attacks on Muslims have periodically taken place, and since the destruction on 6 December 1992 of the Babri mosque in Ayodhya, Hindu extremists appear to have been emboldened to intensify such attacks. In February-March 2002 a massacre of over 2000 Muslims took place in the western Indian state of Gujarat (Prakash 2002; Shukla 2003).

PAKISTAN

Pakistan's travails with its national identity have been marked by inconsistency and confusion. The main question has been whether the country should be a modern, secular, nation-state of Pakistanis or an Islamic state of Muslims; to this question no clear answer has been given.

'Cultural nationalism', based on confessional criteria, was the mobilizing ideology behind the Two-Nation theory on which the demand for Pakistan in pre-Partition, colonial India was based. Yet although Pakistan's founder, Mohammed Ali Jinnah, made religious differences between Hindus and Muslims the justification for the claim to a separate Muslim state, he tried hard to prevent such a state from becoming a theocracy. In an address to the members of the Pakistan Constituent Assembly on 11 August 1947, he said:

> You are free; you are free to go to your temples, you are free to go to your mosques or to any other place of worship in this State of Pakistan. You may belong to any religion or caste or creed—that has nothing to do with the business of the State . . . We are starting with this fundamental principle that we are all citizens and equal citizens of one State . . . I think we should keep that in front of us as our ideal and you will find that in due course Hindus would cease to be Hindus and Muslims would cease to be Muslims, not in the religious sense, because that is the personal faith of each individual, but in the political sense as citizens of the State. (*Speeches*, Vol. 2, 1976 [1947]: 403–4)

Jinnah's early death on 11 September 1948 closed the chapter on secularism and universal citizenship. For the Pakistani establishment ever since, that speech has been an embarrassment, and it was excluded from a compilation of Jinnah's speeches published in 1966 by the Research Society of Pakistan.

Subsequent discussion on national identity began to veer in an Islamic direction, reflecting a classic political identity-crisis: how to distinguish the new breakaway state of Pakistan from the rump state (albeit much larger one) of India. On 7 March 1949, Prime Minister Liaqat Ali Khan moved an Objectives Resolution in the Pakistan Constituent Assembly. God, not the people or its elected representatives, was declared the sovereign in Pakistan. Democracy was going to be observed within limits prescribed by Islam. Similarly, Muslims and non-Muslims were to enjoy fundamental rights 'compatible with' Islam (*Constituent Assembly Debates* 1949: 1–2). Thus, the first constitution of 1956 declared Pakistan an Islamic Republic and made a commitment to bringing all laws into conformity with Islam. The second constitution (1962) initially dropped the appellate 'Islamic' and declared the Republic of Pakistan. The first amendment to this document restored 'Islamic' to the country's name. The third constitution, adopted in 1973, went further towards the Islamicization of national identity by requiring not only the president but also the prime minister to be a Muslim (Constitution of the Islamic Republic of Pakistan 1975).

Symbolic discrimination against non-Muslims began to creep into the constitutional system from quite early times, although until the early 1970's the usual type of liberal civil rights was formally granted to all citizens. However, discriminatory criteria introduced by the government, based on *sharia*, resulted in a differential scale of rights. Religious and gender differences were made the basis of rights policy. The result was state-induced group differences and rights, which carried exclusivist implications for certain categories of citizens. In 1974, as will be recounted below, the Pakistan National Assembly declared the Ahmadiyya community non-Muslims (though its members have always claimed to be Muslims). Under the fundamentalist military ruler General Muhammad Zia-ul-Haq (1977–88), a so-called Islamicization programme was enforced. In 1985 the regime re-introduced separate electorates in Pakistan (the system had been abolished in 1956). The argument advanced in favor of this measure was that non-Muslims stood no chance of getting elected on a general ticket and therefore separate electorates would ensure a fair degree of representation for them. During that period the so-called blasphemy law was also introduced. Thus for example in 1982 Section 295–B was inserted in the Pakistan Penal Code. It read:

> Defiling, etc., of The Holy Qur'an: Whoever wilfully defiles, damages or desecrates a copy of the Holy Qur'an or of an extract therefrom or uses it in any derogatory manner or for any unlawful purpose shall be punishable with imprisonment for life.

In 1986, Section 295–C was added. It stated:

> Use of derogatory remarks, etc., in respect of the Holy Prophet: Whoever by words, either spoken or written, or by visible representation, or by any imputation, innuendo, or insinuation, directly or indirectly, defiles the sacred name of the Holy Prophet Muhammad (peace be upon him) shall be punished with death, or imprisonment for life, and shall also be liable to fine.

The Constitutional Approach to Group Rights in Pakistan

In the mid-1950's the existing provinces of western Pakistan, defined roughly by linguistic criteria, were amalgamated into a single province. However, that policy was abandoned in 1969, and currently Pakistan consists of four provinces—Baluchistan, North-West Frontier Province, Punjab and Sind. Separatist movements have existed in all the non-dominant provinces of Pakistan but only East Pakistan succeeded in breaking away, becoming the separate state of Bangladesh in December 1971. A discussion has been going on for some years to break up the present structure and create smaller provinces but thus far no decision has been taken in that direction.

Notwithstanding the recognition of linguistic nationalism as the basis for distribution of power within a federal structure, the confessional antecedents of the Pakistani polity and the processes of Islamicization that have been underway in the country prioritize groups, rather than individuals, as bearers of differential rights. Thus, all notions of an Islamic polity inescapably link membership in the Islamic community to citizenship rights in the state: the true believer has to be differentiated from the hypocrite, the heretic and the non-believer. As regards the true believer, the fundamentalist version of Islam makes a further division: it segregates the sexes. Consequently the only true bearers of citizenship rights turn out to be Muslim men. These could further be divided into those who follow the official version of Sunni Islam and the various tolerated 'deviations' such as the Shi'as.

The Ahmadiyya

Orthodox Islam is based on the cardinal belief that the Prophet Muhammad was the last of the prophets sent down by God and that after him no more prophets are expected. Mirza Ghulam Ahmad (1835–1908), born at Qadian in the Punjab, started his religious career as a Sunni debater who could confront both Christian missionaries and Hindu reformers with clear arguments in defence of Islam. Mirza gained considerable acclaim from his fellow co-religionists. However, he later staked a claim to being a prophet himself, and made several other controversial pronouncements which were not easily reconcilable with mainstream Sunni doctrines. Upon Mirza's request the Ahmadiyya were shown as a separate sect in the census records (*Report of the Court of Inquiry* 1954: 10). He also made statements that other Muslims perceived as openly pro-British and hostile to Muslim interests.

After his death the Ahmadiyya movement went through a period of internal conflict, culminating in a split into two groups: the main Rabwa group, which regarded Mirza as a prophet, and the minor Lahori group, which acknowledged him only as a reformer. During the colonial period the Ahmadiyya received government protection and were admitted into the army in large numbers. They were able to win converts in Punjab. Elsewhere their influence remained marginal.

In 1911 Mirza's son and later successor and head of the Rabwa sect, Mirza Bashir-ud-Din Mahmood Ahmad, published an article in which he declared that to remain outside the Ahmadiyya movement for a Muslim was to remain outside the fold of Islam (Jones 1989: 200). In return the Sunni *ulama* declared the Ahmadis heretics. In the mid 1940's, as the movement for a separate Muslim state gained popularity, the Ahmadiyya leaders hesitated to support it, fearing that their community would be persecuted in a Sunni-dominated Pakistan. However, Jinnah was able to convince some leading Ahmadis that Pakistan would be a non-sectarian state in which Ahmadis would enjoy equal rights. In particular he was able to win over the support of Sir Muhammad Zafrulla Khan, a leading Ahmadi enjoying British confidence and support. Jinnah entrusted Sir Zafrulla with the crucial task of pleading the case of the Muslim League before the Punjab Boundary Commission, and when Pakistan gained independence appointed him as Pakistan's first foreign minister.

In the early 1950's, the Ahmadiyya controversy again cropped up. The orthodox clerics alleged that Ahmadi officers were misusing their official positions to promote the interests of the sect. Statements by the head of the Rabwa mission, Mirza Bashiruddin, indeed seemed to suggest that he had given orders to Ahmadiyya officers to spread their faith in Pakistan, particularly in Baluchistan. The *ulama* demanded that the government declare the Ahmadiyya non-Muslims and, in accordance with the ideological requirements of an Islamic state, remove them from important positions. Most concretely it was demanded that Sir Zafrulla be removed from the post of foreign minister. In 1953 a violent agitation broke out in Punjab against the Ahmadiyya. Not only the *ulama* but also cadres and officials of the provincial Muslim League government were guilty of fomenting riots in which Ahmadiyya property was looted, the homes of Ahmadis were burnt and many were killed. The central government reacted by imposing martial law and the agitation was crushed (*Report of the Court of Inquiry* 1954).

The Ahmadiyya issue receded into the background for some years, but in 1974 Zulfikar Ali Bhutto, hoping to wrest a populist cause from the *ulama* in the Punjab, took the initiative by getting a bill passed by the National Assembly declaring the Ahmadiyya non-Muslims. During the 1980's many restrictions were placed on their religious freedom and there was a new wave of violent attacks on them. During 1998, 106 cases were registered under various religious laws against them. The editors, printers and publishers of Ahmadi publications faced 191 similar charges. At least five Ahmadis were murdered by religious fanatics (Human Rights Commission of Pakistan, 1999: 7–8).

Christians

Conversions to Christianity took place in the areas comprising present-day Pakistan largely after the British had annexed Punjab and Sind in the 1840's. Most conversions took place from among the poorer sections of society, particularly the untouchable Hindu castes. Some middle-class and elite families also embraced Christianity. At the time of Partition, Christians belonging to the Pakistani areas accepted the new state as their homeland. In fact some of their local leaders in the Punjab co-operated with the Muslim League during the campaign for Pakistan, because Jinnah and other modernist Muslim League leaders had in their public utterances dissociated themselves from the traditional theocratic ideas of the *ulama* (Ahmed 1999b: 147).

Christians in Pakistan lived in relative peace until Bhutto nationalized the missionary-owned educational institutions in the Punjab. This act resulted in Christian protests throughout Pakistan, for the schools and colleges were practically the only places where educated Christians could find employment.

The protesters were beaten up and fired upon by police and casualties occurred. Staff were forcibly evicted from their homes and the property owned by the missions was confiscated. Thereafter the Christians were not heard of again in mainstream politics until General Zia-ul-Haq embarked upon his Islamicization policy. In 1985 the system of separate electorates was reintroduced in Pakistan (it had been inherited from the colonial period and was abolished formally in 1956 when the first constitution came into force). General Zia, in compliance with traditional Islamic law, wanted to separate the primary Muslim-Pakistani nation from the non-Muslims. Initially some Christian leaders welcomed this reform but opinion quickly swung in the opposite direction, for it was felt that separate electorates only served to alienate and marginalize non-Muslims from the majority community.

These apprehensions were borne out by subsequent experience. In the late 1980's several acts of violence were carried out by fanatical sections of Muslim society against Christians. The blasphemy law had been applied mainly against Christians, and lower courts sentenced some to death. In October 1997 retired Lahore High Court judge Arif Iqbal Bhatti was murdered by unidentified members of extremist religious groups. In its annual report of 1998 Amnesty International observed: ' His death was believed to be linked to his role in the acquittal in 1995 of [the Christians] Salamat Masih and Rehman Masih who had been sentenced to death for blasphemy [by a lower court].' Another Christian, Ayyub Masih, was sentenced to death for alleged blasphemy by a session court in 1998. In protest Bishop John Joseph, the Catholic Bishop of the Diocese of Faisalabad, shot himself to death at the gate of the sessions court in Sahiwal on 6 May 1998. In any event on 25 July 2001 the Lahore High Court confirmed the death sentence passed on Ayyub Masih. However, an appeal was filed in the Supreme Court which on 15 August 2002 acquitted him of all the charges. He was granted asylum by the United States and settled in that country.

Cases were also reported of the forcible occupation of church land, dismantling of Christian localities and acts of arson and bombing inside churches (Human Rights Commission of Pakistan, 1999: 7–8). Christian clerics and community leaders have long campaigned against the laws and provisions discriminating against their community in Pakistan. In particular the system of separate electorates has been identified as the main divisive factor in the nation. In a letter of 20 November 2000 to Pakistan's President, General Pervez Musharraf, the Rev. Fr. Emmanuel Yousaf, Administrator of the Archdiocese of Lahore, put this point succinctly:

> It is a fundamental right of any citizen to aspire to represent his/her constituency at any level, be it the Union Council, the Provincial Assembly or the National

> Assembly, regardless of the aspirant's caste, colour or creed . . . The separate electorate system usurps this basic right of the entire population of Pakistan by denying them the right of full franchise because of their religious beliefs.

A leading Christian spokesperson, Group Captain Cecil Chaudhry, a decorated air force officer who had distinguished himself in the wars with India in 1965 and 1971, summed up the disillusionment of non-Muslims with the group-rights policy of the state in the June 2001 issue of *Defence Journal*:

> In Pakistan our political order is based on religious apartheid through the Separate Electorate System . . . The Separate Electorate System, thrust upon the nation by Zia-ul-Haq in 1985, divides the entire nation into five religious groups and does not allow any political interaction between any two of the groups. The seats of the National and the Provincial Assemblies are so divided that Muslims, Christians, Hindus, Ahmadis, and other religious minorities can only contest for and vote within their own group. This system has completely broken down social harmony thus paving the way for sectarianism strife . . . A political system so deeply rooted in religion when allowed to perpetuate will most definitely cause dissensions within each group and give rise to religious extremism, even to the extent of spreading terrorism in the name of religion . . . The non-Muslim citizens have proved that they do not want the Separate Electorates by very effectively boycotting the first two phases of the on-going Union Council elections . . . Having said this let me state that in India the extremist Hindu is targeting the Christians mainly. I also believe this situation will not last and we can already see things improving in India . . . With deep regret I have to admit that there is no comparison. India is a proven secular country and the state of religious tolerance and equality is far better than that of Pakistan . . . If this government allows the present state of gross sectarianism to continue we are doomed as a nation.

Hindus

At the time of the creation of Pakistan there was almost a complete ethnic cleansing of Hindus from what became West Pakistan; only in Sind province did some half a million remain behind. Hindus preferred to lie low and avoid political attention as their religious links with India placed them in a vulnerable position in Pakistan.

Communal attacks against Hindus began to occur in the mid-1980's as the overall ethnic crisis in Sind grew more acute. Following the destruction of the Babri Mosque at Ayodhya in India and the brutal killings of Muslims which accompanied it, there was a fierce reaction in Pakistan. Destruction of Hindu property and temples took place and several hundred Hindus were killed and injured, mainly in Sind but also in Baluchistan. Although the government officially urged the people to exercise restraint, some ministers whipped up mass hysteria through crass demagogy. The Human Rights Commission of Pakistan has published, in its own annual reports, cases of forced conversion of Hindus, including the abduction of young Hindu girls and their forced conversion and marriage to Muslims. The police have generally been uninterested in arresting alleged culprits (Human Rights Commission of Pakistan, 1999: 156).

Minorities' Opposition to Separate Electorates

Less-numerous religious minorities such as the Parsees, Sikhs and Buddhists have also been adversely affected by the increasing theocratization of Pakistan. In the Gilgit and Chitral regions are to be found Ithna Ashari ('Twelver') and Ismaili Shi'as living alongside Sunnis. Here the competition for converts between Iran, the European-based Ismaili mission led by the Agha Khan, and the fundamentalist Zia government backed by the Saudi regime led to several clashes in the 1980's. The tiny community of some 4,000 of the Kalash Kafirs of the Chitral Valley in particular were subjected to aggressive conversion campaigns during the Zia regime. Some *ulama* have demanded that all non-Muslims should be declared *dhimmi* and made to pay the *jizya* tax, although this drastic demand has not received serious attention from the state thus far (Ahmed 1999a: 236).

The leaders of all the minority communities from the four provinces attended an All-Pakistan Minorities Conference in Lahore in October 2000, where they unanimously demanded that joint or undifferentiated electorates be reinstated. They also declared their intention to boycott the local elections scheduled for the summer of 2001 if the voting was held under separate electorates. It is interesting to note that all Pakistani political parties, except the religious ones and the Muslim League, have demanded joint electorates and have included this in their party constitutions. The government of General Pervez Musharraf abolished separate electorates in 2002.

Sectarian Terrorism

When the movement for a separate Muslim state in India gained momentum in the 1940's, some sections of the Shi'a community opposed it, fearing that the future Pakistan might be a Sunni state (Resolution of All-Parties Shi'a Conference 1997: 848–9). However, Jinnah (a Shi'a) and other Muslim League leaders assured the Shi'as that Pakistan would not become a sectarian state ((letter of Syed Ali Zaheer and Jinnah's reply, in Allana ed. 1977: 375–9). This policy was retained so far as the position of the Shi'as was concerned, until Islamicization during the Zia regime inevitably brought in sectarian implications as Zia was seen to represent the Deobandi type of Sunni Islam. The problem came to the fore when the Zia regime began to collect the religious alms tax (*zakat*) from all Muslims. The Shi'as were not willing to pay *zakat* to a state they perceived to be based on Sunni ideology. The difficulties were compounded further when in the late 1980's powerful external actors began to cultivate their lobbies in Pakistan. Thus the Saudi and Iranian governments were believed to be sending large sums of money, as well as books, leaflets, audio- and video-cassettes to propagate their ideologies of Islam in Pakistan. Such propaganda offensives were backed by the inflow of firearms and other weapons. Sunni and Shi'a militias began to menace and terrorize society. Consequently the assassinations of rival Sunni and Shi'a clerics took place, and gun battles and bomb explosions began to become regular occurrences in Pakistan (Ahmed 1998: 176–8).

Women

Prior to General Zia's coming to power successive governments had promoted policies aimed at improving the condition of Pakistani women. For example during the 1960's the Commission on Family Laws argued in favor of introducing registration of marriages with local authorities. It was also decided to introduce traditional *sharia* rules on inheritance that entitled daughters to a share in their father's property, on a ratio of one share to a son and half of that to a daughter. Previously daughters were denied a share in their father's property, as dictated by the customary laws of agrarian communities. This combination of modern reform and traditional law were in that particular situation an improvement on the prevailing practices. These reforms have survived in spite of changes of governments and the rise of fundamentalism, and it seems that there is a wide social acceptance of them.

Complete equality and freedom for women in personal affairs, however, appears unattainable. Attempting this within the confines of the *sharia* is most difficult, for the limits of possible reform within this religious mode of argument are neither wide nor elastic. Prior to Zia, governments had quietly been extending family-planning facilities and girls had begun to attend modern schools in greater numbers. Polygamy had been prohibited in several Muslim countries in the region and a lower age limit for marriage had been introduced. In Turkey and the central Asian Republics, both sexes were receiving equal treatment under the law and equal rights of citizenship. In Tunisia, Syria, Iraq, Algeria and Bangladesh restrictions were imposed on polygamy and an age limit for marriage was maintained.

Under General Zia, however, the overall egalitarian trend was interrupted by Islamic measures ostensibly intended to protect the honour and dignity of women. In 1984 a new Law of Evidence, based on a literalist reading of a

Qur'anic verse, was adopted which reduced the worth of evidence given by a female witness in a court of law to half that of a male witness. Also, since four pious male witnesses were required to testify before a rape could be proven, according to the *Hudud* (Qur'an-prescribed) laws, convictions for this crime became very difficult to obtain. Besides such legal provisions, a campaign to impose an Islamic code of behaviour and dress was launched. In 1980 a circular was issued to all government offices that prescribed proper Muslim dress for female employees, including the obligatory *chador* (a loose cloth covering the head). A campaign to eliminate obscenity and pornography was also announced, but astonishingly this merely took the form of hostile propaganda against the emancipation and equal rights of women. *Ulama* notorious for their opposition to female equality and emancipation were brought onto national television to justify their misogynist opinions (Mumtaz and Shaheed 1987: 77–96).

The annual reports on human rights issued by the Human Rights Commission of Pakistan gave a long list of injustices and violent crimes committed against women (Human Rights Commission of Pakistan, 1998: 184–93; 1999: 209–22). Indeed the imposition of *Hudud* laws and various social, cultural and legal inputs from the state seem to have emboldened ill-doers in this direction. The most notorious development is the growing frequency of so-called 'honour killings'. Close relatives—husbands, sons, brothers—who suspect that a woman has been guilty of an extra-marital liaison, or merely fallen in love with someone unacceptable to the family, invariably take her life.

One case of honour killing received much publicity when members of an upper-class educated family allegedly committed such a murder (Ahmed 2002c: 80–82). On 6 April 1999, Samia Sarwar, 29 years of age and mother of two boys aged 4 and 8, was shot dead in the office of Hina Jilani, a female lawyer specializing in human-rights issues. Married in 1989, Samia left her husband six years later, alleging that he had ill-treated her, and returned to her parents in Peshawar. Now, four years later, she wished to marry another man and therefore asked for a divorce. Her family, however, threatened to kill her if she persisted in this course of action. Samia decided to run away and take refuge at Dastak ('Knock at the Door') in Lahore, a shelter for battered and threatened wives run by Ms. Jilani.

Members of Samia's family pursued her to Lahore and tried to contact her, but Samia was extremely fearful, refusing to meet her father and agreeing to meet her mother only after an assurance that the meeting would convey her family's consent to the divorce petition. She insisted, moreover, that her lawyer, Ms. Jilani, be present during the meeting. Samia's mother and uncle then came to the lawyer's office, accompanied by the family driver who shot her dead. The driver was shot dead on the spot by the guards at Dastak, but neither the mother nor the uncle was convicted, despite them both being accomplices in the crime. There was a 'compromise' between the heirs of the victim and the accomplices in the murder. Such a procedure is permissible under the prevalent Islamic laws of *qisas* and *diyat*. Basically Samia's father pardoned the mother and the uncle. The children were too young to have a say and the husband probably had no objection. Hence no trial took place.

CONCLUSION

In South Asia, cultural groups throughout history have applied their religious law and traditions to internal matters. The pre-colonial state allowed considerable autonomy and the British continued with that tradition but also introduced modern concepts of rights under the law. Independent India continued to follow a mixed policy on this matter but constitutionally gave priority to individual rights, basing its policy on territory rather than culture.

The concessions given to the Muslim group to retain the *sharia* for personal matters, whilst reforms have gone forward in family matters for other communities, have created an exceptionalism which is perhaps not in the best interests of national consolidation in India. Moreover, there is no evidence that the Muslim community is unanimously in favor of maintaining the traditional system, while voices have been raised amongst it in favor of a common or uniform civil code for all citizens. One individual, indeed, quoted above, has given powerful expression to a demand for fuller compliance with the UN convention on the rights of women, enabling Indian women to be treated as equals with men.

The key problem as it exists today is the overweening power of the state as against the autonomy sought by groups, especially when state sovereignty is hedged by religious criteria. It makes the state partisan in terms of conferring rights on citizens, both actual and potential. Thus, for example in Pakistan, while fundamental rights are part of the constitution, the tendency in central government policy has been to establish a differential framework of group rights based on religious distinctions. Differential, in this context, surely means unequal, unfair and discriminatory in respect of all but certain categories of Muslims (Sunnis and Shi'as); and to complicate things further, those two privileged groups are fundamentally at odds with each other on key theological questions. One may fairly ask, therefore, whether a strategy of reform in favor of modern citizenship can succeed at all, if it must simultaneously pay allegiance to rigid interpretations of religious scripture, especially in the light of the fact that nowhere in the Muslim world is there complete agreement on Islamic principles or the interpretation of Islamic religious texts.

What is perhaps even more challenging in modern multi-ethnic and culturally diverse societies such as India and Pakistan is how to arrive at a consensus on what belongs to the public and what to the private sphere. Cultural groups in general and minority cultural groups in particular need help from the state to preserve their special identities. Equally, it is clear that they do not want to preserve a *stigmatized* group identity. Thus in a general sense one can say that minority or non-dominant religious groups aspire to equality of religious identity, but are against the maintenance of the dominant culture, whether based on caste hierarchy and other racial and ethnic prejudices.

Considered in these complicated terms, the issue of group rights in South Asia becomes a challenge for the overall concern for human rights. However, at present the dominant faith communities—Hindu in India, Sunni Muslim in Pakistan—seem to be gripped not simply by illiberal ideas but even by openly-hostile and violent habits of behaviour towards deviating members and the groups identified as threats and enemies. In post-independence India, there is very little evidence that communitarian leaders representing Hindu culture have voluntarily agreed to remove caste oppression, tolerate dissenting individuals or seek accommodation with other groups. It is therefore imperative that the Indian state should continue to act on behalf of oppressed groups and introduce special laws that alleviate their suffering while actively incorporating them into egalitarian and universal citizenship. The evidence from Pakistan should leave no doubt that a polity based on faith is a poor guarantee of tolerance of dissent from within or of peace between communities, claims to 'authenticity' notwithstanding. What we should note is that religious minorities in Pakistan favor inclusion in the general category of citizens, with equal rights, so that they can be included in the Pakistani nation. This they want to achieve without compromising their religious beliefs.

The application of the principles of the European Enlightenment to the deeply-religious cultural milieu of South Asia appears to have been a problematic enterprise but India has benefited greatly from the inputs by the Nehruvian regime. On the other hand, seeking the foundation of individual and group rights in 'authentic' culture, whether Hindu or Islamic, is surely a course of action fraught with disaster. Rather, it is important that reform should comply with international norms on individual and group rights established through the key UN declarations and conventions. Whatever politicians and activists may claim, to leap to ideals of universality along with the rest of humanity is surely a more generous impulse than the artificial creation of differential structures that are merely discrimination and oppression in disguise.

REFERENCES

Aggarval, B. R. ed. (1986). *The Shah Bano Case*. New Delhi: Arnold-Heinemann.

Ahmed, I. (1987). *The Concept of an Islamic State: An Analysis of the Ideological Controversy in Pakistan*. London: Frances Pinter.

—— (1988). *State, Nation and Ethnicity in Contemporary South Asia*. London/New York: Pinter.

—— (1999a). 'South Asia' in Westerlund and Svanberg eds.

—— (1999b). 'The 1947 Partition of Punjab: arguments put forth before the Punjab Boundary Commission by the parties involved' in Talbot and Singh eds.

—— (2002a). 'The fundamentalist dimension in the Pakistan movement'. *Friday Times* (Lahore), 22–28 November.

—— (2002b). 'The 1947 Partition of India: a paradigm for pathological politics in India and Pakistan'. *Asian Ethnicity* 3, No. 1 (March).

—— (2002c). 'Globalization and human rights in Pakistan'. *International Journal of Punjab Studies* 9, No. 1 (January-June).

—— (2002d). 'The post-colonial Indian discourse on secularism'. *Daily Times* (Lahore), 1 December.

Alavi, H. (1989). 'The politics of ethnicity in India and Pakistan' in Alavi and Harriss eds.

—— and J. Harriss eds. (1989). *Sociology of 'Developing Societies': South Asia*. London: Macmillan.

Allana, G. ed. (1977). *The Pakistan Movement: Historic Documents*. Lahore: Islamic Book Service.

Amnesty International (1998). *Annual Report 1998*. London.

Anderson, M. R. (1990). 'Islamic law and the colonial encounter in India' in Mallat and Connors eds.

—— and S. Guha eds. (1998). *Changing Concepts of Rights and Justice in South Asia*. Calcutta: Oxford University Press.

Antonova, K., G. Bongard-Levin, and G. Kotovsky (1979). *A History of India: Book 1*. Moscow: Progress Publishers.

Bhatia, S. (1987). *Social Change and Politics in Punjab: 1898–1910*. New Delhi: Enkay Publishers.

Brass, P. R. (1974). *Language, Religion and Politics in North India*. Cambridge: Cambridge University Press.

Chaube, S. K. (1989). 'Ethnicity, regionalism and the problem of national identity in India' in Hassan, Jha and Khan eds.

Chaudhry, C. (2001). 'Remembering our Heroes'. *Defence Journal* (Karachi) 4, No. 11 (June).

Farquhar, J. N. (1967). *Modern Religious Movements in India*. Delhi: Munshiram Manoharlal.

Faruqi, Z. H. (1980). *The Deoband School and the Demand for Pakistan*. Lahore: Progressive Books.

Hassan, Z., S. N. Jha and R. Khan eds. (1989). *The State, Political Processes and Identity: Reflections on Modern India*. New Delhi: Sage Publications.

Human Rights Commission of Pakistan (1998). *The State of Human Rights in Pakistan 1997.*

Human Rights Commission of Pakistan (1999). *The State of Human Rights in Pakistan 1998.*

Jinnah, M. A. (1976). *Speeches and Writings of Mr Jinnah*, vol. 2. Lahore: Sh. Muhammad Ashraf.

Jones, K. W. (1989). *The New Cambridge History of India: Socio-Religious Reform Movements in British India*. Cambridge: Cambridge University Press.

Kunda, R. (1989). 'Common civil code' in Shakir ed.

Mahajan, G. and D. L. Sheth eds. (1999). *Minority Identities and the Nation-State*. New Delhi: Oxford University Press.

Mallat, C. and J. Connors eds. (1990). *Islamic Family Law*. London/Dordrecht/ Boston: Grahman and Trotman.

Mallick, R. (1998). *Development, Ethnicity and Human Rights in South Asia*. New Delhi/Thousand Oaks/London: Sage Publications.

Mumtaz, K. and F. Shaheed (1987). *Women of Pakistan: Two Steps Forward, One Step Back*? Lahore: Vanguard.

Naqvi, M. (1995). *Partition: The Real Story*. Delhi: Renaissance.

Prakash, V. (2002). *Hindutva Demystified*. New Delhi: Virgo Publications.

Shakir, M ed. (1989). *Religion, State and Politics in India*. Delhi: Ajanta Books.

Shukla, I. K. (2003). *Hindutva: An Autopsy of Fascism as a Theoterrorist Cult and other Essays*. Delhi: Media House.

Singha, R. (1998). 'Civil authority and due process: colonial criminal justice in the Banaras Zamindari, 1781–95' in Anderson and Guha eds.

Smith, D. E. (1963). *India as a Secular State*. Princeton, NJ: Princeton University Press.

Talbot, I. and G. Singh eds. (1999). *Region and Partition: Bengal, Punjab and the Partition of the Subcontinent*. Karachi: Oxford University Press.

Talha, N. (2000). *Economic Factors in the Making of Pakistan 1921–1947*. Karachi: Oxford University Press.

Westerlund, D. and I. Svanberg eds. (1999). *Islam Outside the Arab World*. Richmond: Curzon.

Archdiocese of Lahore (2000). Rev. Fr. Emmanuel Yousaf, Letter entitled 'Request for an Audience', 22 November.

Constituent Assembly of Pakistan Debates, Vol. 5. (1949). Karachi: Government Printing Press.

Constitution of India (1992). New Delhi: Universal Book Traders.

Constitution of the Islamic Republic of Pakistan (1975). Lahore: Publishers United Ltd.

(1954). *Report of the Court of Inquiry constituted under Punjab Act II of 1954 to enquire into the Punjab Disturbances of 1953*. Lahore: Government Printing Press.

(1971). *The Laws of Manu*, trans. W. Doniger with B. K. Smith. New Delhi: Penguin Classics.

Index

Abacha, Sani, 165
Abbasid Empire, 60
Abdülhamit, Sultan, 103
Abubakar, Yakubu, 156
Adivasis (India), 190, 197, 198
Advani, L. K., 180, 184
African Charter on Human and Peoples' Rights, 18
Agabi, Kanu, 161
Age, Chief Bola, 157
Ahmad, Mirza Bashir-ud-Din Mahmood, 204, 205
Ahmad, Mirza Ghulam, 204
Ahmadiyya (Pakistan), 203–5
Ahmed, Datti, 166
Ahmed, Hocine Aït, 140, 142
Akcura, Yusuf, 103, 105
Akhil Bharatiya Vidyarthi Parishad (India), 170
Aldebe, Mahmoud, 70, 71
Alevi (Turkey), 101, 106, 109, 113–15, 123, 124
Aligarh movement (India), 194
All-India Muslim Personal Law Board, 175
Ambedkar, Bhimrao Ramji, 193
American Convention on Human Rights, 18
Amnesty International, 206
Amsterdam Treaty (EU), 76
Arbitration Act (Ontario), 5
Arya Samaj (India), 176, 194
Asad, Muhammed, 72
Atatürk (Mustafa Kemal Pasha), 104, 106, 124
Augsburg, Peace of, 13
Azmi, Shabana, 200–201

Babangida, Ibrahim, 159
Babayaro, Hadiza, 163
Babri Masjid mosque, 185, 201, 207
Baer, Lars-Anders, 44
Bafarawa, Governor (Sokoto state, Nigeria), 155
Bahiyan Samaj (India), 197
Bajrang Dal (India), 170
Bakht, Sikander, 177, 186
Baobab for Women's Rights (Nigeria), 157
Bauer, Bruno, 25
Bauman, Zygmunt, 42, 43, 47
Baykal, Deniz, 120
Ben Badis, Abd Al-Hamid, 143
Ben Bella, Mohammed Ahmed, 142
Benjedid, Chadli, 133, 136
Berbers, ch. 6 *passim*. *See also* Kabyles

Bernström, Mohammed Knut, 72
Bharat Mazdoor Sangh (India), 170
Bhatti, Arif Iqbal, 206
Bhutto, Zulfikar Ali, 205
BJP (*Bharatiya Janata Party*, India), 23, 169–71, 175, 176, 177–82, 183, 184, 185–87
Bosnia-Herzegovina, 79, 81, 83, 85–87, 88, 94, 96; UN High Representative to, 94
Bosnian migrants, 64, 66
Boumedienne, Houari, 132, 133, 136
Bouteflika, Abdelaziz, 130, 138, 146
Boyd Report (Canada), 5
Brahmo Samaj (India), 194
Buhari, Mohammadu, 154

Camus, Albert, 144
Carlsson, Ingvar, 72
caste system (India), 1, 8, 10, 31, 189–90, 194, 197–98
Ceaucescu, Nicolae, 80
Celebi, Faruk, 67
Cem Vakfi (Turkey), 115, 123
Chandhoke, Neera, 24
Chaudhry, Cecil, 207
Christian Association of Nigeria, 161
Christian Democratic Party (Sweden), 69
cizye tax. *See* Islam, taxation
Collectif Contre la Répression en Algérie, 136
communitarianism, 20–21, 29, 181–84
Comte, Auguste, 106
Conference of Berlin, 13
Congress Party (India), 170, 175, 179, 185, 193, 194, 195, 196, 198
consociational democracy, 2
Constituent Assembly (Nigeria), 153, 155, 159
Constitutional Court (Turkey), 110, 111, 112, 116, 119, 120
Contact Group (NATO/Russia), 83; Stability Pact for South-Eastern Europe (1999), 83
Conventicle Act (Sweden), 61–62
Copenhagen Political Criteria. *See* European Union
Council of Europe, 6, 51, 76, 93, 94, 101; European Charter for Regional or Minority Languages (1992), 35, 51, 76, 83, 86–87; European Convention on Human Rights (1950), 77, 82; Framework Convention for the Protection of National Minorities (1995), 17, 35, 51, 76, 83, 84, 85, 86–87, 88; Venice Commission, 87
Crusades, 60
CSCE (Conference on Security and Co-operation in Europe). *See* OSCE

Dagen newspaper, 70
Dalits (India), 190, 197, 198
Daniel, Isioma, 166
Darsh, Sheikh Syed, 3
Dastak (Pakistan), 210–11
Dayi, Alhaji Nasir Bello, 157–58
Dayton Agreement, 76, 85, 86, 94
Descartes, René, 11
dharma-karma theory (Hinduism), 189–90
dhimmi. *See* Islam
differentiated citizenship, 2, 7, 8, 21, 23, 24, 130
Diyanet (Turkish Ministry of Religious Affairs), 106, 107, 108, 109, 120, 121, 123
Djindjic, Zoran, 85
Dravida Kazam (India), 194
Dubashi, Jay, 178

Edelman, Murray, 53
Ekueme, Alex, 164
El Kseur Platform (Algeria), 139, 146
Erbakan, Necmettin, 110, 111
Erdogan, Recep Tayyip, 111, 112
European Charter for Regional or Minority Languages (1992). *See* Council of Europe
European Commission, 85, 123, 126

European Convention on Human Rights (1950). *See* Council of Europe
European Council (of Ministers), 101, 124, 125, 126
European Court of Human Rights, 5–6, 101, 111, 113
European Parliament, 126
European Union, 76, 77, 83, 90, 91, 98, 101; and Turkish accession, 101, 125–26; Copenhagen Political Criteria, 101

Falk, Richard, 31
Family Worship Centre, Abuja, 153
female circumcision, 6–7, 28
FFS (*Front des Forces Socialistes*, Algeria), 140, 142, 143, 144
FIS (*Front Islamique du Salut)*, Algeria), 141, 143
FLN (*Front de Libération Nationale*, Algeria), 129, 142
Framework Convention for the Protection of National Minorities (1995). *See* Council of Europe

Gandhi, Indira, 170, 196–97
Gandhi, Mohandas K. (Mahatma), 193, 194, 197
Gandhi, Rajiv, 175, 179, 200
gays, 10
Georgievski, Lyubcho, 90, 91
Gerle, Elisabeth, 68–69
Gökalp, Ziya, 103, 105
Guermah, Massinissah ('Momo'), 137–38, 141
Gurr, Ted, 28

Habermas, Jürgen, 56
Hadj, Messali, 134
Harff, Barbara, 28
Herder, Johann Gottfried, 12
Higgins, Rosalyn, 26
High Commissioner on National Minorities. *See* OSCE
Hindu Code Bill, 172–73
Hindutva, 176, 181, 184, 187
Hobbes, Thomas, 11
Hobsbawm, Eric, 25, 26
Human Rights Commission (Pakistan), 24, 205, 208, 210
Husaini, Safiya, 156–57

Ibn Fadlan, 60
Ibn Khaldun, 130
Ibrahim, Abdulkadir, 157
Idahosa, Bishop, 153
indigenous peoples, 1, 8, 9, 10, 14, 30, 31, 190, 197
Inönü, Ismet, 105
International Court of Justice, 14
International Labor Organisation Convention no. 169 (1989), 51
International Tribunal for the Former Yugoslavia (Hague Tribunal), 85
Internet, 10, 66, 73
Iranians (immigrants in Europe), 66
Islam: and blasphemy, 203; and secession, 131–32, 203; and secularism in Turkey, 105–9, 110–13, 120–21; *dhimmi* (non-Muslims), treatment of, 3–4, 7–8, 153–55, 161–64, 190–91, 202, 205–208, 212; in Nigeria, 153–67; in Ottoman Empire, 102–4; in South Asia, 190–95, 198–209; in Sweden, ch. 3 *passim;* in the Balkans, 78–79; *jihad*, 6; ritual slaughter, 28; *sharia* law, 3–5, 24, 27, 192, 193, 195, 200, 202; *Süleymaniye* movement, 67; *Tablighi* movement, 67; taxation under, 3, 78, 107, 190, 209; women's dress code, 5–6, 112–13, 121, 210. *See also* women, position of
Islamic Foundation (Leicester), 67
Islamiska informationsföreningen (Islamic Information Association, Sweden), 67, 68
Islamiska samarbetsrådet (Islamic Co-operation Council, Sweden), 70
Istanbul Declaration (1999). *See* OSCE

Jaitley, Arun, 178, 179, 180
Jamaat-e-Islami (India), 175
Jamaat-i-Islami (Pakistan), 67
Jana Sangh (India), 178, 181
Janata Dal Party (India), 175
Jengede, Buba Bello, 155
Jews, 2, 4, 5, 7, 14, 25, 61; and ritual slaughter, 28
jihad. *See* Islam
Jilani, Hania, 210
Jinnah, Mohammed Ali, 195, 201–2, 204, 205, 208
jizya tax. *See* Islam, taxation
Johns Hopkins University, 162
Joseph, Bishop John, 206

Kabo, Sheikh, 162
Kabyles, in Algerian society, 131, 132, 133, 134–35, 142, 144–47
Kani, Chindo, 162
Kant, Immanuel, 11
Karlsson, Ingmar, 70
Kavakci, Merve, 112
Khan, Agha, 208
Khan, Arif Mohammed, 175
Khan, Liaqat Ali, 202
Khan, Sir Muhammed Zafrulla, 204, 205
Khan, Sir Syed Ahmed, 194–95
Kingsway Ministries, 152
KLA (Kosovo Liberation Army), 81, 89, 90
Kosovo, 76, 79, 80, 81, 89, 90, 96, 97
Kostunica, Vladimir, 85
Kristdemokterna (Christian Democratic Party, Sweden), 69
Kukathas, Chandran, 55
Kuper, Leo, 29
Kurds, 16, 131, 139; (in Turkey), 104, 105, 107, 109, 110, 115–19, 122–24, 125–26
Kutan, Recai, 111
Kymlicka, Will, 21–23, 31, 36, 38–39, 77, 93–98, 123, 124

Lausanne Treaty (1923), 104
Lawal, Amina, 157–58
League of Nations, 13, 14, 48
League of Prizren (1878), 79
Lenin, Vladimir Ilich, 13
Léotard, François, 91
Lijphart, Arend, 27
Locke, John, 11
Lounès, Matoub, 137
Lugard, Lord, 163

Macedonia, Republic of, 87–93, 96–98; Lake Ohrid agreement, 91, 92, 93; NLA (National Liberation Army), 89–92; Tetovo, 89, 96; VMRO party, 90
MacIntyre, Alasdair, 182
Madhok, Balraj, 180
Mahasabha, 183
Mahmud II, Sultan, 103
Majlis-e-Mushawarat (India), 200, 201
Malkani, K. R., 180
Mammeri, Mouloud, 136
Manu, 189
Marx, Karl, 25
Masih, Ayyub, 206
Masih, Rehman, 206
Masih, Salamat, 206
Mazrui, Ali, 160, 164
Mill, John Stuart, 21,
Miller, Reverend, 163
Milosevic, Slobodan, 81, 85
Mohand, Issad, 138
Mouvement Culturel Berbère (Algeria), 136
Muhammed, Yahaya, 158
Musharraf, Pervez, 206–7
Muslim League, 175, 183, 195, 198, 205
Muslim Women's Bill (India), 175, 176, 179, 200
Muslims. *See* Islam
Mustafa Kemal Pasha. *See* Atatürk

Nandy, Ashis, 24
National Human Rights Commission (Nigeria), 158
nationalism, in Europe, 12–13

NATO (North Atlantic Treaty Organisation), 76, 77, 83, 90, 91, 98, 101
Nehru, Jawaharlal, 194, 196, 198, 212
Nehru, Motilal, 194
Nwabueze, Ben, 155, 159–60

Obasanjo, Olusegun, 159, 165, 166
Öcalan, Abdullah, 117–18
Odua People's Congress (Nigeria), 165
Okin, Susan Moller, 37, 42
Omaku, Mr & Mrs (Family Worship Centre, Abuja), 153
Onaiyekam, Archbishop John, 161
Ontario, 5
OSCE (Organization for Security and Co-operation in Europe), 82, 93, 94, 101; High Commissioner on National Minorities, 76, 77, 82; Istanbul Declaration (1999), 82
Otterbeck, Jonas, 67
Ottoman Empire, 3, 13, 62, 63, 78–79, 88, 93, 94, 102–4, 105
Ouhayia, Ahmed, 146
Owen, David, 83

Pardew, James, 91
Parekh, Bhiku, 19, 35
Partition (of India, 1947), 169, 186, 189, 195, 196, 201, 205
Persson, Göran, 72
Petkovski, Tito, 89
pillarization, 2
Poona Pact, 194

Québecois, 22

Ramaswami Naicker (India), 194
Rawls, John, 18, 31, 37, 38, 181–82
RCD (*Rassemblement pour la Culture et la Démocratie*, Algeria), 136, 140, 143, 144
Redeem Christian Church, 152
Reindeer Farming Act (Sweden, 1971), 46, 50
Reindeer Grazing Acts (Sweden): (1886), 44; (1928), 47
Rex, John, 19
Robertson, Geoffrey, 26
Roma people, 14, 85, 87
Rousseau, Jean-Jacques, 11
RSS (*Rashtriya Swayemsevak Sangh*, India), 169, 170, 177, 201

Sahin, Leyla, 5, 113
Said, Sheikh, 104
Salaam magazine, 67–68
Salhi, Mohamed Brahim, 145
Sami people, in Sweden, 44–52
San Egidio centre, 143
Sandel, Michael, 182
Sarwar, Samia, 210–11
Savarkar, Veer, 176, 186
Scramble for Africa, 13
secession, and group rights, 9, 22, 26, ch. 4 *passim*, 131, 132, 134, 159
self-determination, 13, 15, 26, 43, 52, 54, 89, 141
Senior Advocates of Nigeria, 158
separate electorates (South Asia), 193, 203, 206, 207, 208
Shagari, Shehu, 154
Shah Bano case, 173–75, 178, 179, 180, 181, 185, 199–200
Shahabuddin, Syed, 200
Shiv Sena (India), 170
Shue, Henry, 30
Singh, Om Prakash, 186
Soummam Platform (Algeria), 129, 135
SSR (National Union of Swedish Sami), 48
Stability Pact for South-Eastern Europe (1999). *See* Contact Group
Staya Shodhak Samaj (India), 194
Stefan, Orthodox Patriarch (Macedonia), 91
Sufism, 67, 106, 113, 151, 152
Süleymaniye movement, 67

Supreme Council for Sharia (Nigeria), 164, 166
Swaraj, Sushma, 178, 179, 180

Tabi'u, Muhammeed, 160
Tablighi movement, 67
Tamazight (Berber language), 135, 137–40, 143, 145
Tatars, 63
Taxed Mountains case (Sweden), 50
Taylor, Charles, 39–40, 182
Tito (Josip Broz), 80, 87, 88, 94
Trajkovski, Boris, 93
Turkey, political parties: AKP, 111, 112, 124; CHF, 104; CHP, 120, 124; DEHAP, 119; DEP, 119; DKP, 119; DP, 116; FP, 110, 111; HADEP, 119; HEP, 119; ITF, 104; MNP, 110; MSP, 110; OZDEP, 119; PKK, 117–18, 122; RP, 110, 111; SHP, 119; SP, 111; TIP, 116
Turks (immigrants in Europe), 7, 28, 64

United Nations, 12, 14, 16, 17, 164; Charter, 14, 15, 16, 18; Commission on Human Rights, 9; Declaration on the Rights of Persons belonging to National or Ethnic, Religious and Linguistic Minorities (1992), 16–17, 32; Draft Declaration on the Rights of Indigenous Peoples, 9; treaty instruments adopted on human rights, 16
Universal Declaration of Human Rights (1948), 15, 16, 62

Vance, Cyrus, 83
Venice Commission. *See* Council of Europe
Versailles, Treaty of (1919), 13, 14
Vienna, Congress of (1815), 13
Vikings, 60
Vishwa Hindu Parishad (India), 170, 201

Walzer, Michael, 21, 182
Westphalia, Peace of, 13
Wilson, Woodrow, 13, 14
Wolin, Sheldon, 55
women, position of, 1, 2, 5, 6, 8, 10, 12, 16, 18, 30, 31, 172, 174–76, 200–201; in India, 198; UN Convention on the Elimination of All Forms of Discrimination Against, 16, 200; under Islam, 5, 6, 8, 65, 112, 113, 121, 155–59, 166, 174, 178, 179, 181, 199, 200, 201, 209–11
Women's Rights Advancement and Protection Alternative (Nigeria), 158

Yan Hizba (Nigeria), 162
Yawuri, M. A., 158
Yerima, Governor (Zamfara state, Nigeria), 154
Young, Iris, 40–41, 54
Yousef, Rev Fr Emmanuel, 206

Zaheer, Syed Ali, 208
Zetterstéen, K. V., 72
Zia-ul-Haq, Muhammed, 203, 206, 207, 208–9